DAN ROONEY

DAN ROONEY

MY 75 YEARS WITH THE PITTSBURGH STEELERS AND THE NFL

AS TOLD TO **ANDREW E. MASICH** AND **DAVID F. HALAAS**

DA CAPO PRESS

A Member of the Perseus Books Group

Designed by Jane Raese
Set in Janson by The Perseus Books Group

Cataloging-in-Publication data for this book is available from the Library of Congress.

First Da Capo Press edition 2007
First Da Capo Press paperback edition 2008
HC ISBN: 978-0-306-81569-0
PB ISBN: 978-0-306-81745-8

Published by Da Capo Press
A Member of the Perseus Books Group
www.dacapopress.com

Da Capo Press books are available at special discounts for bulk purchases in the U.S. by corporations, institutions, and other organizations. For more information, please contact the Special Markets Department at the Perseus Books Group, 2300 Chestnut Street, Suite 200, Philadelphia, PA 19103, or call (800) 810-4145, ext. 5000, or e-mail special.markets@perseusbooks.com.

10 9 8 7 6 5 4 3 2 1

To all the Steelers who played or coached, the support staff,
and those who managed the team—for 75 years.
And to our fans—the Steelers Nation—
the best in the National Football League.

CONTENTS

The story of Dan Rooney is the story of the National Football League.

When Dan was born in 1932, the NFL was still in its formative stages, a struggling league of eight teams that was considered a minor attraction on the American sports scene. The following year, Art Rooney, Dan's father, took a leap of faith based on his love of football and bought one of three new franchises in the NFL. He called his team the Pittsburgh Pirates and later changed it to the Steelers to better reflect the city.

Dan Rooney, the Steelers, and the NFL grew up together. There were the normal growing pains, but as they flowered into maturity over the past seventy-five years, all three became unparalleled stories of inspirational success.

Football was my passion as a kid growing up in the 1960s and 1970s in Washington, DC, and the New York City area. But I had no real appreciation for the Steelers until I attended Washington and Jefferson College in Western Pennsylvania in the late seventies. That's when I experienced the tremendous influence that the game of football, the Steelers, and the remarkable Rooney family have on the entire region.

The Steelers were in the process of winning an unprecedented four Super Bowls in the seventies, with Chuck Noll, Terry Bradshaw, Joe Greene, and many other supremely talented contributors leading the charge. It was an amazing phenomenon—the region's passion for football, the way the Steelers united the community, and the love and respect that the fans had for Art, Dan, and the rest of the Rooney family. It was clear that it was all very special.

A few years later in 1982, I had the good fortune to land an internship with the NFL commissioner's office in New York. It didn't take long to figure out that Dan Rooney held a unique place among the NFL's leaders.

Dan was an owner who was active in league affairs. He was a man of integrity and dignity who was always willing to be involved and helpful. He was deeply immersed in the NFL's labor negotiations, playing a key role for decades. He was seen as a voice of reason during many difficult discussions because he had a strong sense of the best interests of the game; he was practical; and he knew how to forge a consensus.

At league meetings, you could see how the other owners and the commissioner valued Dan's opinion. He knew the game and league as well as anyone. He had good football and business sense. He understood the complex partnership aspects of a sports league. He was a good listener. He gave sound advice and fought for his beliefs, but he was always supportive when decisions were made. You could see how Commissioner Rozelle and then Commissioner Tagliabue relied on Dan.

Now Dan Rooney is the patriarch of the league. He has been there longer than anyone else. He knew the NFL's pioneers and listened to their stories. He is like a father figure to many of us in the NFL. He praises us when we do something good. More important, he lets us know when he disagrees with a decision and always offers alternatives. He is the conscience of the league. He reminds us of the special values that the NFL and the game of football represent.

I have been so privileged to have Dan as a mentor. As he has done for so many others, he helped bring me along with his support and his wisdom. When he became co-chairman of the search committee to find a new commissioner to succeed Paul Tagliabue, I knew that Dan would not do me any favors. I knew he would simply do what was best for the NFL by managing a fair and thorough process for all of the NFL owners.

At the end of that process, I was sitting in my hotel room in Chicago where the league owners were meeting to choose the new commissioner. There was a knock at the door. I opened it and there was Dan Rooney. He said, "Commissioner." It is a moment we shared that I will never forget.

What a journey it has been for Dan Rooney, his wonderful family, the Steelers, and the NFL. This is a story that captures the rich history of America's passion for football, the importance of family, and the unique success of the National Football League. Enjoy the ride and thanks for the memories, Dan. Let's keep them coming.

NFL Commissioner Roger Goodell
August 13, 2007

PREFACE
By Paul Tagliabue

Dan Rooney's life has been dedicated to the Pittsburgh Steelers and the National Football League—first observing league affairs as a wide-eyed youngster and then actively participating for decades as an owner, team executive, and league committee member.

In the mid-1940s, Dan watched his father, Art, and other league owners select Bert Bell as the league's first post–World War II commissioner. Last year, Dan co-chaired, with Carolina Panthers owner Jerry Richardson, the league committee that recommended Roger Goodell to be the NFL's current commissioner.

Between these events, Dan worked inexhaustibly with his father, his fellow owners, and with commissioners Bell, Rozelle, and me for six decades to help shape NFL football into America's sports passion. He and his family will continue to do so with Commissioner Goodell.

Dan and the Rooney family have also lead the Steelers through decades of great black and gold football, creating legends (e.g., the "Immaculate Reception") and legendary players (too many to name) along the way.

Over the decades, Dan's leadership has extended to an extraordinary array of subjects, initiatives, and changes as the NFL evolved and became the globe's strongest sports league.

When I first met Dan Rooney in the early 1970s, the Steelers had just begun play in the American Football Conference. They had switched conferences along with the Baltimore Colts and Cleveland Browns to join the ten teams of the former American Football League in the AFC, rather than stay in the NFC. The Steelers' alignment in the AFC was not entirely popular with Steelers fans or within the Rooney family. But Dan saw that while it involved unsettling change, it reflected the NFL's growth and was critical for fan interest nationwide. So he worked intensely to make a success of the Steelers' new AFC divisional alignment.

Dan's leadership did not stop there, however. He was deeply involved in resolving disputes and reaching agreements with the NFL Players Association from the 1970s into the present decade. His integrity and understanding of both football and team economics made him invaluable in negotiations on the college draft, the need for competitive balance on the football field, free agency, and player safety matters.

Dan often served as a spokesman for the league, locally and nationally. Dan's personal qualities, wide experience in and out of football, and commitment to Pittsburgh's people, neighborhoods, and community organizations prepared him well for this role. When the league faced congressional issues in the 1970s and 1980s, for example, Dan was usually the first person to be called by Commissioner Rozelle to join him in Washington to explain the league's position. And Dan would frequently bring not just himself or other Rooneys, but allies and supporters of the Steelers from across the political spectrum—Pittsburgh's leading companies, not-for-profit organizations, and labor unions.

New stadiums were another of Dan's longtime priorities. Understanding what Three Rivers Stadium had meant to the Steelers, Dan pushed in the eighties and nineties for league policies that could help all teams build state-of-the-art stadiums. As an increasing number of NFL teams became frustrated in the nineties with difficult new stadium issues, Dan offered bold ideas. I'll never forget Dan telling me, "We can't have the Patriots leaving Boston and their fans just because some local politicians are creating trouble. All of us in the NFL need to put up some money to help all clubs build new stadiums and stay where they belong." Shortly thereafter, the league's membership endorsed an innovative program for leaguewide financial support of new stadium construction.

But Dan Rooney is not just an innovator, consensus builder, and peacemaker. He is a fighter who relishes a good argument or—when his convictions or core interests are challenged—even a tough lawsuit. For Dan, his right to fight to defend his principles, his Steelers, or his NFL in a courtroom is as crucial as a Steelers Super Bowl victory. Many pretenders and adversaries have learned this, including the USFL, the NFL Players Association, and others both inside and outside the NFL.

Dan Rooney's love of the Steelers and the NFL grows out of his love for football, especially Pennsylvania football. "Do you know," he would ask me, "that Pennsylvania leads all states in having the most Pro Football Hall of Famers?" "So what," I would counter, "they didn't all play for the Steelers."

It didn't matter to Dan. Often the objects of his admiration are athletes or coaches, especially those with ties to the Steelers, Pittsburgh, or Pennsylvania. Mention Unitas, Noll, or Dungy; Joe Paterno, Roberto Clemente, Mel Blount or Joe Greene; Tony Dorsett, Dan Marino, or Joe Namath—and Dan Rooney will recall a story or incident featuring their talents on the playing field or leadership in the community.

But Dan's serious heroes are patriots, explorers, revolutionaries, poets, and men and women of faith. Mention Jefferson, Lewis and Clark, Michael Collins, Yeats, or Mother Teresa and you will have begun an illuminating conversation with Dan Rooney.

For Dan, these are the visionaries and achievers who inspire his leadership, not just in Pittsburgh or in the NFL, but in other lands and walks of life—such as with the American Ireland Fund and the Rooney Prize awarded annually to outstanding young Irish poets and fiction writers.

For Dan, these are the visionaries and achievers who provide the inspiration, values, and example that he believes we should all strive to display, whether in the NFL or in other aspects of our lives. These individuals understand history and tradition but are not irrationally bound by it. They combine conviction with openness to new ideas. And they have understood that the right course sometimes requires peacemaking—and sometimes fighting.

The story of Dan Rooney's life focuses on the Rooney family, football, the Steelers, and the NFL. But it is a story that teaches much more. Whatever our career or interests, it is a story that offers invaluable lessons not just for our time but for generations to come.

Paul Tagliabue
NFL Commissioner (1989–2006)
August 15, 2007

All of us wonder, at one time or another, about our purpose in life. Some people are lucky enough to discover their life's work, while others struggle to find meaning. This is the story of a man who has a clear sense of himself, and his purpose. Dan Rooney is a man of family, faith, and football. The clarity of his vision attracted us to this project. We are honored and privileged to work with a man who has been at the very center of building the Pittsburgh Steelers, one of the most beloved and successful sports franchises in history. At the same time, he has been an integral part of the growth of the National Football League as football evolved into America's game.

When Dan first mentioned to us that friends and colleagues had suggested his story should be told in a biography, we encouraged him to pursue the project, not as a traditional biography but as an autobiography. We thought the story should be told from his point of view. At first he resisted the idea. He is a genuinely humble man and said, "That's just not me." But we at the History Center, his family, and his friends persisted. His story is important. He has made history.

Over the course of the last two years, we spent thousands of hours interviewing him, traveling with him, and just plain getting to know him. We talked to his family, who shared their experiences and insights as well. In addition we met with players, coaches, colleagues, and friends. We pored over archives, old newspapers, and scrapbooks to fill in missing pieces and confirm Dan's recollections. All in all, his memories are remarkably accurate and vivid, considering they span seventy-five years—years of great change filled with a bewildering array of people and events. We found a man devoted to his family and friends, a man of abiding faith, and a man of uncompromising dedication to football. Football to him is more than a game. In many ways, it symbolizes the strength and vitality of the people and place he loves—Pittsburgh. You can't really separate Dan Rooney from Pittsburgh any more than you can separate him from football. It's in his blood; it's part of his character. As we worked with the Steelers organization—at the South Side complex, at Heinz Field, on the road—we saw his mark everywhere. The closeness of the organization, from the team and coaches and secretaries to the front office and grounds crew, feels more like a family than a corporation. Steelers center Jeff Hartings said it best: "We honestly love each other. I honestly felt that I would rather lose a game like this with this team than win a Super Bowl with a team I didn't enjoy playing with."

We found this attitude remarkable, considering this is a five-time Super Bowl championship team with the best record in the NFL over the past twenty years. It's also a very successful business. This didn't just happen. Dan likes to say there are four things that make a winning football team—talent, coaching, closeness, and management. He doesn't talk much about the management part. But make no mistake. From top to bottom, the Pittsburgh Steelers organization reflects Dan Rooney's business acumen, values, integrity, and character. And perhaps most important, it reflects his determination to win. You can see it in the Steelers mission statement: "The mission of the Pittsburgh Steelers Football Club is to represent Pittsburgh in the National Football League, primarily by winning the Championship of Professional Football."

Consider: Five Super Bowl championships. Six conference titles. And twenty Steelers elected to the Pro Football Hall of Fame. Dan has been named NFL Executive of the Year, Dapper Dan's Sportsman of the Year, and he's been inducted into the Football Hall of Fame.

He leads off the field as well, serving on the boards of the United Way of America, the American Diabetes Association, Senator John

Heinz History Center, and the University of Pittsburgh Medical Center. Dan has assisted American Indian nations in education and youth recreation programs. He was the driving force behind the American Ireland Fund, now the world's largest private organization funding constructive change in Ireland.

Tony O'Reilly, former Heinz Company chairman and co-founder of the American Ireland Fund, described Dan Rooney as "a singular man. The level gaze, the humorous yet watchful eyes, the quiet authority that he exudes are products of many tough battles, many triumphs, and some failures."

This is the man we have come to know.

Andrew E. Masich
David F. Halaas
Senator John Heinz History Center and
Western Pennsylvania Sports Museum,
Pittsburgh, PA

PROLOGUE
By Dan Rooney

George Halas and the founders of the NFL were there at the Hup-mobile dealership in Canton, Ohio, when the league was founded in 1920. Then Tim Mara, Charley Bidwill, George Marshall, Curly Lambeau, Bert Bell, Ole Haugsrud, and of course Art Rooney joined the league and brought organization and entertainment values with them. Besides these pioneer owners, the NFL was blessed with out-standing commissioners who joined the league at times of need, when their unique talents provided leadership.

I urged the league to record and preserve the history of the NFL for posterity. But now we have lost them all—the first generation who knew how it happened and put it all together. The story as I know it hasn't been recorded. This led to my purpose in writing this book—to tell the history of the NFL, the Steelers, and me, as I know it from being there and listening to my father and other men who were there from the beginning—the men who started the league, who worked, scraped, spent their money, and hammered it into reality.

So as the last man standing, the last to know from hearing, witness-ing, and experiencing that history, I guess its up to me to tell the story as best I can. Recently the league and sports world lost a key man from the past. He provided the way, the integrity, the motivation, and criticism—a giant of a man—Wellington Mara.

The Steelers of Pittsburgh, the Eagles of Philadelphia, and the Redskins, who began in Boston and then moved to Washington in 1936, all came in 1933. Their entrance was significant because it put the league in premiere cities in the east—the big market cities with not only the most people and resources, but the most knowledgeable operators who could manage the league and its teams. This story tells or recalls the difficulties the teams and owners faced to keep going, even meeting the payroll. They helped each other, and they guided those who followed later, particularly the commissioners. That first generation did what had to be done—you will see and hear what they did.

About the Steelers. How they were special. How Pittsburgh was the birthplace of professional football. Immigrants from Europe came to Pittsburgh and located along the river valley towns. Their sons became excellent football players with great high school teams. The mills and mines had teams and paid the best players so they could win. It began in Western Pennsylvania and Eastern Ohio. They forged modern football and made rules so everyone played the same game.

They began on a shoestring. John Brown, a Steelers offensive tackle in the 1960s and early 1970s, told me he began to play on cinders and finished on a carpet.

Pittsburgh grew, and football was its passion. Every young man who could play, did play. They learned the game as boys. They became the most knowledgeable fans in the National Football League.

Steelers football is special. Here's a letter I received following the Steelers-Chargers game in 1995:

January 15, 1995
Dear Steelers:

I watched as the last few moments of the AFC Championship game drew down to one play. The Chargers deflected the pass, the game was over. And as I watched the players leave the field I saw the pain in their eyes. I am a Charger fan, I'm elated that the team I love most is going to the bowl of bowls. But I'll tell you what. The city of Pittsburgh should be proud to have such a team. The players and their young coach are young, enthusiastic, talented, focused, spirited, and together. And the hospitality that poured out to the visitors—to the ENEMY was nothing short of awe inspiring. Championship is not measured by the wins or losses. True championship in pro ball requires talent, heart, courage, teamwork, and professional conductance. I could not believe what I was seeing on that field today. I saw a team that even in defeat would not let go of their championship heart. As I watched the players leave the field I said a prayer for your team. You guys are true professionals. No one can say that the Pittsburgh Steelers are anything other than a truly class A football team.

In the short term there is no remedy for the pain of a loss other than time. But as time goes by, you will realize that what I'm saying to you all today is the absolute truth. Today, in my opinion, the real champions of the AFC lost the football game, but they did not lose the championship. You have broken my heart, and you have a new fan in San Diego. Give me a towel.

Sincerely,

Patrick J. Morris

San Diego, CA

The Steelers stood together in the steel mills ready to fight World War II. They played together those weekends. After working a full shift, they practiced. They all wanted to win.

The league continued to grow. In 1960 Lamar Hunt put together the AFL. In 1966 the two leagues merged, forming a unified National Football League. In 1970 the merged league played as one. The Steelers, the Browns, the Bengals, and the Ravens joined in a division in the AFC North. You will read how this happened.

I respect all the owners and the people on the thirty-two teams. They are all friends who want the league to thrive. Jerry Richardson always says, "Protect the shield," the NFL logo. The commissioners have been vital. The players are special. They are the game. They make it. Fans love them—at least in Pittsburgh they do.

I will tell about growing up with my brothers, sometimes our arguments, but mostly our love.

Our mother was a wonderful lady. Our father was the "Chief." He directed us. He gave his advice. He sure didn't spoil me.

I'll give you some thoughts on my family. My wife, Patricia, our nine children and sixteen grandchildren. My nieces and nephews, my grandparents, uncles and aunts. It's a lot, but they were fun to be with.

In the end, I'll try to sum it up—give a view of the future NFL. Roger Goodell will probably be the last commissioner I will know. He will provide the leadership to carry on. I hope I can help him. With God's blessing, maybe.

Dan Rooney

Chapter 1

IMMACULATE RECEPTION

DECEMBER 23, 1972, dawned cold and gray, but today no one seemed to care about the weather. It had been a long time coming, the kind of day I dreamed about all my life—the first NFL postseason game to be played in Pittsburgh since 1947.

Before the kickoff, thousands of fans gathered downtown under the banners of their heroes—Dobre Shunka (Good Ham) for linebacker Jack Ham, Gerela's Gorillas for kicker Roy Gerela, and Franco's Italian Army for rookie running back Franco Harris. Other fans—those who couldn't get tickets, and there were only 50,350 who did—packed themselves in cars and buses in search of televisions outside the seventy-five-mile blackout radius. They crammed into motel rooms in East Liverpool, Ohio, and Meadville, Pennsylvania, or chartered buses and drove to Erie and jammed local American Legion and VFW halls. Anywhere with a television set. In some places, people

1

were selling seats in their own living rooms to frantic Steelers fans desperate to see us in the playoffs.

Now, as the big game against the Oakland Raiders began, the built-up emotion and excitement spilled out of Three Rivers Stadium with a volume and intensity that could be heard all the way across the Allegheny River into downtown.

"Here we go, Steelers, here we go!
Here we go, Steelers, here we go!"

Inside the stadium the noise was deafening. The concrete deck heaved so violently with every stomp of the crowd, I worried the structure might give way. For most of the game it seemed we were going to win. It had been a fierce defensive struggle; first downs were difficult to come by and both teams punted a lot. Daryle Lamonica had started as quarterback for the Raiders, but we intercepted him twice and beat him up so badly they took him out and replaced him with their young backup, Ken Stabler. Gerela's two field goals had given us a 6-0 lead when late in the fourth quarter Stabler dropped back to pass, couldn't find a receiver, and so slipped outside and ran 30 yards for a touchdown. With the extra point, the Raiders had a one-point lead.

Now the packed stands were hushed. The scoreboard told everything: Raiders 7, Steelers 6, fourth-and-10 . . . 22 seconds on the clock. It looked like we didn't have a chance. What a shame—the best season we ever had, and our first playoff game. I really wanted to beat Al Davis's Raiders.

As Terry Bradshaw and the Steelers offense broke huddle, I knew this was the last play. But when our players lined up on our 40-yard line, they didn't look like a beaten team. Bradshaw still had his swagger, still seemed as confident and fearless as ever. Turning his head from side to side, he begins the count, then takes the snap. Bradshaw's back, out of the pocket, running to his right. He ducks one pursuer, his eyes downfield, looking for a receiver. He shakes loose from the rush, then fires at Frenchy Fuqua cutting across the middle. The ball, Frenchy, and Raiders safety Jack Tatum arrive at the same place at precisely the same time. I hear the collision even from where I'm sitting—four levels up, just above the press box. That's it . . . the game's over . . . but wait! There's Franco Harris with the ball—where did he come from?—running for all he's worth along the near sideline toward the end zone—Go Franco!—stiff-arming the Raiders' Jimmy Warren, somehow staying in bounds, then in for a touchdown. Unbelievable! The crowd goes crazy—is it really a touchdown? Fans swarm the field, mobbing Franco and Bradshaw. I know there's going to be controversy, so I run down the stairs into the press box where the reporters sit stunned, looking at each other in disbelief.

Everybody is talking, yelling, trying to piece together in their minds what their eyes just saw. They're saying the ball ricocheted off Tatum's pads, shot back 10 yards where Franco made a shoestring catch. Where's the Chief? Seconds before the snap, I remember seeing him head for the elevator so he could be in the locker room to console the players when they came off the field. He missed the whole thing! The most incredible play I ever saw.

Just then the press box phone rings. It's on the wall right where I'm standing, so I answer it. It's Jim Boston, our man on the field, calling from the baseball dugout. He tells me he's got Fred Swearingen, the referee—the guy in charge of the crew officiating the game—standing right next to him. Boston says Swearingen wants to talk to Art McNally, the supervisor of the officials. I can see McNally in his usual place at the other end of the box. So I yell, "Art McNally! Art McNally! They want to talk to you!" He comes over, takes the phone, and I hear every word he says. The noise in the press box still hasn't died down, so McNally is pressing the phone to his ear so he can hear what Swearingen is saying. I don't know what the ref said, but

McNally shouts into the phone, "Well, you have to call what you saw. You have to make the call. Talk to your people and make the call!" Of course, no one had seen the television replay yet—it all happened too quick. So I turn back to the field. The officials are huddled together at the 30-yard line. I know the rule: If the ball bounced off Tatum before Franco caught it, then the play stands and it's a touchdown. If the ball bounced off Frenchy, then the pass is incomplete, the game's over, and the Raiders win. I'm straining to see the replay on the TV suspended overhead in the press box and trying to hear what the commentators are saying. They're debating the call: "Did Frenchy touch the ball? Was the catch good?" Finally, Swearingen steps away from the other officials and raises his arms to signal touchdown. The press box goes wild, papers fly, reporters yell at each other—and I run for the elevator.

Now, I don't know if the Lord is worried about every football game that's played, but in this case it sure seemed like a case of divine intervention. The locker room is a madhouse. I look for my son Artie, but he's still out on the field picking up the team's equipment and running interference for the players making their way through the swarming fans. Across the locker room I see number 32—Franco. I'm not a touchy-feely kind of guy, but after I shove my way through the crowd I can't help but give him a big hug. "Franco, that was the greatest play I ever saw!" And I mean it, too. Then there's the Chief, standing with Coach Noll, players all around them—Joe Greene, Andy Russell, Gerela, Ham, Rocky Bleier, Bradshaw, Frenchy—helmets off and grins as big as can be. Dad doesn't say anything, but Chuck steps up and makes a little speech, "You guys played a great game—I'm really proud of you! Now next week we have another big game, so don't celebrate too long." Chuck is all business. Can you believe it? He could keep his cool even during the "Immaculate Reception." That's what Myron Cope, the voice of the Steelers, later called it. At first I thought it was sacrilegious, but over time it kind of grew on me.

The Immaculate Reception is one of the greatest touchdowns in the history of football, even though Al Davis and coach John Madden complained bitterly about the call and how it destroyed their season and the Raiders dynasty that might have been. Frenchy—ever the showman—added to the controversy by refusing to give a straight answer about whether or not he had touched the ball. But Chuck Noll summed it up: "Well, if Frenchy didn't touch the ball . . . and Tatum didn't touch the ball . . . well, the rule book doesn't cover the hand of the Lord."

The Immaculate Reception changed not only the history of the Pittsburgh Steelers but the NFL itself. The Steelers went from forty seasons as the "lovable losers" to a great, great football team. Maybe the best that ever played. The national television audience for that game was huge, one of the largest ever to see a football game. The excitement of that one play captured the imagination of fans everywhere, especially throughout the far-flung Steelers Nation. The moment was so powerful, so memorable that millions of people who saw the game on TV honestly believe they were in the stands at Three Rivers Stadium that day. The Immaculate Reception immediately entered the realm of sports legend. It is still one of the greatest plays in NFL history and, for that matter, all of sports. This play and this playoff game helped establish pro football as America's passion, surpassing baseball, "America's pastime," as the number-one sport.

Of course, there are other milestones in the history of the NFL. I saw most of them, because I celebrated my first birthday the same year the Steelers played their first season in 1933. In some ways I think of myself as the Last Steeler, the last of the founding generation of the NFL. I've had the good fortune to know and work with the men who started the league—Wellington Mara, Curly Lambeau, Tim Mara, George Halas, Walter Kiesling, George Marshall, Charley Bidwill, Bert Bell, and, of course, the Chief—men who knew and loved the game and shared with me their values of hard work and sportsmanship and fairness. The National Football League has come a long way since its beginnings, and I'm honored to have been a part of it.

Pro football was born* on the muddy fields of Pittsburgh's North Side in 1892—just three blocks from where I was born forty years later. I guess you could say the game is in my blood.

---

*Sports historians agree that the first professional football game was played at Recreation Park on Pittsburgh's North Side on November 12, 1892, when the Allegheny Athletic Association squared off against their archrivals, the Pittsburgh Athletic Club. It is believed that both teams paid their players—Allegheny Athletic Association paid all-American guard William "Pudge" Heffelfinger $500 cash—ushering in a new era of professional sports in America.

CHAPTER 2

GROWING UP ON THE NORTH SIDE

I WAS BORN IN MERCY HOSPITAL in Pittsburgh on July 20, 1932, the first Rooney to be born in a hospital. The Sisters of Mercy came from Ireland during the great potato famine of the 1840s to care for the people of Pittsburgh, and I've always been proud of the fact that Mercy Hospital was the first hospital west of the Allegheny Mountains.

The Pittsburgh of my youth is hard to describe. The Great Depression of the 1930s gave way to the boom years of World War II. The city of the 1940s was a remarkable mix of natural beauty and urban ugliness, peaceful parks and industrial energy. Here, two great rivers, the cool green Allegheny and the muddy Monongahela, wind through the forested hillsides and rocky bluffs of Western Pennsylvania to merge at the point of land where Pittsburgh was established by George Washington in 1758. The two rivers form a third, the mighty Ohio, one of the world's busiest and most important waterways. At

7

the confluence of these three rivers, the city of Pittsburgh grew and prospered, becoming by the time of the Lewis and Clark expedition in 1803 the "Gateway to the West."

By the end of the nineteenth century it was one of America's great manufacturing and industrial centers. And by the time I came along, Pittsburgh was the City of Steel, building a worldwide reputation as the "Arsenal of Democracy." During the war years Pittsburgh forged its steel into shells and ships, jeeps and big guns, and every article and implement imaginable to support the war effort. Towering stacks above the mills and red-brick factories spewed black soot around the clock. As a boy I often thought day and night seemed reversed. Smoke blocked the sun during the day, causing street lights to blink on at noon, while at night, the orange glow from the blast furnaces lit the sky.

Not everyone saw this industrial energy as a good thing. One early visitor, overwhelmed by the noise and smoke and sulfurous stink, declared Pittsburgh wasn't a city at all but "Hell with the lid off." But for Pittsburghers the smell and smoke meant jobs and money. White-collared businessmen gladly changed their soot-grimed shirts in the middle of the day, while hundreds of thousands of blue-collared mill workers walked or rode inclines and trolleys from their crowded hillside homes to the factories below.

From around the world—England and Ireland, Italy and Germany, Slovakia and Russia and Poland—men and women migrated to Pittsburgh to build a better life for themselves and their families. They settled in unique neighborhoods—ethnic communities reflecting the language, culture, and character of their homelands. Although their accents hinted of their origins, these newcomers quickly adapted to their surroundings and became Americans. Yet to this day Pittsburghers identify themselves by their neighborhoods.

My neighborhood, the North Side, was different than most. It was a wonderful coming together of all these immigrant groups, although when I was growing up, Germans, Italians, and especially the Irish held sway. Sometime in the 1880s, my great-grandparents Arthur and Catherine Regan Rooney came to America from Newry, a small town in Northern Ireland. Arthur worked as a bricklayer in the Pittsburgh steel mills with his son, Daniel, my grandfather and namesake. Daniel married Margaret Murray, and in 1905 they moved with my father, Arthur J. Rooney, and his two younger brothers to the North Side, then known as Allegheny City. This thriving community, situated directly across the river from the Point and Pittsburgh's downtown, stretched northward from the Allegheny River to the hills beyond. Though the people of old Allegheny bitterly fought to remain an independent city, sprawling Pittsburgh annexed it in 1907. My father and most of his contemporaries refused to recognize the "hostile takeover" and for the rest of their lives continued to call our neighborhood Allegheny.

I knew it as the North Side, pronounced as one word: *Norseside.* We thought ourselves separate from Pittsburgh, in fact separate from anywhere. We were different and proud of it. We had our own style and our own language. Though our family never spoke what is called "Pittsburghese," there is a unique dialect that I and everyone else on the North Side understood. People would say *yunz* instead of *y'all.* In this dialect *Pixburgh* was *dahntahn.* Neighborhood parks were the most *bee-you'-tee-full.* When hungry, people asked for some *snik-snaks.* They drank *pop,* ate *jumbo* (baloney) *sammiches,* and in the summer they cooled down with flavored shaved ice from Gus the *icy-ball* man. We bundled things with *gumbans* (rubber bands). And when people stuck their noses in our business, we called them *nebby.*

I can pick out a Pittsburgh or North Side accent anywhere I travel. In Florence, Italy, at a dinner one time, a young woman started talking and my ears pricked up immediately. She talked just like me! I knew right away she was from the North Side. Our peculiar dialect has good points and bad. On one hand it defines us and gives us a sense of belonging and community, but I'll be the first to admit our way of talking can sound coarse and a little strange to a refined ear. Sometimes people jump to the conclusion that we're uneducated, but *nuh-uhh*, we're a lot smarter than people think.

My father and his seven brothers and two sisters lived in an apartment above grandfather's "Dan Rooney's Café and Saloon." My grandfather owned the entire building, located just a block from Exposition Park, a field for football, baseball, and any other game or match you can imagine. My father grew up strong and tough and streetwise. A natural athlete, he loved to compete. Baseball, football, boxing, you name it, he played it. And he played to win.

By the time he was eighteen he was out of the house and on his own. His intelligence and winning smile caught the attention of local politicians, like state senator James J. Coyne. Before he was twenty-one, Dad became chairman of the old Ward (actually Pittsburgh's 22nd Ward, but all the old timers insisted on calling it the 1st Ward, its Allegheny City designation). Dad had the Irish gift of gab, but he wasn't just a smooth talker—he genuinely loved people and they loved him. He liked nothing better than helping others and he learned to work the system to get the most for his friends and constituents. At the same time, he was a young man and actively participated in sports of all kinds, but in these early years boxing was his passion.

Carnivals came to town twice a year with professional boxers, pugs who would challenge the local talent. A tough mill worker could make $3 for every round he could go with the pros. The carney boxers usually made short work of the yokels—except when they got to our neighborhood and took on the Rooney brothers. My father and his brothers beat the carneys so many times and made off with so much money, the promoters banned them from the boxing tent. In fact, Dad was such a skilled boxer that he attracted the attention of the U.S. Olympic Committee, which in 1920 invited him to represent the United States at the Antwerp Games. My grandmother, however, was against the whole idea. Dad would have liked to go, but he was so busy with ward politics and other enterprises he declined the honor. The Olympic Committee then tapped Sammy Mosberg, a good New York fighter who Dad had just beaten in a big tournament a few weeks earlier. To everyone's surprise, Mosberg came home with the gold medal. Just to show the home crowd who was best, Dad challenged Sammy to a rematch—and whipped him again. That was Dad. I still have the silver trophy he won for beating Mosberg at the 1920 Pittsburgh Athletic Association tournament, which he prized above all others. It's not a very flashy trophy, but to him it kind of represented Olympic gold.

Boxing, football, baseball—he loved them all. But he was more than an athlete. He was a skilled organizer and a great promoter. While still a teenager he started the Hope-Harveys, a regional semi-pro football team that played home games in Exposition Park, sometimes before crowds of more than twelve thousand people. "Hope" was the name of the fire station that provided locker rooms for the team, and "Harvey" was the doctor who tended to the players' bruises, sprains, and broken noses. The Hope-Harveys hit hard, won more than they lost, and as the best football club in the region developed a loyal and vocal following in the Pittsburgh area.

As he grew older, Dad turned to baseball. He was good at it, real good. Soon he was making money by both playing for and managing teams like the Wheeling, West Virginia, Stogies. He even signed with the Boston Red Sox for $250 a month, but found he could make twice as much barnstorming with semi-pro teams in the Midwest. For more than fifteen seasons he traveled the baseball circuit, holding his own with such Hall-of-Famers as Honus Wagner and Joe Cronin, not to mention Smokey Joe Williams and Buck Leonard of the Negro League. Of course, Honus Wagner was past his prime—"athletically old," Dad said—but still the best player he'd ever seen. Cronin broke into the majors with the Pittsburgh Pirates but made history as a slugger for the Boston Red Sox. He could belt the ball a mile and made a great impression on Dad. So did Williams and Leonard, two of the Negro Leagues' greatest players. In 1925, playing in the Mid-Atlantic League, Dad batted .369 and led the league in runs, hits, and stolen bases.

He said he once tried to hold down a "real" job in a steel mill but quit at noon on the first day, wondering how anyone could work day in and day out under such harsh conditions. He had nothing but respect for the hard-working steelers who could do it, but this kind of job wasn't for him. He was back on the baseball diamond the next day.

By 1930 Dad had made a success of everything he tried: as a baseball barnstormer, a ward leader, a sports promoter, and as a horse handicapper. He saw his first race when he was eighteen years old and quickly developed an uncanny ability to pick winners. This wasn't luck. He studied the sport, knew the animals, the trainers, the jockeys, the owners. Dad always told me that betting on horses wasn't just a game of chance—he wouldn't have done it if it were—it required knowledge and skill. Some people say he was the best thoroughbred handicapper in the country. Maybe he was. All I know is that by the time he was thirty years old he had earned enough money to think about marriage and starting a family of his own.

He met my mother, Kathleen McNulty, a girl from the Point who had just moved with her family across the river to the North Side. In June 1931, after a brief courtship, they married and then honeymooned in San Diego and New York, where on a hot sunny afternoon they watched the thoroughbred Twenty Grand win the sixty-fourth running of the Belmont Stakes. Mom and Dad didn't stay away from Pittsburgh very long. Soon they moved into a small apartment above a North Side furniture store on Western Avenue, just a block from Exposition Park.

I came along the next year, the first of five brothers: Arthur J. Jr., Timothy J., and the twins, Patrick J. and John J. The Rooney clan tends to recycle the same names over and over, generation after generation, so our family tree gets a little confusing at times.

I'll admit Dad did get a little fixated about the "J"s. His "J" was for St. Joseph—the patron saint of workers—and all my brothers got the same middle name. Being the first born, I somehow escaped the "J" brand. My middle name is Milton, for my father's longtime friend, Milton Jaffe. Dad may have felt a little guilty about winning Milton's golf clubs in payment for a bet they made the first time they ever played golf together. It's a shameful fact that in many American communities of that day anti-Semitism had become institutionalized. Pittsburgh was no different. Jewish people were barred from many golf courses, so Dad took Milton to his club, Wildwood. It turned out Milton was an awful golfer. Dad said he was doing him a favor by taking his clubs. They had a great relationship and remained close for the rest of their lives.

The little garret was soon overrun with Rooney boys tracking tar, picked up from the second-story courtyard, through the house. Mom was hard-pressed to keep the place clean and us in line. Dad often was away on business, so my mother called in her sister, Alice, to help out.

I always received special treatment—a fact my brothers were not very happy about—because I was not only the oldest boy in our family but the first grandson of the extended Rooney clan. With Irish families, firstborn sons are favored, and from the beginning I was the cock of the walk. I tried to live up to those expectations, and my mother often allowed me a longer leash than my little brothers.

This sometimes got me in trouble. My earliest memory, as vivid as if it happened yesterday, is of an outing to a restaurant on Babcock Boulevard when I was about five years old. Mom, Dad, and Alice corralled Art and me—it must have been like herding cats—but I got away and found my way to a pond in front of the restaurant. I was busy floating scrap-paper boats when somehow I lost my footing and splashed head over heels into the water. The pond was small but deep—well over my head. The thing I remember most clearly is that I didn't panic. I sank to the bottom and pushed off with my feet, propelling myself to the surface, allowing me just enough time to gulp a breath of air before sinking back to the bottom again. This bobbing went on for some time until finally I let out a yelp every time I broke the surface. "Help!" . . . "Help!" . . . "Help!" Luckily, my cries attracted a man who at first thought I was a drowning dog. When he finally fished me out, I ran—without so much as a thank you—into the restaurant, jumped soaking wet into my mother's arms, and told the story. They were horrified but thankful I never lost my cool and managed to keep my head above water. They made a big deal of that, and I could tell my father was proud of me. I've always remembered the look he gave me and that special smile of his. I also remember the next time we went to the restaurant the owner had filled in the pond with rocks.

Dad had been spending a lot of time with his new football team, the NFL "Pittsburgh Pirates," which he had bought for $2,500 in the summer of 1933, about the time of my first birthday. NFL commissioner Joe Carr approached my father because the league saw Pittsburgh as a good expansion opportunity, now that Pennsylvania's "blue laws" prohibiting Sunday play were about to be repealed. Carr and the NFL owners knew Art Rooney to be the best promoter in Western Pennsylvania. They also appreciated the fact that he was a real football man—he understood the sport and would be just the guy to cultivate a fan base in the Pittsburgh market. Dad and Carr met in New York to discuss the terms for buying the franchise. Joe said he could have the team for $2,500.

Dad raised his eyebrows and repeated, "Two thousand five hundred dollars?"

"Well, if that's too much," Carr said quickly, "something can be arranged."

"No, Joe," Dad said, laughing. "Twenty-five hundred dollars is fine."

And that's how my father became the proud owner of the NFL franchise then known as the Pittsburgh Pirates.

Let me say right here, there's been a lot of talk over the years about how Dad came to buy the franchise. It's been rumored that a big $250,000 payday at Saratoga enabled him to purchase the team. That's nonsense. Dad's legendary day at the racetrack occurred in the summer of 1937, a memorable opening day at Saratoga. Thunderheads darkened the sky and a lightning strike killed several horses in a holding paddock. It was a fateful day all right—the biggest payday Dad ever had at the racetrack—but it had nothing to do with buying the team. He made the deal with the NFL three years earlier, on July 8, 1933.

As I've said, my father had many business interests by this time. While twenty-five hundred dollars might have been a lot of money during the Depression, there's no question he had the financial wherewithal to close the deal without a racetrack windfall. That's one of the reasons Joe Carr came to him in the first place. He was a good promoter and businessman, and he had money. The big payday at Saratoga might have helped keep the team afloat during the lean years of the late 1930s and 1940s, but there's absolutely no truth to the story that he bought the Pirates with his Saratoga winnings.

My father always enjoyed telling the story of the Pirates' first game. The blue laws were still in effect then, and several of the city's religious leaders threatened to shut us down if we played on Sunday. So Dad went to Pittsburgh's Irish superintendent of police, Franklin T. McQuade, and asked him if he was going to support the preachers and stop the game.

"Nonsense," he said, "I'll be sitting right next to you at kickoff—nobody will find me there."

Dad loved to tell stories, and always told us to tell the truth, but to be honest, the Pirates' first game was played on a Wednesday (the Giants beat us, 23-2), not a Sunday. The McQuade story applied to the *ninth* game of the season, which was the first professional football game ever played on a Sunday in Pittsburgh.

We didn't see Dad a lot in those days. He was on the road much of the time, visiting racetracks, promoting fights, and working hard to make the football Pirates a success. Mom thought it would be good for Dad to spend some time with us boys, but she wasn't wild about the idea of us hanging out at Dad's office at the Fort Pitt Hotel or on practice fields with rough athletes.

Once, against her better judgment, she allowed my father to take my brother Arty and me to the football training camp at St. Francis College. Dad was supposed to watch us, but he left us on the sidelines to fend for ourselves. The players kept us company. I would laugh my head off when they grabbed our hands under our legs and flipped us over. But when one of the water boys tried this stunt with me, instead of landing on my feet, I fell flat on my face and broke my nose. That same day, Arty came home with a terrible sunburn. When my mother saw us, she was quite upset and told Dad, "You'll never take these kids again—you're supposed to be watching them!" But of course, she relented and the next week we were back at training camp loafing with the players.

We did have our share of close calls. One time, a big running back got tackled right on the sidelines where I was kneeling. I would have been crushed if another player hadn't grabbed me by the collar and yanked me out of the way.

Because I was the oldest, I occasionally got to go along with Dad when the team was on the road. In 1939 the Pirates were playing a preseason game against George Halas's Chicago Bears in Erie, Pennsylvania. The Pirates had never beaten the Bears, a real powerhouse in those days. On the night of the game my father and I were in the hotel where both teams were staying. As we walked down the hallway, we heard a loud commotion coming from the Bears' meeting suite. George Halas was giving a fiery pep talk to his players. Dad always loved a good joke, so he pulled me aside and whispered instructions. As Dad ducked around the corner, I knocked on the door.

Coach Halas himself answered and looked down at me. "Young Rooney," he said, "you're in the wrong room. Your daddy's room is down the hall."

I didn't bat an eye. I was on a mission and spoke right up, "Mr. Halas, I know where our room is. My old man sent me here to tell you to take it easy on our team tonight."

Everybody in the room, including Halas, broke up laughing and the Bears' strategy session ended right there. Pittsburgh defeated the Bears 10-9, and Halas later reported to the press that I was the reason for their loss. "Young Rooney was the best offensive weapon Pittsburgh had," he said.

It might have been true. The Pirates were perennial losers. As competitive as my father was, he really didn't take the football team very seriously in those early years. He only bought it so Pittsburgh would have a major league football franchise, something he thought important for any first-class city. And nobody loved Pittsburgh more than my father. Still, he never thought professional football would vault college football and major league baseball to become America's most popular sport.

My father's reputation as a boxing promoter continued to grow even after he got into the football business. He started by organizing charity bouts on the North Side at the St. Peter Catholic School yard. In August 1933 he gained national attention when he brought the heavyweight champion of the world, Primo Carnera, to Pittsburgh for an exhibition fight—just at the time he was negotiating with the NFL for the football team. A few years later, Dad met Braddock fight-promoter Barney McGinley, and in 1937 they formed the Rooney-McGinley Boxing Club for the promotion of world-class fight cards. The two enterprising young men worked well together and became fast friends.

Meanwhile, my mother knew our little apartment was just too small for us. Just six weeks after the twins were born, while Dad was out of town, she made an offer on a big old house on North Lincoln Avenue. Only a block away, it was located between the once grand Thaw residence and the opulent Scaife mansion. Everyone knew Harry Thaw as the guy who shot the famous architect Stanford White in a jealous rage over Evelyn Nesbitt, the "girl on the red velvet swing." Charles Scaife was a rich industrialist who moved out of the North Side after the Allegheny City annexation. This street was once known as "millionaire's row," but now during the Depression in 1939 it had lost much of its luster. The house my mother had her eye on was the smallest on the block, but compared to our old second-floor apartment on Western Avenue, it seemed a palace. It had twelve rooms with high ceilings, a good-sized bathroom, and a yard in the back where we could play, a big improvement over our tarred rooftop courtyard. Mom put down $500 of her own money to close the deal on the $5,000 house. She always reminded my father that he never paid her back. Of course, she continued to run the house and everything in it, including us boys. She gave us chores, and we helped the best we could.

Dad was the disciplinarian when he was home, and he could be pretty tough. He was fair and sympathetic for big problems, but he could be difficult for smaller, everyday issues. We never cried in front of him because then he would really give it to us. "You're a big boob," he'd say, or "You're a big baby." He rarely spanked us. I remember him whacking John, who had been playing with his friend Johnny Bluecoat too close to the Allegheny River. It was winter and John might have drowned, dressed as he was in boots and a heavy winter coat.

Dad always worried about us playing near the water. He himself nearly drowned during the 1912 flood while rowing a boat in flooded Exposition Park. The boat overturned and his heavy coat almost pulled him under near the third-base line. He never let us forget it.

Sometimes Mom had to tell him to go easy on us. Don't get me wrong, my father loved us, but Mother really raised us. He was always busy, managing baseball and football teams, promoting fights, and running the Ward—anywhere there was an opportunity. He had to make a living, and he did just that.

When he was home, he loved to play with us, and play meant sports: throwing footballs, hitting ground balls, and boxing. Sometimes he would lace the gloves on us and teach us how to bob and weave, jab and hook. In the winter he flooded the backyard so we boys and all the neighbor kids could play hockey. I remember he never babied us.

A bloody nose? "Shake it off."

A hard hit ball and a sprained finger? "You're not crying are you?"

A black eye? "What did the other fella look like?"

I have to say, when he smacked grounders to us, he never held back. It was like he was playing with Ty Cobb. He didn't know how to play half-speed with kids, and when we bobbled a ground ball or complained that our hands hurt, he'd say, "What are you, a baby?" It got so we didn't like to play baseball with him.

Baldy Regan and I managed our own baseball team, the "Rooneys." We signed up my brothers and some of our neighborhood friends. We thought we were pretty good, until the day Dad came out to the field at Monument Hill to see us play. Tim popped a ball over the second baseman's head and started running for all he was worth.

At first base he turned right.

"You don't play it like that," Dad said, shaking his head in disgust.

"We play differently now," Tim objected, "not the way they played in the olden days."

Things went downhill from there.

The next inning a fly ball sailed deep into the outfield, over the heads of Tim and Colman Daly. Instead of going after it, the boys stopped and argued about whose ball it was. Meanwhile a runner scored, and my father kept shaking his head and shouted, "What are you guys doing out there?" Pat and John did the Rooneys proud that day, but it wasn't enough to make up for our team's poor play.

Pat was pitching a good game. He struck out three players in a row, which should have ended the inning, but the catcher dropped the ball on the final strike and the boy beat the throw to first base. So Pat had to strike out a fourth player.

The next inning the same thing happened. Pat threw his glove down and walked off the mound, yelling back over his shoulder, "I can't do this anymore!"

That was enough for Dad. Shaking his head, he shouted to us, "None of you guys know a thing about the game! Don't say you are Rooneys," and he walked off. We never saw him back at Monument Hill.

Our North Side group was made up of all kinds of kids. My very good friend, Richie McCabe, was an Irish boy. Then there were Babe Hugo, Dan Laughlin, and Don McGerry—they loved mischief as much as anyone. And up the block, two African-American kids, Joey and Clarence White, rounded out our little band.

I remember in 1941 we were all sitting around our kitchen table listening to the Billy Conn–Joe Louis world heavyweight fight at the Polo Grounds. Now, Billy was from Pittsburgh—they called him the "Pittsburgh Kid"—and a regular visitor to our house. He was like family and asked Dad to be godfather to his son. He was actually closer to my father than he was to his father-in-law, with whom he engaged in fistfights and kitchen brawls. Dad was a calming influence on the hot-tempered Conn and often traveled with him. In fact, he was with him that night at the Polo Grounds when he fought Louis. For thirteen rounds it seemed like Conn had the "Brown Bomber" on the ropes. Most of us were going wild, cheering for Billy, but Joey and Clarence were quiet. Then, in a sudden reversal, Louis caught Conn with a right hook that floored him and ended the fight.

Now we heard from Joey and Clarence, who were cheering. I couldn't understand it and turned to them and asked, "What are you guys cheering about? Conn's been knocked out!" They just smiled and said, "We've got to go home." They wanted to celebrate the victory with their family.

This was a real eye-opener for me. Joe Louis was their hero because he was black and they identified with him. Joey and Clarence remained friends, but in this case race trumped neighborhood loyalty. I know this sounds impossible but in those days growing up on the North Side, we didn't think about your skin color, or your accent, or what church you went to. What mattered was that you lived up to your word, pulled your own weight, and looked out for your friends.

The North Side could be a rough place. Mom warned us away from the crap games and street toughs who hung out near the playing field at Monument Hill. One time, my friends and I were playing on the Hill when a flasher accosted us. We had never seen anything like that before, so we pelted the degenerate with stones and ran for home. My Dad's youngest brother, Tom, happened to be there at the time. He was only ten years older than I, and more like a big brother to me than an uncle. When he heard the story, he grabbed my mother's car keys and screeched off for the Hill, me beside him on the front seat. The flasher was still there, dressed in a suit and tie, leaning against a telephone pole. Tom ran up to him, grabbed him by the knot of his tie and pinned him against the pole. I thought he was going to kill the guy. But Tom just looked him in the eye and said, "If I ever catch you around here again, you won't be able to walk down that hill!" The flasher never came back.

You had to know how to take care of yourself. I remember my first real fistfight. It was about even and neither of us quit. You couldn't quit—you'd lose respect. We all had our share of fights with each other, but we stuck together. We didn't worry about other boys. Our real rivalry was with the green-uniformed park police—we called them the "Grasshoppers." We would jump over the four-foot chicken-wire fence protecting the precious grass in West Park. When the Grasshoppers spotted us on the grounds, they'd chase us, especially me, whom they regarded as the leader. But I was too fast for them and never got caught, although I think they knew who I was and where I lived.

If Mom had known what we were really up to she might have worried more than she did. We worked up a routine to get pocket change to buy popsicles and snik-snaks. We'd go out to Allegheny Avenue where there was lots of traffic and make like we were beating up one of the smaller boys. Babe Hugo was a fine actor and could cry on demand. Invariably a passing motorist, usually a woman, would see the fight, slam on her breaks, and chase us "bullies" off. Babe, bawling his eyes out, would sob, "They took my lunch money!" The kind-hearted woman would give him a handful of change to make up for his loss. This scam worked fine—until the day Babe overplayed his hand. This time the Good Samaritan smelled a rat and insisted on taking Babe home to his mother. After all, she explained, "The bad boys are sure to come back and take your money again as soon as I leave." Babe beat it out of there in a hurry. After that, we learned to get our popsicles at Hite's Drug Store through other means, by hook or by crook.

Our house was the hub of activity for all the neighborhood kids. It made sense. We had a big enough backyard to accommodate all the sports, and my father used our basement to store equipment for his baseball and football teams. Plus, the five Rooneys provided enough kids for a team in any sport—though the twins, Pat and John, mostly got in the way in the early years. One time poor Pat caught a hockey stick square in the face, knocking out two of his front teeth.

Sometimes our play went beyond sports. The backyard was perfect for war games. During World War II we excavated trenches in our backyard. What we knew of war came from World War I movies, like *Sergeant York* starring Gary Cooper, so we dug trenches instead of foxholes. This wasn't a particularly good idea. When the rains came, as they always do in Pittsburgh, the trenches filled with muddy water or washed away, so we really never had grass in the backyard, just dirt and asphalt. In truth, we were oblivious to the seriousness of the war effort. While other kids got involved in scrap drives and other patriotic activities, we played war games. It only hit home how dire the situation really was when we learned that Billy Conn had thrown his silver and bronze boxing trophies into the scrap pile at Lake Elizabeth, the drained pond at West Park. That really made an impression on us.

The war arrived on our doorstep when we learned that Uncle Tom, who had survived Guadalcanal, Tarawa, and all the heavy fighting against the Japanese in the South Pacific, had been killed in the first assault wave on the beaches of Guam. Tom had always been my favorite uncle. He had enlisted at the age of eighteen in the marines right after Pearl Harbor. We exchanged many letters while he was away. Although he couldn't tell me much about the war or where he was, he never failed to offer good advice, urging me to study hard and stay in school. It took months for the navy to return his body to Pittsburgh. The marines turned out for the ceremony at North Side Catholic Cemetery and fired a rifle salute as the bugler played taps. My mother took Tom's death especially hard. He was so young, more like one of her children than a brother-in-law, and so close to me in age that I think it reminded her of how vulnerable we all were.

Our house was headquarters for much of our mischief on the North Side. We got on top of the carriage houses and garages and jumped across alleys from roof to roof making all sorts of racket. We made so much noise that our cranky neighbor, old man Hausen, would yell out his second-floor window, "Pipe down you kids and play someplace else." This spurred us on to even louder and more raucous play. Hausen told my father that we were "hoodlums" and needed to be controlled. He threatened to call the County Child Delinquency Department, but my dad just laughed it off and told us to stay out of Hausen's way. Even Aunt Alice, who stayed with us to help my mother, would shout back in our defense when Hausen went off on one of his tirades. She knew we were just having fun.

But I have to admit we did sometimes carry our pranks a little too far. One day we found a dead cat down by the river. We all looked at each other with the same idea in mind: "Let's get even with Hausen!" As we dragged the carcass back to Lincoln Avenue, we came across a bucket of tar, which Babe Hugo pointed out was just the thing we needed to glue the cat to old man Hausen's porch. The deed was done quicker than you could skin a cat.

It's difficult to describe the pandemonium that resulted. Hausen went berserk and my father looked pretty upset. Our cantankerous neighbor had been right all along. His Irish temper flaring, my father gave me a whack—the only time I can remember him spanking me. I never saw him so mad. He banished the whole crowd from the house and grounded me for a week. But Mother once again came to the rescue, saying to my father, "You're not going to let Old Hausen beat us, are you?" Dad gave in, the kids came back, and it was business as usual for the Rooneys, much to Hausen's disbelief and dismay. Eventually he moved away. To this day I'm not sure whether we drove him out or he left of his own accord.

These were happy-go-lucky days for us kids, but remember the late 1930s were hard times. We didn't know how tough things were, that so many people were out of work and going hungry. We always knew we had a place to eat and a roof over our heads, but some North Side families didn't.

I'll never forget the day a strange man came to the door and asked my mother for help. He said he was hungry, and she sent him around to the back door. Watching through the window, I saw her give him a plate of food. He turned away from me but I could see him eat. He was very hungry but he was still proud. Mom asked if he wanted more, but he shook his head no and thanked her for her kindness. She slipped him a couple dollars and I could see he was grateful. This hungry man made a big impression on me. I can see him even now—I'll always remember the face of real hunger and the value of charity.

I was often in charge of my younger brothers, but I didn't always do such a good job of watching them. Art was three years younger and he always wanted to tag along.

Mom would say, "Take him with you."

And I would say, "Mom, I don't want to take him. He's just a little kid."

Timmy was two years younger than Art, and the twins, Pat and John, younger still. Whenever my little brothers got into trouble, I was blamed, like the time we went for an outing at Senator Coyne's farm in Alison Park. Tim, Arty, and I, along with some friends, were out by the horse barns. The senator's son, Jimmy, had just mounted a high-spirited horse and was about to ride for the fields to check the fences. Somehow Timmy got under the horse, and the animal reared. Jimmy yelled, "Somebody get him!" So while the horse was still on its hind legs, I dashed in from the side, grabbed Tim, and pulled him out of the way. When we got home, Mom was furious. She blamed me for not watching little Tim more closely. She wouldn't accept any excuses, accident or no, it didn't matter—he was my responsibility. What bothered me most about the incident was that I had let my mother down.

My mother's reliance on me shaped my character in ways that stayed with me for the rest of my life. She taught me how to accept responsibility, even though my brothers often gave me a hard time and resisted my authority. Maybe that's why I've always been more comfortable being in charge and making decisions than taking orders and following along. My mother was the most important influence on my life during these formative years. When I think of her now, I wish I had been nicer to her and helped her more. I wish I had told her how I really felt—that I loved her very much.

My parents instilled in us their values. My father always said integrity and character are everything. Mom and Dad expected us to do the right thing. If my dad ever caught us saying something disparaging about a person, he would come down hard on us. "That isn't going to do you or that person any good talking like that," he would say. What my father cared about most was treating people right. If he ever caught one of us acting like a "big shot," he'd give us a hard time. He made sure we would never use the Rooney name to get special favors or to make someone else feel small. We never swore in front of our parents. Occasionally when I'd slip and swear around my friends, they would look surprised, even though any one of them could curse a blue streak with only the slightest provocation. But they knew such language wasn't me. It's kind of strange considering the locker rooms and sandlots I grew up in, but even today I rarely resort to profanity.

Our family went to church at St. Peter's every Sunday and on holy days. Mom would have gone more often but she always had little ones at home to care for. We were a Catholic family, and the church was especially important to me. I wanted to be like Father Campbell, a man who did good work and people looked up to. From the time I was in seventh grade at St. Peter's School, I thought seriously of becoming a priest myself. I started going to mass four or five times a week. No one in my family insisted, but I could tell Mom and Dad were pleased. But they didn't push me one way or the other. It was something I'd have to figure out for myself.

———————

After eight losing seasons as the Pittsburgh Pirates, coached by Dad's friends—Jap Douds, Luby DiMelio, Joe Bach, Johnny Blood, and Walt Kiesling—my father was desperate to win. It's not like he didn't invest in the team. He had broken the salary barrier in 1938 when he hired Byron "Whizzer" White, the great University of Colorado running back, receiver, and kicker, for the unheard price of $15,800— three times the going rate for the top players in the league. The other owners were furious. George Preston Marshall accosted Dad, saying, "What are you trying to do, ruin the league?" But as I said, Dad was desperate. His losing team was not only losing fans, it was losing money. He thought the Whizzer could turn the team around, but although his new star impressed fans and opponents, even he couldn't overcome the erratic coaching and general poor play of the Pittsburgh team. To make matters worse, the Whizzer only played one season, then went on to Oxford as a Rhodes scholar, then law school, and eventually to a seat on the U.S. Supreme Court. Byron White was a gentleman, scholar, and one of the greatest athletes I've ever seen.

Having failed at finding the right coach and the best players, Dad tried a different strategy: he'd rename the team and start the 1940 season with a clean slate. A public naming contest generated "Steelers," and Dad thought it a perfect fit for Pittsburgh's hard-working fans. But even a name change wasn't enough to turn the "same old Steelers" into winners. The team finished a dismal 2 wins, 7 loses, and 2 ties.

At the end of the season, wealthy New York financier Lex Thompson offered to buy the team for $160,000. Dad knew that Thompson would move the team to Boston, leaving Pittsburgh without an NFL franchise. So he and his friend Bert Bell, owner of the Philadelphia Eagles, and Thompson came up with a scheme whereby Thompson would buy the Steelers and move them to Boston, which was without a team at the time. Dad and Bell would join forces and make the "Keystoners" a team for all of Pennsylvania—a team that would play half its games in Philadelphia and the other half in Pittsburgh.

The league approved the sale, but a group of franchise owners led by George Preston Marshall of the Washington Redskins blocked the move of the Pittsburgh franchise to Boston. He wasn't about to allow my father and Bell to control an entire state. Thompson was miserable and so was my father, who found himself and Pittsburgh without a team.

None of the partners was happy with the situation, so before the opening kickoff of the 1941 season, Dad and Bell pulled a switcheroo and traded the Eagles to Thompson for the Steelers, which Thompson had renamed the "Iron Men." Dad threw out the name Iron Men and kept the Steelers in Pittsburgh, which is all he ever wanted, and Bert Bell became half owner and coach.

Bert Bell was quite a character and oddly complemented my father. The son of a wealthy Philadelphia family, Bell received the unlikely name of deBenneville, which out of necessity he shortened to Bert. Like the "boy named Sue," deBenneville learned to fight in schoolyards and locker rooms and grew up tough and strong. He excelled as an athlete, especially in football. Cut off from the family fortune once it was clear he was going to make a career of football, Bert always had money problems. He borrowed cash from his fiancée, Frances Upton (who had starred with Eddie Cantor in the popular film *Making Whoopee*) to purchase the Eagles franchise in the summer of 1933, the same year Dad bought the Steelers. Dad and Bert hit it off from the first, and I believe the whole Eagles-Steelers flip was a result of Bert's financial difficulties and my father's desire to help him out.

Now, I was just a kid when this was going on. My mother tried to explain these dealings to me, but no matter what she said, I fretted about Pittsburgh losing the Steelers.

Mother got Dad on the phone and said, "You'd better talk to Danny, he's worried you're going to sell the team."

I listened while they talked for a while.

Finally, Mother said in a firm voice, "No, I think *you* should talk to him."

So she handed the phone to me, and Dad said, "Don't worry, Danny. We're not going to sell the team. This is just something we have to work out."

To this day, the complexity of this crazy deal makes my head spin. But I can tell you, I was sure relieved when Dad told me he wouldn't sell the team. Then and there, I realized just how much football meant to me.

I was nine years old when all this happened. I played football every day after school. In fact, we called our sandlot team the "Rooneys." Joe Goetz, the man who sold Dad uniforms and equipment for the Steelers, fixed us up with brown jerseys with "Rooneys" printed on the front and a big number on the back. I can't tell you how excited we were when the jerseys first arrived and we pulled them from the box. The first one out was number 98. This was Michigan all-American Tommy Harmon's number and we all wanted it. Then Art pulled out a second shirt, and it had the same number: 98. The kids began pulling out the jerseys—all had 98 on the back. Every single shirt had the number 98 printed on it. Did Goetz's supplier make a mistake? No, there was no mistake. Goetz had an oversupply of Tommy Harmon shirts and he just wanted to get rid of them. At first we didn't know what to do. But then it came to us. We'd call ourselves the "Rooney 98s."

In the off season I worked out by hitting the tackling dummies my father stored in the basement, along with all the other Steelers equipment. One day, I got a little rambunctious and dove for an overhead pipe, intending to swing into the dummy feet first. But I missed my grab and came down hard on the cement floor. Off to Mercy Hospital we went, where the doctor set my broken left arm. My mother was nearly in tears, but I got her to take a picture of me, my arm in a sling, bruises all over my face, and a leather Steelers helmet on my head. I looked like a pretty tough customer, and it's still my favorite picture.

During the season I spent every available hour as the team's water boy. I'd do anything and everything I was asked: carry water, sweep the locker room, paint helmets, run errands.

For the 1941 season, Bert Bell coached the Steelers. It was a disaster. After four losses in a row, Bert called my father and said, "We gotta do something drastic!"

Dad said, "I know, Bert, did you ever think of changing coaches?" Dad knew this would be a hard decision for his friend and partner—football was his life.

The next day, though, Bert made a little speech to the press. "I believe it to be in the best interests of the Pittsburgh fans that I resign." With that, he moved into the front office with Dad and together they hired Duquesne University head coach Aldo "Buff" Donelli. But Donelli didn't leave Duquesne—he split his time between the two teams. NFL commissioner Elmer Layden got wind of the deal and voiced his displeasure in no uncertain terms. While Buff's Dukes racked up victory after victory, his Steelers suffered defeat after defeat. The Steelers began to question Donelli's allegiance. On one game day, the players asked, "Where's the coach?" The response came back, "He's out of town with the Dukes!" This was the final straw for Layden, who demanded that Donelli make up his mind. "Either coach the Steelers or Duquesne, you can't do both!" For

Donelli the decision was easy: he'd stay with the winning Dukes. So Dad turned again to his old pal Walt Kiesling. Kiesling won only one game that season. Oddly enough, it came against the Brooklyn Dodgers, coached by famed University of Pittsburgh head coach Jock Sutherland. Somehow Kiesling's Steelers prevailed, 14-7, playing in brutal conditions on an iced-over Forbes Field, home of the baseball Pittsburgh Pirates.

————————

In 1942 the Steelers drafted Bill Dudley, an unconventional player but a real talent. Behind big tackle Ted Doyle, who spent his days welding navy landing craft at the defense plant on Neville Island, Dudley led the Steelers to a 7-4 record, the franchise's first winning season. Dudley did everything wrong—he couldn't throw, he couldn't kick, he wasn't fast, and he wasn't very big—but he hated losing and led the league in rushing yards and interceptions. Dudley was intelligent and explosive and could have led the Steelers to more winning seasons, but he was lost to the war effort.

People wondered whether the NFL would survive World War II. So many men were called up for active duty that the teams were soon stripped of their talented players. Those left behind were generally 4-F, while others received deferments as strategic "war workers," men who worked in steel mills and defense plants.

The Steelers of the war years were a mixed crew, and it soon became evident that they would not be able to hold their own against other teams in the league. The Philadelphia Eagles were also hard-pressed to field a team fit enough to compete in the NFL. Because of the scarcity of players, the league revised its team player limit to twenty-eight, down from its prewar standard of thirty-three. This meant that many players had to play both offense and defense, with few opportunities for substitutions.

By 1943, the situation in the NFL was desperate. Necessity, they say, is the mother of invention, and never was it more necessary to be creative if the league were to survive.

By pooling their resources, the two understrength clubs might field one competitive team. The Eagles could dress nineteen players, while the Steelers had only six players under contract. NFL commissioner Elmer Layden worried the Pittsburgh franchise might not make it. He discussed the situation with my father, and soon after Dad and Bert Bell went to Lex Thompson in Philadelphia and proposed the unholy Steelers-Eagles union. They argued that it might be the only chance for the survival of the two franchises—and possibly for the NFL itself. Although shocked by the boldness of the plan, Thompson soon came to appreciate its merits. And so the "Steagles" were born, a crazy amalgamation of the Pittsburgh Steelers and the Philadelphia Eagles.

Not that bringing these two rivals together was easy. It wasn't, not for the owners, the fans, the players, and most of all the coaches. Pittsburgh coach Walt Kiesling and Philadelphia's Earle "Greasy" Neale clashed almost immediately. The hard-headed Kiesling and the flamboyant Neale successfully merged the teams, but they couldn't agree on anything—strategy, assignments, uniforms, not even what brand of coffee to drink. The whole thing would have broken apart had not Bert Bell stepped in. He proposed that Greasy run the offense, while Kies handled the defense. The men continued to battle over who would coach the guys who could play on both sides of the ball, but all in all the arrangement worked.

The Steagles couldn't even fill the twenty-eight-man roster. On a good weekend they were lucky to dress twenty-five. When tackle Al Wister came limping off the field during a close game, Greasy Neale confronted him and barked, "What's wrong with you?"

"I *think* I broke my leg, Coach!"

"Well, get back in there until you find out for sure!"

Though the Steagles didn't reach the championship game, they managed to finish the season with a winning 5-4-1 record. The problem of the merged team wasn't just with the coaches. The owners had their share of disagreements. The training camp was located in eastern Pennsylvania, and twice as many home games were played in Philadelphia. Lex Thompson dominated the partnership and insisted the Steagles headquarters remain in Philly.

This was too much for my father. He was losing his team and the Pittsburgh fans. Yes, it was true that most of the Steagles team roster consisted of former Eagles players, and Thompson had the better players when the partnership was formed, but Dad wasn't about to be maneuvered out of the business by the smooth-talking Philadelphia playboy. Dad demanded that Pittsburgh become Steagles headquarters, beginning with the 1944 season. But Thompson refused, so my father went in search of a new partner.

That's how the "Card-Pitts" were born. Pittsburgh merged with the Chicago Cardinals, a union that resulted in one of the most unfortunate team names in football history. Fans suggested that "Car-Pits" was a fitting moniker since other teams walked all over them. The miserable 0-10 season accurately reflected the talent of the combined teams. The Card-Pitts fielded medically discharged veterans, several 4-Fs, and even a few high school players. Kiesling, who promised fans that the Card-Pitts would give all rivals a "real battle," had to share coaching duties with the Cardinals' Phil Handler and Buddy Parker. This arrangement brought even more problems than the Kies-Greasy combination of the year before, but for different reasons. Kies hit it off so well with Handler that the two spent more time at the racetrack together than they did with the team. Parker's role was unclear, and to confuse matters even more, Dad brought on Jim Leonard to keep a good Irish eye on the whole coaching staff. Leonard had been a two-sport (baseball and football) standout at Notre Dame, and then played three seasons for the Philadelphia

Eagles. After leaving the Eagles, he began his coaching career by establishing the football program at St. Francis College in Loretto, Pennsylvania, then came to the Steelers as assistant coach during the war years. But not even Leonard's oversight could bring order to the coaching chaos. My father summed up the shutout season: "Merging the two teams didn't make us twice as good—it made us twice as bad!"

When the war ended in 1945, the men came streaming home and the Steelers began the rebuilding process, now under new head coach Jim Leonard. The 2-8 season convinced Dad that the team needed a real coach. In the past he had been content to hire friends and cronies, guys he could hang out with and who didn't take their card playing too seriously. Now he set his sights on Jock Sutherland, the legendary University of Pittsburgh gridiron master.

Dr. John Bain "Jock" Sutherland came from Scotland, attended the University of Pittsburgh, and graduated with a degree in dentistry. The first football game he ever played at Pitt was coached by the grand old man of American football, "Pop" Warner. Jock's real talent was not as a player, or a dentist for that matter. He was a natural-born coach. In 1919 he took charge of the football program at Lafayette College, a tiny school in Easton, Pennsylvania. In the five years he was there, he never had a losing season. In 1923, his last year at Lafayette, sportswriters named his 9-0 team the best college team in the country.

When Pop Warner resigned at Pitt, Jock Sutherland took the helm and steered the Panthers to fifteen years of dominance. Four times his teams went undefeated, and three times received the country's number-one ranking. Sutherland's single-wing attack overpowered defenses and the Pitt juggernaut rolled over all opposition, until the university's administration determined to deemphasize the football program in order to focus more attention on academics. Pitt would not attain national standing again until 1976, under Coach Johnny Majors.

Jock turned to the NFL, coaching the Eastern All-Stars against the New York Giants in 1939, then signed the following year with the ne'er-do-well football Brooklyn Dodgers. In two seasons he turned the club around, finishing a strong second behind the Eastern champs, the Washington Redskins.

In late 1941, the war interrupted Sutherland's pro coaching career. He accepted an active duty commission in the Naval Reserve and served ably until 1945. That's when Dad and Bert Bell caught up with him and talked him into taking on the Steelers. Jock played hard to get, but the co-owners double-teamed him. He didn't have a chance. Dad and Bert signed Jock to a five-year deal that included a big salary, options, and profit sharing. This was a turning point for the Steelers. George Halas remarked that Sutherland's hiring was not only good for the Steelers but a great step forward for the league. The day after the newspapers reported that Sutherland had signed with the Steelers, season ticket sales went through the roof, from 1,500 the previous year to 22,000 in 1946.

Jock Sutherland's first Steelers training camp began in mid-August, 1946, at the municipal field just outside Hershey, Pennsylvania. I was there. Already there was a fall crispness in the air enhanced by the sweet smell of chocolate that permeated everything for miles around the Hershey factory. Everyone was excited about Dr. Sutherland—that's what we called him, no one called him Jock to his face—and the new brand of leadership he would bring to the team.

We were a little worried, too. Frank Scott, the equipment man, was in awe of the man and could barely function in his presence. Just an hour before the first practice was scheduled to begin, Frank came to me with a look of sheer terror in his eyes.

"I can't find Dr. Sutherland's blackboard!"

Everybody knew that the blackboard was an extension of Jock's being, the very symbol of the man. He used it on the field to diagram every play, offense or defense.

"What do you mean you can't find the blackboard?" I asked.

"I've lost it! It must be back in Pittsburgh!" he moaned. "You gotta help me—can you drive?"

Now, I'm only fourteen at the time, but I tell him, "Sure I can drive, but I don't have a license."

Without hesitating, Frank pulled out a twenty-dollar bill and pressed it into my hand.

"That doesn't matter. Get to the department store as fast as you can and buy a board. There's no time to lose!"

I took off in Frank's old Ford and drove for town. I was a little nervous driving through the heavy downtown traffic—I'd only driven a car for short stretches in the country on family trips to Ligonier— but I found the department store okay, illegally left the car in a loading zone out front, dashed through the glass doors like a madman, and asked the first person who looked like a clerk where the blackboards were. I was directed to the basement, where I found just what I was looking for: a wood-framed blackboard about two feet by three feet, and a big box of chalk. I paid the seven bucks, threw the board in the backseat, then drove through the traffic back to camp just as Dr. Sutherland and the players jogged onto the field. Frank Scott was the happiest man I'd ever seen. He hugged me and told me to keep the change, then nonchalantly propped the blackboard up as if it had been there all the time. I'd saved the day and made thirteen dollars to boot. The Steelers used that same blackboard for the next fifteen years.

Jock turned the team around, all right. We went 5-5-1 in 1946, and in 1947 he led us to our best season ever, 8 wins and only 4 losses. We tied the Eagles for the Eastern Conference championship. On the off-week before the playoff game, our players struck for more pay. Jock and Bert held firm and would make no concessions. The players lost their bid for more money, and what's more lost their focus. The Eagles beat us and went on to the championship game.

Jock brought to the Steelers not only his commanding presence and strict discipline, but also his single-wing formation. Bert Bell introduced to the team the Chicago Bears–style T formation back in 1941, and the coaches who followed him—Donelli, Kiesling, Neale, Handler, and Leonard—stuck with it. But Sutherland was a firm believer in Pop Warner's single-wing, a run oriented offense in which the center snapped the ball to one of two backs. By 1946 the single wing was popular only with youth football and a few college teams, because most of the pros had abandoned it for the T formation. Despite the trend away from this old style of play, Jock made it work. I remember we had some great players that year: Halfbacks "Bullet" Bill Dudley and Johnny "Zero" Clement, tight end Elbie Nickel, and receiver Val Jansante.

I loved being out there, loafing with the players and working with the team. I did whatever needed to be done and didn't get paid much to do it, but I felt part of the team—I was a Steeler.

CHAPTER 3

JOHNNY U AND ME

North Catholic Halfback Problems Are Over—
Dan Rooney Is Coming

THAT'S THE HEADLINE that appeared in the *Pittsburgh Press* in the summer of 1946, soon after I graduated from St. Peter's grade school. While playing both halfback and quarterback on the sandlot, our team posted a winning record. The coach always told me I was one of the fastest boys in the school, and I was big for my age, tipping the scales at more than 135 pounds and standing five feet eight inches tall in my bare feet.

But as for solving North Catholic's halfback problems, that was a tall order. All this attention embarrassed me, and I took a lot of ribbing from my friends and teammates: "Who is this guy who thinks he's a star?" I wondered whether one of my father's reporter friends had written the story. As the Steelers' water boy, I'd met and gotten to know most of the sportswriters on the sidelines during practice. I guessed these guys were just having some fun at my expense. Even if it was a put-up job, the headline made me want to prove that I really was a good football player. I wanted to show what North Catholic could do.

Let me tell you something about Pittsburgh and Western Pennsylvania football. More great football players and coaches—from sandlots to the pros—hail from this region than from any other place on earth. Sportswriters have named Pittsburgh the "Cradle of Quarterbacks." More than forty NFL quarterbacks have come from the area, including such Hall of Famers as George Blanda, Jim Kelly, Dan Marino, Joe Montana, Joe Namath, and, of course, maybe the greatest quarterback of all time, Johnny Unitas. Willie Thrower, the first African American quarterback to play in the NFL, came from New Kensington, just up the river from Pittsburgh.

Why Western Pennsylvania—is it something in the water? I don't pretend to have all the answers. But I do know that the people of our region take their football seriously. They know and love the game. The hard-working people, many of immigrant stock, adopted the game and made it their own. The sport that evolved in Western Pennsylvania bore little resemblance to the high-brow college game that came from Princeton and Yale at the end of the nineteenth century. Western Pennsylvania–style football was physically tough, straight-ahead, and hard-hitting, reflecting the often brutal and sometimes violent realities of work in the steel mills and coal mines. Dad believed the tradition here was "Jock Sutherland, rock'em–sock'em coal miner football," which provided the people with a safety valve to blow off pent-up steam.

In this densely populated, urban industrial environment, each mill and mine forged its own self-reliant community, its own school, and its own football team. Every Friday night these schools filled their stadiums with thousands of spectators, fifteen, in fact, for every student enrolled in the school. They cheered as loud for a good block as for a good catch or run. They were knowledgeable, they understood the subtleties of the game, and God help the officials who made the wrong call.

It wasn't just a game—it was an obsession. And from the 1930s to the 1960s and beyond, Western Pennsylvania became a football factory, turning out each year hundreds of outstanding athletes bound for colleges and universities coast to coast. For many of these sons of mill and mine workers, football was the only ticket out of the hard industrial world of their parents.

Competition between the schools was intense—Monaca Indians vs. Rochester Rams, Aliquippa Quips vs. Ambridge Bridgers, Charleroi Cougars vs. Monessen Greyhounds, Westinghouse Bulldogs vs. Peabody Highlanders, Clairton Bears vs. Duquesne Dukes, and, of course, Central Catholic Vikings vs. the North Catholic Trojans. Often separated by only a hill or valley, rivalry between these schools brought the quality of play to a level unknown in other American cities. While New York and Philadelphia may have had the tax base and population density of Pittsburgh, they never had the real estate necessary for stadiums and practice fields that teams in Western Pennsylvania enjoyed.

Whatever the reasons, it seems to me, the stars aligned perfectly to make Western Pennsylvania the place for football to evolve into America's passion. And every able-bodied boy of my generation dreamed of becoming a football player, not just to suit up and be on the field, but to excel—and win.

All that summer of 1946 I lived and breathed football, working at the Steelers camp with Coach Jock Sutherland. It was hard labor but I enjoyed it, moving the team equipment on and off the field every day, lugging the heavy rag-stuffed tackling dummies, and dragging around canvas laundry bags. In addition, I exercised every day—pushups, sit-ups, pull-ups, running, and throwing footballs for accuracy and dis-tance. And I continued to play sandlot games on Monument Hill against teams like the Mt. Lebanon Bulldogs, organized by Bob Prince, the future voice of baseball's Pittsburgh Pirates. By summer's end I was in top physical condition. I may not have been the biggest or the best player entering North Catholic that fall, but I was sure in better shape than any other boy.

North Catholic was a huge school with an active athletic program where football came second only to God, though I suppose the Mari-anist brothers would argue that academics ranked pretty high, too. But if you asked any boy on campus, he'd set you straight: football was tops.

The first day of tryouts, however, took me by surprise. For some reason I didn't realize that I'd have to run against the other boys to qualify for the team. The coaches weren't going to automatically place me on the squad just because of a headline. As I walked by the practice field with my new books, Coach Al Lesniak, who was super-vising the 40-yard qualifying race, spotted me.

"Rooney, why aren't you running with the rest of the boys? Get out here!"

"But Coach, I'm not dressed for it."

"Don't give me that! You think you're too good to try out for the team? Drop your books and line up!"

I felt awkward and a little nervous being out there, since I hadn't counted on running that day. I wanted to do my best, but I felt all the other boys would have an advantage dressed in their gym gear and football shoes. I lined up wearing my regular school clothes: leather-soled oxfords, slacks, dress shirt, and a tie.

The whistle blew and I took off like a rocket, tie whipping back over my shoulder. When I crossed the finish line, I looked around and found myself all alone—I'd outrun the field.

This success kind of went to my head, so much so that the other guys gave me a hard time, "You really think you're a big shot, beating everybody, don't you!"

Their taunts bothered me, and that night I had a hard time sleeping. But the next day when I got to school everything was fine, especially when I discovered a complete uniform, from helmet to cleats, laid out for me in the locker room. Coach Lesniak had named me the starting halfback of the North Catholic Trojans' freshman squad. I've never been so proud of a uniform—not since the Rooney 98s—white jersey with a black number 11 emblazoned on the back, and white pants with black, high-top shoes. The first time I saw myself in the mirror decked out in full pads and uniform, I thought I was something, a real football player.

After just a few weeks, Joe Thomas, head coach of the junior varsity team, noticed me on the freshman squad. At our first practice, Thomas instructed the freshmen, talked about X's and O's, and shot questions at us. "Okay, who knows what the strong safety does?"

I raised my hand and told him, "He protects deep against the pass and covers short passes over the middle as well." I then proceeded to explain the assignments for every position on the board: safeties, linebackers, linemen, detailing their every move. Thomas was so impressed he moved me up to the JV team the next day. In no time I became the starting halfback on the JV squad, running sweeps out of the single-wing and Wing-T formations.

With Coach Thomas's guidance I developed as a player and a person. He taught me a disciplined work ethic, as well as the importance of integrity and character. Just as Mother and Dad had, Thomas cultivated my leadership skills. He made me responsible for team equipment and schedules, and showed me how to lead without being overbearing. He said you can be at the top of your game without being cocky or acting like a big shot. His own life was a lesson in humility.

Everyone at North Catholic knew that Thomas was the most talented coach at the school, yet the administration withheld from him the honor of being head football coach. Instead of giving him the football job, they put him in charge of the basketball program. This was a bitter pill for Joe, but he handled it with dignity and grace. To his credit, he brought home three state titles in basketball, even though football was his real passion. There was some sort of power struggle within the administration that I was too young to comprehend. They didn't want to pay Joe the salary a head football coach commanded and couldn't agree on a contract.

I remember the day he came to me and said he was leaving the school to accept a job at Chaminade, a Marianist brothers Catholic high school in New York. I was crushed and couldn't understand how North Catholic could let such a great coach and teacher get away. It didn't make any sense to quibble about a few dollars when you had a guy like Joe, who knew what it took to win and at the same time could inspire, build character, and change lives.

Actually, Coach Thomas was not much older than the students he was teaching. Like my uncle Tom, he had served in the Pacific during World War II, and he loafed with the high school players like one of the boys. But he mentored us both on and off the field, and next to my own parents, had the most profound influence on me. On the field, he encouraged me to develop my throwing skills to complement my running game. He told me I had real potential as a quarterback and got me as much playing time as he could. When the freshman squad went up against Millvale, he suggested I play as halfback/quarterback. Even though I was technically on the JV, I was still a freshman and eligible to play on the freshman team. The game was a real mismatch, and I felt like we could run circles around the Millvale players. By the end of the game, I had scored six touchdowns.

Standing in the end zone, Joe Thomas saw everything. As I scored the last touchdown, I saw him laughing. It was embarrassing for the Millvale team and the freshman coach should have pulled me from the game, but both he and Thomas wanted to see what I could do. That was the last game I ever played with the freshmen.

In fact, about three weeks after the Millvale game, Thomas had my good friend Miles Bryan and me dress for the varsity game. We didn't get much playing time but we learned a lot. At the end of the season we wondered if we'd get our varsity letters and were a little disappointed when we didn't. But the coaches made the right decision. They knew we could wait and that our heads would swell if we got those letters too soon. We still had our whole high school careers ahead of us.

During my freshman year I played halfback out of the single-wing. In my sophomore year I played quarterback in the Wing-T formation, because the coaches knew I could throw. In the Wing-T the quarterback, flanked by a fullback and wingback, takes the ball from the center, and can throw or run, but usually hands off. I really enjoyed running the ball—I was fast and had good moves. Though they made me quarterback, I would have preferred playing tailback, where I could both throw and run the ball.

We had a good season my sophomore year, going 7-1, but just as school closed for the summer, I came down with rheumatic fever. The illness really laid me low. I was confined in a hospital for two months and hated being there. I felt sorry for myself, and I know I made life miserable for my entire family, especially my mother. The only bright spot in my hospital stay was that a Steelers backup quarterback, Joe Gasparella, often visited me. We talked for hours about art and architecture. He'd been an excellent student at Notre Dame and an accomplished artist and architect, and taught me the fundamentals of drawing and design. I remember he brought sketchpads and I would refine my drawing skills, perfecting shading and perspective. I began to think that an architecture career might be in my future.

When they took me to the hospital I was nearly five feet ten inches tall and weighed 147 pounds. When I finally got out, I found that though I had gained weight, I had stopped growing. In fact, I never grew another inch.

It hurt having to sit out my junior year, but I came back strong as a senior, helping lead the team to a winning season. I played quarterback, but the coaches also used me on defense, either as corner or safety. By this time I had muscled up to 163 pounds, and had regained my speed and stamina.

In the fall of 1949 we played one of our toughest games against the Aliquippa Quips on their field, a dark hole in the ground we called the "Pit." Now, they were pretty smart and knew that the lights only worked on one side of the field—the Aliquippa grounds crew fixed it that way. Their coaches opted to wear dark brown uniforms, while we had to wear our white jerseys. They could see us, but we couldn't see them. When the Quips pulled a reverse on the first kickoff, I honestly didn't know who had the ball until their runner crossed the goal line. It was a seesaw battle. I had a pretty good game and our whole team played their hearts out, but we lost by a touchdown.

Later we played Ambridge, a mill town just across the Ohio River from Aliquippa. These guys were tough, the sons of steel workers. They had scouted us and the word was they had to stop me to win the game. We played them to a standstill, but we were short-handed—my friend Richie McCabe, a great running back, was out sick. Our coach, John Karcis, emphasized the running game and wouldn't let me pass the ball.

With the score tied, I shouted to the coach on the sidelines, "Let me throw!"

"All right, throw from the A formation!" he yelled back.

Although we hardly ever practiced from the A formation, we moved steadily downfield. We got close enough to kick a field goal, but our kicker shanked it in the final seconds and we tied the game, one we should have won. It was a heartbreaker.

The last game of the season we played Central Catholic, a match up that would determine the City Catholic championship. We pulled out all the stops for this game, trick plays we hadn't tried all season. We scored the winning touchdown when I faked the handoff to Miles Bryan, driving up the middle, and flipped the ball to Ray Dilalla, the halfback. Ray ran up the left side for the winning score and the North Catholic crowd went wild. Winning the Catholic championship for us was better than winning all-city. There was a real rivalry between Catholic schools in those days.

Central Catholic was our main competition. With 1,300 boys, they had a big talent pool to draw from. North Catholic had 1,000 boys, and we always gave Central a run for their money. But during my senior year, St. Justin's, a little Catholic school perched atop Mt. Washington just across the Ohio River from the North Side, produced one of the best quarterbacks to ever play the game. About 250 boys attended St. Justin's and they weren't in the same league as the big schools. We never played them except in exhibition games. The kids at North Catholic considered St. Justin's a "B-league team."

Their quarterback was a gangly six-foot junior named Johnny Unitas. The local sportswriters at first thought him awkward and his throwing style clumsy. But this kid could get the job done. Coaches marveled at his drive, and spectators thrilled to his impossibly long passes. His Lithuanian immigrant father, a coal truck driver, died when Johnny was only five, and his mother worked two jobs to keep her five children fed and clothed. Johnny wore the same hand-me-down shirt and pants to school every day. They were poor, but then so were many other people who lived in the blue-collar Brookline–Mt. Washington neighborhood where he grew up.

Johnny was a year behind me in school. An indifferent student, he starred on the St. Justin's football team from the start. Some people said he was too skinny to play and thought he'd get hurt. But he had these enormous hands that seemed to wrap around the ball, enabling him to do amazing things, like his patented jump pass over the middle.

Just before the start of school in 1949, his junior year, Johnny accidentally shot himself through the middle finger of his right hand—his throwing hand—with a gun he had borrowed when he learned a burglar might be prowling the neighborhood. On the first game of the season, his bandaged and splinted finger stuck straight up from the ball like a baseball bat. Incredibly, on the first series of downs, he let loose with a pass that must have traveled fifty yards in the air, resulting in a touchdown. Little St. Justin's triumphed that day and the Unitas legend began to grow.

I regret to this day that I never got the chance to play against Johnny Unitas. North Catholic played St. Justin's in an exhibition game during my junior year, when I was still convalescing. Johnny had dismantled our defense and embarrassed mighty North Catholic. Everybody at school talked about this upset and how well Unitas played. I realized what a talent he was when I watched the game film.

When the Pittsburgh All-Catholic Team was named at the end of the 1949–50 season, many of my friends expected to see my name as the first team quarterback. I'll admit I expected it, too. I got razzed pretty good by my buddies for only making the second team. But looking back on it, it shouldn't have come as a surprise to anyone that Johnny Unitas, this phenomenal young athlete from St. Justin's, was voted first team quarterback instead of me.

Actually, I didn't take it too hard. I had other things on my mind. At the Arch Pharmacy, working behind the counter dispensing ice cream cones, I noticed a girl I'd known at St. Peter's in seventh grade. I thought she was pretty cute, with her red hair and green eyes. My heart skipped a beat every time I saw her, and I looked for excuses to go to the drugstore. This was the only place I saw her, because after St. Peter's she attended St. Mary's Catholic Girls School, while I went on to North Catholic, an all-boys school.

One day Richie McCabe's older brother, Jumbo, asked me, "Don't you have a girlfriend?"

"Well," I said, "there's a girl who works at the corner drugstore—Patricia Regan—and I wouldn't mind going out with her."

Jumbo didn't waste any time fixing me up. Soon, I got a call from Patricia. She asked me if I'd escort her to the St. Mary's junior prom.

"I don't know how to dance," I said.

"I'll teach you."

"Okay, I'll try. We'll see how it goes."

After that I'd walk her home from work, and sometimes we'd sit on the porch of her house, just across the street from Allegheny High School, and talk for hours. We never did practice our dancing, but it didn't matter. When I picked her up on the night of the prom she looked like a million bucks. She wore a long, yellow dress and a white orchid, and I came dressed in a formal white jacket. I can't say whether we looked good on the dance floor, but a number of friends commented that we made a nice-looking couple. My good friend Joseph "Bud" Rieland and his girl accompanied us. Bud couldn't drive a lick, so I drove Mom's Buick.

And so we started dating. Aunt Alice, who watched over us kids like a sergeant, wasn't happy about this. She didn't think the Rooney boys should have anything to do with girls. She delighted in enforcing the midnight curfew and would tell Dad if I didn't make it. The twins stuck up for me and always swore that I'd gotten in a minute before the big grandfather clock chimed twelve.

Everyone in the family knew I was getting serious about Patricia, maybe a little too serious. My mother told me I should date other girls, and I dutifully went on some double dates. One time I went on a date with Miles Bryan's sister Mary. Miles and his girl were in the front seat, while we sat in the back. Mary squeezed my hand, but I wouldn't squeeze back. The next day, Miles said to me, "Mary tells me you're the worst date she's ever had—you must really like that redhead."

On summer nights, I'd borrow the keys to Mother's Buick (my parents always bought Buicks from McNulty's North Side Buick), pick up Patricia, and drive out to North Park. We told our parents we were going to see the stars, but in those days, the sky was totally obscured by dense clouds of smoke from the steel mills. We took it on faith there were stars up there, but we never actually saw them. It didn't matter. The real show was the city lights and the red glow of the mills reflecting off the clouds. And the sounds—blast furnaces, heavy equipment, and the banging of coupling freight trains—echoing against Pittsburgh's hillsides, a constant reminder that this was the city of steel, the industrial strength of the nation.

By the time of our senior proms, Patricia and I were definitely an item and everyone knew it. The question was which prom to attend, the one at St. Mary's or North Catholic? Both schools had scheduled their events on the same night, so we decided we'd just have to go to both. Bud Rieland kidded me in front of our homeroom class, "Rooney can go to two proms—but he can only get one girl!"

This excited a lot of comment. Remember, Father Campbell had been counseling me on becoming a priest, and I had been attending morning mass quite often. I took my faith very seriously, but the more I saw Patricia, the less appealing the priesthood seemed. My faith wasn't diminished, but my career choice was in serious doubt. This change of heart was not lost on the priests at school.

In my religion class, the priest announced, "There's a guy in this class who's losing his vocation, just because some little girl smiled at him." All the boys turned in their seats and looked at me with big grins. I guess it was obvious who he was talking about. Needless to say, I did not pursue a religious calling.

Once I graduated from high school I set my sights on college. And not just any college—I wanted to play football. Now, my dad was never very keen on college. He believed there was plenty of honest work that didn't require a degree. He wasn't opposed to education, but Pittsburgh was a hard-working, blue-collar town, and there were lots of good jobs and money to be made for anyone willing to work. Dad owned a piece of a construction business at this time and since I shoveled and mixed cement in the summers, he asked if I wanted a job with the company.

I told him, "No! I'm not working a shovel the rest of my life!"

"Well, do you want to work at the racetrack?" he said.

"No, I'm not interested in horses."

This conversation took place in Dad's office in the Union Trust Building in downtown Pittsburgh. People were coming and going all day because that's where the Steelers sold their tickets and where my father conducted business for his other enterprises. That day it just so happened that longtime family friend and business associate George Anderson was in the office. He overheard my father tell me that I didn't need to go to college.

"You have to be kidding, Art!" he said. "It's obvious your son is a bright young man. You're making a big mistake. He's capable of succeeding in college, and these days he'll need a college education no matter what he's doing—including football. He has to go to school!"

For the next few weeks, with my mother and several teachers as allies, Anderson worked on my father until he finally gave in and allowed that a college education might be a useful thing—so long as I went to a good Catholic school. Of course, there was never any question about that. I considered College of the Holy Cross in Massachusetts, St. Bonaventure in southwestern New York, and St. Vincent College and Duquesne University in the Pittsburgh area. I ruled out Holy Cross pretty quick because it was too far away from home. My father and Uncle Dan—Dad's brother who was ordained Father Silas, a Franciscan priest—took me to St. Bonaventure for a look around. Father Silas was the athletic director at the college and cleared the way for my enrollment.

As we drove through the campus, Father Silas, with a sweeping gesture toward a dormitory, said, "And here's where Danny will be staying."

I knew then and there the fix was in. They had already decided that I would be attending St. Bonaventure in the fall—without even talking to me. My father usually got his way, but I was pretty strong-willed myself and told them St. Bonaventure was out—I wouldn't go there.

Dad relented and said, "Then you can go to St. Vincent. They have a decent football program."

St. Vincent College had financial trouble in the 1930s, and Dad had guaranteed a note that kept them going. Whatever strings he pulled, I got enrolled there right away and spent time at their summer football training camp. I wasn't happy being there, mostly because it wasn't my choice. What's more, the football coaches there had the most complicated playbook I'd ever seen. Just imagine, when the quarterback called a play in the huddle, he didn't call just one play. He had to give each running back explicit instructions on his assignment. Instead of just calling out, "Fox Green on three," a play everyone would understand, I'd have to say, "Fullback block, halfback two, wingback eight, pass on three." It was unnecessarily complicated. In a real game the refs would have flagged them for delay of game twenty times a half.

It didn't take very long before I'd had enough. I returned to Pittsburgh, and on my own signed up at Duquesne University. This school was close to home, and it had a football program. When I told Dad about it he wasn't pleased. He had worked hard behind the scenes to get me into St. Bonaventure and then St. Vincent, only to have his efforts undone by his thankless son.

He told me to go to the Steelers training camp, at that time held at St. Bonaventure, and report for work—all the kids who worked there were back in school. After two weeks of exile I came home again.

Of course, he knew my principal concern was being near Patricia, but he felt I shouldn't be making decisions affecting my career and livelihood based solely on affairs of the heart. To his dismay, I stood my ground. With the help of the Duquesne dean of admissions and graduate assistant Merle Gilliand (later PNC Bank chairman and life-long friend), I arranged my class schedule so I could attend football practice in the afternoons.

It worked out. My first year at Duquesne went well, both academi-cally and on the football field. Professor Ebert, my business law in-structor, told the class, "We've had a lot of Rooneys coming through here, but none of them were as smart as this guy." He had taught my father, my uncles, and a host of Rooney cousins. Who knows if he was just laying it on thick so I would work harder or whether he really meant what he said. But in any case, my youthful dream of becoming an architect or businessman had given way to football.

Then I learned that Duquesne would drop its football program af-ter the season. This news was disappointing. I had made the decision to attend Duquesne partly because of its football program.

Villanova representatives had come to Pittsburgh to recruit while I was still in high school. They were interested in North Catholic ath-letes. They asked Miles Bryan, Dave Winter, and me to come to a ho-tel to discuss the possibility of attending Villanova. As we wrapped up the meeting they asked me to stay and Miles and Dave left. They of-fered me a scholarship to play for Villanova. I told them I'd let them know. I didn't tell anyone but my teammates. After a couple of days I called and thanked the Villanova recruiters but told them I was going to Duquesne.

After Duquesne dropped its football program, I received another call from Villanova. They said the scholarship was still there if I would come and play for them. I discussed this with Patricia. She said she would back me in any decision I made. I called the coach at Vil-lanova and thanked him but said I was staying in Pittsburgh.

At Christmastime 1950 I surprised Patricia with an engagement ring, which my mother had helped me select the week before. We married two months later, during Duquesne's winter break.

The wedding was a Rooney affair from beginning to end. Uncle Dan, better known as Father Silas, married us at St. Peter's Church, with Father Campbell and Father McAnulty (later president of Duquesne University) attending at the altar. Bud Rieland, my North Catholic classmate and good friend, stood as best man, while Art served as my groomsman. The twins, Pat and John, were the altar boys. Tim filmed the proceedings. Barbara Foley served as Patricia's maid of honor, and her sister Mary Regan (later my dad's devoted secretary for almost forty years) acted as bridesmaid. As soon as we exchanged our wedding vows, we turned to see St. Peter's packed with our friends and family. It seemed the whole North Side had jammed into the old stone church. In fact, more than half the people in the church were related to us—parents and siblings in the front pews, behind them uncles and aunts, and scores of cousins. Also in attendance were neighbors, the mayor, ward leaders, Coach Kiesling, Billy Conn, and Dad's business associates. Patricia's father, Martin Regan, brought the builders union, Local 249. As we walked down the aisle to leave the church, Uncle Paddy Muldowney stepped out of the back pew, grabbed Patricia, and gave her a big kiss. I was afraid all the guys would line up and do the same thing, so I took her by the arm and steered her out the front door, where we were pelted with rice. Tim, with a 16 mm camera on his shoulder, walked backward recording every detail, for I was the first Rooney son to be married—a pretty big deal for our family. Even Aunt Alice, who wasn't too keen about us getting married so young, wanted the event recorded for posterity.

One thing I was sure about: this was the right decision, the best I ever made.

———————

In the summers I worked for my father's construction business, but I also continued to go to the Steelers training camp, not as a water boy, but as the camp manager. Jock Sutherland had died suddenly after the 1947 season, and John Michelosen had taken over as the Steelers head coach, never deviating from Jock's single-wing formation even though the rest of the league had adopted the more versatile T formation. During the four years Michelosen coached, the Steelers lost more than they won, but we had many talented players, including running back Bobby Gage, running back–punter Joe Geri, and Hall of Fame defensive tackle Ernie Stautner.

I handled the payroll, wrote the checks for laundry and other services, arranged schedules, sent the water boys on errands, and even negotiated player contracts—mostly draft choices, since in those days the majority of players signed before camp began. I was only nineteen at the time and not legally old enough to sign a contract. But I did the negotiating just the same. I'd call Fran Fogarty in Pittsburgh, our business manager, and he'd give me advice on how much I could spend. Then I'd sit down and talk with a player. "You're now making a hundred dollars," I'd say. "We'll give you a hundred and ten." After I had negotiated the salary, along with incentives and benefits, I took the contract to the coaches to sign, because Dad was hard to pin down. He'd be at his office in Pittsburgh, at the racetrack, but almost never at the St. Bonaventure camp.

Patricia and I set up housekeeping in a small apartment. Married life was good for both of us. She helped me become a better student and challenged me intellectually. My grades improved and I even made the dean's list.

Though I was married and had many responsibilities I don't think you could say that I was yet a mature adult. I remember the first time

I brought Patricia home to my parents' house after we were married. My mother had prepared a beautiful dinner. Dad and my brothers were arrayed around the big round dining table at their usual places. Our father held court. "Now, we can't talk football all night," he said, so we tried to change the subject, but after about ten minutes of current events and small talk, the conversation always came back to football. The family was on its best behavior, as Mother and Aunt Alice wanted to make a good impression on Patricia. Everything seemed to be going just fine, until my mother brought out the dessert: vanilla ice cream, my favorite.

That's when things started to go downhill.

Fourteen-year-old Tim piped up, "You have vanilla ice cream for him, don't you! How come you don't have chocolate! You never think about us!"

"What are you talking about?" I asked.

But Timmy wasn't backing down. He stood up, his chair falling over backward, and put up his fists. I jumped up, too, and squared off with him. We were both ready to fight. But before any punches were thrown, my mother came between us and swept Timmy back with a broom, knowing him to be the instigator.

All the while Dad just laughed, while my mother shook her head, mortified by our boorish behavior in front of her new daughter-in-law. Dad never did mind our sibling rivalries—in fact, he seemed to encourage them.

In some ways Patricia and I grew up together. We had met in grade school, started dating in high school, then married at age nineteen while I was still in college. There's nothing like the responsibilities of marriage to hasten maturity. We made mistakes, of course, but we learned and matured together.

About this time, Father Campbell came to me and asked if I would help out at St. Peter's by coaching the boys' football team. My twin brothers, Pat and John, were stars on the team, Pat as a receiver and John as halfback. Coaching these kids taught me a lot about football, and about people. Most of the boys came from working class families. Their parents wouldn't, or couldn't, come to our games or practices. The fathers worked long days, and the mothers stayed at home with kids and never-ending chores. The kids learned to look out for them-selves. More than anything, these boys needed their self-esteem bol-stered, and they turned to me for guidance and encouragement. To-gether, we fixed up a locker room they could be proud of. Inevitably, some of the boys would get banged up—football is a contact sport and these kids often played with wild abandon. So when they got hurt, I'd take them to either Allegheny General or Divine Providence Hospital, where they never charged us for emergency room visits and the doctors were very kind to them. Sometimes I provided first-aid myself. Maybe I shouldn't have. I recall, one boy had his finger dislo-cated and I pulled on it and manipulated it back into place. It worked out okay, but I later learned this was dangerous. His ligaments might have gotten out of alignment, requiring surgery. But somehow we got along without serious mishaps.

As young as I was, in some ways I became a father figure to the boys. We practiced under the North Side's street lights on a field in West Park, near Lake Elizabeth. One night I noticed some of my older players harassing a youngster. They wanted his money, and the little guy wasn't able to defend himself.

I confronted the oldest boy and said, "Mike, I'm really disap-pointed in you. Bullying a little kid isn't you. Just stop it!"

Another kid hanging out in the park came up to me and, looking me straight in the eye, sneered, "Just who are you to be telling us what to do?"

I stared him down and said, "Listen you little punk, you'll end up down at the police station if you don't watch yourself. Let this kid go!"

My boys hung their heads and retreated. I never saw them bullying anybody ever again. These weren't bad kids; they just needed direction and a firm hand.

Patricia and I had to see to all the team's needs, including getting the boys to the games. We piled kids and equipment into our beat-up Chevy station wagon. It must have looked like a clown car, but we made it work. We sewed numbers on old, repaired Steelers' jerseys, which had to be altered for the little guys. I painted the receivers' helmets white so the quarterback could see them, and the linemen's helmets green so he'd know they were ineligible to catch passes. Patricia asked the family living in the apartment above us if we could use their washing machine. She wanted to dye a batch of uniforms. She filled up the machine with green dye and crammed in twenty pairs of pants. The pants turned green all right, but you can guess what happened the next time our neighbors did their wash. For weeks after that, we saw their green-tinted sheets and underwear flapping on the clothesline outside our apartment. But they were Irish, too, so nobody seemed to mind.

My first season coaching went well. St. Peter's won nine games and lost only one. The loss came from St. Joseph's and Coach Danny McCann—he was a real character and I know played a ringer or two. The most frustrating part of coaching these youngsters was that I knew too much about the game and expected too much of the boys. I always wanted to kick the ball in obvious kicking situations, but they didn't always have the leg for it. I also tried to teach them a "gap-8" defense, which required great discipline: the players had to stick to their positions and not get distracted. Unfortunately, the rival coach at St. Cyril's also knew the gap-8 and mowed us down with his bigger players. Once I figured out how to use the talent we had, we started winning. We even beat St. Bernard's, the powerhouse of the league.

I was proud of my boys. They never cried, and they learned to take their losses like men. Those kids didn't know it, but I was learning as much from them as they were from me. These lessons would stick with me the rest of my life and prepare me for my career with the Steelers.

While I was coaching at St. Peter's, Father Campbell was keeping an eye on me. He continued to counsel me on spiritual matters, while I advised him on the sports program at the school. I remember when the new gym was built. No provisions had been made for installing backboards on the basketball court. Father Campbell asked me to put them up, attaching them directly to the wall at both ends of the court. But I knew they couldn't be hung that way, because the players needed to run under the basket. When Father Campbell saw us installing them two feet away from the wall, he asked, "What are you doing?"

When I explained the rules of the game to him, he said, "You don't know anything about basketball. You're a football player!"

"We're putting them up right," I countered.

"No you're not!"

"Well," I said, laughing, "we have a book that tells us where the baskets go."

"The book is wrong," he said, "but go ahead and do it your way, but don't make a mistake." He reminded me of my father.

Father Campbell was a great man and a real inspiration to me. He instilled in me the confidence I needed to run a sports program. I may have given up any hope of being a priest, but he taught me the importance of give and take in working with people.

My coaching at St. Peter's, under Father Campbell's guidance, gave me the opportunity to work with children. I remember 1952 was a busy year for me. I was a junior at Duquesne taking a full load of classes, working part-time jobs, and acting as manager for the Steelers summer training camp. That year our first son, Art II, was born—another major milestone for the Rooneys and a time of celebration for our extended families. To me, having a family has been more important than anything else in life. More important than lifting the Lombardi Trophy over my head at the Super Bowl or being inducted into the Hall of Fame.

While I attended Duquesne and began a family, Johnny Unitas, a year behind me in school, explored several universities with strong football programs. First, Notre Dame looked him over, but the coach there told him, "I like what you do, but you're so skinny! I mean, you're five eleven, and a hundred thirty-some pounds—we're liable to be sued for manslaughter if we played you." Turned down there, Johnny went to Indiana University in Bloomington with the same result—they didn't want him. All the coaches thought he had talent but believed he just wasn't big enough to survive in a top-flight college football program. They suggested he try Ivy League schools which, with their smaller players, might be able to use him. But Johnny knew in his heart that his academics weren't up to Ivy League standards. The University of Pittsburgh, in his own hometown, offered him a scholarship. So with my friend Richie McCabe, he went to take the entrance exam. Richie passed, but Johnny didn't, something that bothered him for the rest of his life.

Finally, the University of Louisville in Kentucky, not known as a big-time football school, picked him up in 1951. Coach Frank Camp started the gangly freshman quarterback in the fifth game of the season against St. Bonaventure. Johnny's team gave this strong football school a run for its money, losing only in the final seconds by a field goal. Despite the loss, Unitas led Louisville to a winning season. The university deemphasized football the next year, however, and reduced the size of the squad to only nineteen, requiring players to play both offense and defense. In the single-platoon system, the rules allowed for the substitution of only one player, usually the quarterback, but Johnny excelled at defense, too, hauling in more interceptions and making more tackles than any other player. He carried Louisville on his broad but skinny shoulders.

At first Johnny was placed on academic probation, but once he settled in, he applied himself to his studies and turned into a better than average student. Despite his obvious football talent, the Louisville team couldn't compete with other schools. By the time he graduated in 1954, the team's record was undistinguished, but Johnny racked up 3,000 yards in passing, despite the fact he spent much of his senior year on the injured list. A hairline fracture of his right ankle limited his playing time, forcing him to wear high-top shoes that became his trademark in later years.

When the 1955 NFL draft took place in January, Unitas wasn't on anybody's—not the coaches' or the sportswriters'—radar.

At that time, Ray Byrne and I managed the draft for the Steelers. Ray was a part-time undertaker at his family's funeral home, and the butt of many jokes. People would ask, "What are you doing, drafting a bunch of stiffs?" But we had a good system. Ray was a thorough researcher, corresponded with all the college coaches, and kept detailed records of all the players. I'd telephone the top kids around the country, using the operator as a kind of secretary to connect the calls. Weeks ahead of time, we developed our priority list and strategy for our draft picks. Of course, we ran these by Dad and Walt Kiesling, whom Dad had brought back to coach in 1954, but by and large they deferred to our judgment.

Now, the Steelers already had three quarterbacks. The starter, Jim Finks, was pretty good—in 1952 he had thrown for 2,307 yards and led the league with twenty touchdowns. His backup, Vic Eaton, was a versatile player who could do just about anything but wasn't outstanding in any position. In 1953 Wellington Mara, owner of the Giants and my father's good friend, had revealed that New York hoped to acquire quarterback Ted Marchibroda, the St. Bonaventure and University of Detroit standout, if he was available. So Dad snatched him up in the first round that year, even though we knew he would sit out two years for compulsory military service and rejoin the team in 1955.

The Steelers were now quarterback rich. Even so, as the draft unfolded I kept an eye on Johnny Unitas. I knew he had great talent. With his wiry strength and those big hands he could fire a football like a bullet and knock down any receiver who wasn't ready for the power of his passes.

By the ninth round, Johnny still hadn't been selected, so I told Ray Byrne, "We gotta get this guy now 'cause we don't want him playing against us."

Kiesling thought we were nuts. Though Johnny's six-foot-one-inch frame had filled out with 170 pounds of muscle, he still looked scrawny. But it didn't make any difference. Kies didn't like him, believing he was "too dumb to play."

We took him anyway, the 102nd overall draft pick. Can you believe it? The best quarterback in the history of football, and we got him in the ninth round for $5,500. Given Kiesling's dislike for him, that money wasn't a sure thing.

Just weeks before the draft, Johnny had married his high school sweetheart, Dorothy Jean Hoelle. Dorothy wisely advised that they should move in with her mother in Pittsburgh to save rent money. They really didn't know where their next meal would come from. The Steelers contract seemed a blessing, but it wouldn't kick in until the season began, so John worked a construction job between college and the opening of the Steelers camp in July.

When camp opened, Johnny and Dorothy were expecting their first child. Patricia and I now had three children: Art, Patricia, and

Kathleen. I was working hard, juggling babies and jobs. I was so busy Dad thought I should give up my volunteer coaching job at St. Peter's, even though he knew how much this meant to me. But he was right; I had too much on my plate. At the camp I was negotiating contracts, taking care of all the logistics, and working out the game schedules with Kiesling.

I'll say this about Kiesling. He was a real football mentor for me; he knew the game inside and out. In his playing days, he was an ox of a man whose leather helmet never looked quite big enough for his enormous head. He was a legitimate Hall of Famer as an offensive tackle, and a lot smarter than he's given credit for. He was an extremely able mathematician, and it always amazed me how he could work out complex calculations in his head. At the same time, that head of his was awfully hard. When he got an idea, he latched on to it like a pit bull and no one could change his mind.

Unfortunately, he had made up his mind about Unitas—even before camp began. I was responsible for drafting him, but that didn't mean Kies was going to play him, a fact that became painfully clear as the summer progressed. Every day Johnny showed up on time, eager to play and show what he could do. He would have his uniform on, helmet in hand, standing on the sidelines. He'd do the exercises and run with the team. He did his homework and learned the plays, but Kies never let him take a snap. For some reason he thought John wasn't smart enough to quarterback a team in the NFL. Just a dumb kid from Mt. Washington. Jim Finks and others had taken to calling Johnny "Clem Kadiddlehopper," after the goofy country bumpkin made famous by comedian Red Skelton on his popular television show.

I didn't see all that was going on that summer because I wasn't out on the field, but my brother Tim and the twins, John and Pat, were out there every day watching the players and following their progress. Especially Unitas. At the end of the day, Johnny stayed on the field and ran the boys through the passing plays that the team had just practiced. My brothers were all good receivers and were amazed at the precision of his passes and power of his arm. They came to me all the time, talking about how good he was. They had watched the other quarterbacks—Finks, Marchibroda, and Eaton—and believed that Johnny was the best of the bunch, hands down. They urged me to talk to Kies, and I did.

But remember, I just turned twenty-three and I'm arguing with a guy, a Hall of Famer, mind you, who's twice my age and who had taught me just about everything I knew about professional football. My father's admonition to "let the coach . . . coach" rang in my ears as I pleaded with him to give Unitas a chance. Nothing doing. Kies could not be persuaded.

Finally, I saw it was no use and gave up, but my brother Tim didn't. He was furious and hand-wrote a twenty-two-page letter to Dad. My brother Art was in the office when the letter arrived. He said Dad just shook his head as he read through the pages of Tim's diatribe. "That fresh punk thinks he's some sort of football expert," he said, then wadded up the letter and banked it into the trash can against the wall. Art allowed that Tim had a point, but Dad wouldn't hear it. "I like John, too," he said, "but Kies is the coach, let him do his job."

It might have been better to have let Kies cut Johnny at the beginning of camp rather than stringing him along through the final preseason game before letting him go. Now he didn't have a chance to sign on with another team, at least for that year. I know Johnny unloaded on Kiesling when the coach asked him to turn in his notebook and clear out. He told Kiesling that it wouldn't have been so bad to have been cut if he had screwed up, but he never had a chance to show what he could do. Kies said that in a thirty-three-man squad, he couldn't afford to have four quarterbacks. Someone had to go, and he had to stick with the more experienced men. Johnny never forgave him.

Without any prospects in the NFL, Johnny grabbed a job on a pile-driving crew at a steel mill in Aliquippa. He also signed on with the Bloomfield Rams, a semi-pro sandlot team in the Steel-Bowl Conference. They played at Arsenal School in Lawrenceville, on a grassless field covered with gravel and lead musket balls that still remained from the explosion of Allegheny Arsenal at that very site during the Civil War. The conditions were brutal. I can't imagine how hard it must have been for him, with his wife and new baby, his hopes for an NFL career crushed.

Sometime later that year, I was driving my father and Kies down West Liberty Avenue on Pittsburgh's South Side in the old Chevy station wagon. Dad was in the front and Kies in the back. A car sped past us. I recognized Unitas's distinctive flat-topped crew cut and prominent ears.

"That's John Unitas in that car," I said.

"Catch him!" Dad said.

At the next red light I pulled up next to him. I could see John had his wife, Dorothy, and their daughter, Anna, with him.

Dad rolled down his window and yelled out, "John!"

"How are you doing, Mr. Rooney?"

"I hope you catch on with a team and have a great career!"

"Thank you, Mr. Rooney," John replied, genuinely pleased.

Kies slumped in the back seat, looking like he'd just swallowed a large spoonful of vinegar, and growled, "He'll never amount to anything."

The light changed and we both pulled off, going our separate ways.

After a year of sandlot ball and backbreaking physical labor, John finally caught a break. He had written to every team in the league begging for a tryout. Somehow one of his letters surfaced on the desk of General Manager Don Kellett, just at the time the Baltimore Colts were looking for a backup for their rookie quarterback sensation out of Oregon, George Shaw. Johnny signed on for $7,000, $1,500 more than I had offered him to play for the Steelers. He told Dorothy, "Look at it this way, hon, I didn't get cut, I just got a fifteen hundred dollar raise." In preseason, Johnny impressed scouts and sports-writers, but it didn't look like he was going to get any playing time as long as Shaw held the number-one quarterback slot. But in the fourth game of the 1956 season, Shaw got buried in a pile of Chicago Bears linemen, tearing ligaments in his right knee, knocking him out for the rest of the year.

Johnny got the call, and the rest is history.

His career with the Baltimore Colts is the stuff of legend. In my mind, he's by far the greatest quarterback in football history. His brand of football—brilliant play-calling, pinpoint passing, showman-ship, and never-say-die intensity—changed the game just as television came into its own. The 1958 NFL championship game between the Baltimore Colts and the New York Giants remains one of the greatest games ever played. Nationally televised, forty-five million Americans watched transfixed as Unitas drove his team downfield in overtime to defeat the powerful Giants. Unitas threw that day for 349 yards, sur-passing Redskins' Sammy Baugh's title game record that had stood for more than twenty years. Johnny's two last-minute drives brought home viewers to their feet, cheering, and made America passionate about Sunday football. The game would never be the same.

I was one of the forty-five million people watching the game on television that historic day, and I remember thinking, "How did we ever let Johnny Unitas get away?" The Unitas story stays with me as a reminder that sometimes you have to trust your instincts, even if those around you, people you know and trust, don't agree. In this case, my brothers and I were right; Kies and Dad were wrong.

CHAPTER 4

COMING OF AGE:
"THE GAME'S CHANGING, DAD"

SINCE THE LATE 1940S and early 1950s the game had been changing. The upstart All-American Football Conference, a serious rival to
the NFL, boasted teams like the Baltimore Colts, San Francisco
Forty-Niners, and Cleveland Browns. These teams looked to capture
a piece of the NFL fan base, so they opened their play books—nothing was sacred—and experimented with innovative offenses and defenses. The Cleveland Browns, coached by Paul Brown, had pioneered a new pass offense, one that confounded opponents and
wowed the fans. The Browns broke the game wide open with their
aerial attack, which by itself could win games.

In 1949, after much soul-searching and debate, the NFL owners
agreed to merge with the rival AAFC, but only the three strongest

teams—the Colts, Forty-Niners, and Browns—would be brought into the fold. These teams brought with them their exciting new play.

In the summer of 1950, my father arranged for the Browns to play one of their first NFL games against the Steelers. This preseason contest would be played in War Memorial Stadium in Buffalo. So far the Browns had annihilated the opposition, averaging 35 points a game and racking up a 4-0 record. They shouldn't have taken us by surprise, but they did. They never stopped passing. They went on to beat us 41-31, but the game was never close.

Later, in the regular season, we played the Browns again, this time on our home turf at Forbes Field. At halftime as I walked off the field into the tunnel with Bob Davis, our wide receiver and defensive end (they played both ways in those days), Davis yelled over to the Browns players, "Hey, you guys pass so much you should be playing with the Celtics!" They just laughed, and went on to beat us again, 17-0.

On our bye week, Coach Kiesling and I decided to see for ourselves how the Giants' defense would handle the Browns' passing game. I gassed up Dad's Buick (the one that advertised on the doors, "North Side Buick" in gigantic letters and "Pittsburgh Steelers" underneath in barely readable print) and drove the two hours to Cleveland. I enjoyed that trip, especially spending time with Kies as he talked about the defensive options the Giants might use against the Browns. Our coach, John Michelosen, had utilized a 6-2-3 defensive formation (six men on the line, two linebackers, and three deep backs) in our game against the Browns. It didn't work. They picked us apart.

But the Giants-Browns game was a real eye-opener for me. The Giants' coach, Steve Owens, pulled the two ends off the front line to protect against the short pass, while the safeties covered long. The four guys up front had to stop the run. This is the first time we'd seen a 4-3 defense. It was a revolutionary change. They shut down the Browns' passing attack, forcing them to rely on only their ground game. The Steelers—and everybody else—saw the writing on the wall and had to adapt. The passing game was here to stay, and the 4-3 defense was the way of the future.

When we got home to Pittsburgh I told my father all about what I'd seen in Cleveland. "The game's changing, Dad," I said, "and we've got to change, too!"

Years later I learned that a young Johnny Unitas had also watched the Cleveland Browns play that season. He saw the same thing I did, but while Kies and I focused on defense, Johnny was inspired by the offensive opportunities. And he was just the quarterback to apply the new style of play introduced by the Browns and the other NFL newcomers.

But change came hard to the Steelers. Dad continued to defer to the coaches and, let me tell you, these guys weren't on the cutting edge of football theory. Coach Michelosen held on to Jock Sutherland's old single-wing, while everyone else had gone to the more versatile T formation. But as hard as he tried, Michelosen was not Jock Sutherland. His team lacked the punch and creativity that Jock's exhibited.

After Michelosen went through two losing seasons among his four as coach, my father decided to replace him, this time with Joe Bach, who had last coached the Steelers in the mid-1930s. He was a tough customer back then. He had the brass to stand up to my father and once squared off with him during a four-day train ride home from Los Angeles. The Los Angeles Bulldogs, a West Coast semi-pro team, had badly beaten and embarrassed Pittsburgh in an exhibition game. Dad hated to lose, especially to these bums. The fight broke out when he tried to tell Bach how to do his job, and only ended when Dad delivered a right cross to Bach's jaw, knocking him out cold. Back in those days, my father hadn't made up his mind to let coaches do the coaching. Dad fired him at the end of a disastrous season. Actually, Joe threatened once too often to resign, and this time Dad called his bluff and accepted.

Don't get me wrong, Bach was a pretty good coach in those early years, but time had passed him by. In his second stint with the team, 1952–53, Bach had lost the old fire, racking up an unimpressive 11-13 record. Suffering from loss of stamina and the effects of diabetes, Bach remained mired in the past, grudgingly adopting the new T formation over the single-wing.

In 1954 Dad brought Kies back for the third—and last—time. With him came his old coaching staff, those who were still around. Remember, these are the same guys who let Unitas go. They were a conservative bunch. It seemed like every play was right up the middle. Bob Drum of the *Pittsburgh Press* invented a little ditty that he'd sing in the press box at the start of every Steelers game:

"Hi-diddle-diddle, it's Rogel up the middle."

Kies was as predictable as the Pittsburgh streetcar schedule. And it was true: every team in the league knew running back Fran Rogel was coming up the middle. Kies saw the game as a test of strength and will. We didn't need to outsmart or outmaneuver the other teams— we'd drive straight ahead and overpower them with Pittsburgh-style football.

By now Dad had decided not to interfere with the coaches' play calling, but even he grew frustrated with Kies' one-dimensional attack. He pressed the coach to try a pass on the first play of the game.

"Look Kies," he said, "I want you to throw on first down."

The coach resisted. "No, you don't throw the ball on first down!"

But Dad insisted and was so certain that this opening play would make Steelers history, he told all the boys in the press box to watch for a pass.

Drum said, "I'll believe it when I see it."

Dad chomped his cigar and smiled. "You just watch—I guarantee it."

Pittsburgh quarterback Jack Scarbath faked to Rogel, dropped back, and fired a long pass to Goose McClaren, who caught the ball and streaked down the field for an 80-yard touchdown. But the refs called the Steelers offsides, and the ball came back. Kiesling reverted to his old routine, and on the next play Rogel ploughed up the middle for a one-yard gain.

Drum chanted, "Hi-diddle-diddle, Rogel up the middle."

Nothing would change on Kiesling's watch, although he accepted the T formation and the new defenses that would allow the Steelers to be competitive in the new NFL.

———

The NFL had come a long way since its humble beginning at the Jordan and Hupmobile car dealership in Canton, Ohio, in 1920. The days of Jim Thorpe and Joe Carr were long gone. Carl Storck came in as the third president of the NFL in 1939. He was barely able to hold the fractious owners together. According to my father, the only contribution Storck brought to the NFL was the big box of candy he brought to every league meeting. Otherwise, the league was in a holding pattern until Elmer Layden took over in 1941. Layden, one of the Four Horsemen of Notre Dame fame, was a real football guy who had coached at Duquesne University and Notre Dame itself. Right out of the chute he set out to correct the league's negative public image.

At this time college football was king, and the press corps had little respect for the professional game. Layden put an end to ill-considered player and team endorsements of liquor, cigarettes, and laxatives. He obsessed over details as minute as socks, sloppy uniforms, and the color of stripes on the officials' shirts. The league's tarnished image needed to be polished and protected. The owners charged Layden with holding the league together during the difficult war years when the demand for manpower stripped the teams of their best players. Try as he might, however, he failed in his effort to get President Roosevelt to officially endorse football as a morale booster, as he had professional baseball. Baseball had seen a surge of interest following the president's call for Americans to attend games and continue with traditional recreational pursuits. He said, "The enemy will have won if we give up our American way of life." But the president didn't give professional football the same consideration he gave baseball, and Layden and the owners worried the league's survival hung by a thread. The commissioner encouraged the Pittsburgh-Philadelphia partnership that gave birth to the Steagles and, later, the disastrous Chicago-Pittsburgh "Card-Pitt" union.

When the AAFC announced its launch in 1945, the owners expected Layden to combat the rival league, which threatened the very existence of the weakened NFL. Following the owners' lead, he opposed any consolidation with the new league, but he really didn't have the stomach for an all-out fight with the well-financed and well-organized AAFC.

By 1946 the discouraged owners—all of them, including my father, had lost a good deal of money—clamored for change. Layden was exhausted and ready to call it quits. But the Redskins' George Preston Marshall wasn't about to wait for Layden's resignation. Marshall wanted him out, the sooner the better.

The owners agreed not to renew Layden's contract and turned to Steelers co-owner and my father's friend, Bert Bell. Bell's personal finances had suffered during the war years. By 1945 my father had purchased some of Bert's share of the Steelers and gained controlling interest. He did this not to control the team, but because he wanted to help Bert out any way he could. When Bert agreed to become NFL commissioner, however, he knew he'd have to surrender his stake in the Steelers to avoid a conflict of interest. Dad suggested, "Let Barney have it!" As nearly as I can figure, when the deal was done, Barney

McGinley, Dad's old friend and boxing club partner, became part-owner of the Steelers.

The details of this arrangement never mattered much to my father. When Barney died, his interest went to his four children. His son, Jack McGinley, was the most involved of any of the McGinley family in the Steelers organization. Jack had married my father's youngest sister, Marie, the same Aunt Marie who watched me as a young boy. In many ways, Uncle Jack reminded me of my father—his love of Pittsburgh, his sense of humor, his devotion to family, his belief in the goodness of people, and his integrity.

We all got along, and it's always seemed to work. Today, the Steelers' board of directors is still composed of Rooneys and McGinleys.

Bert Bell lifted the league to a new level. First, he set out to bring unity and collegiality to the owners. He was, after all, one of the guys. He knew them, and he knew how to work with them. United, they could take on the AAFC. Bert brokered a compromise with the AAFC strongmen, millionaires like actor Don Ameche and producer Louis B. Mayer, cutting loose the weaker teams and bringing the Colts, Forty-Niners, and Browns into the NFL. The Browns were owned by Mickey McBride, a friend of my father's, and he had money. These well-financed teams represented big markets with growing fan bases. The AAFC was dissolved. The new NFL in 1950 comprised thirteen teams, representing cities from coast to coast: Chicago Cardinals, Cleveland Browns, New York Giants, Philadelphia Eagles, Pittsburgh Steelers, Washington Redskins, Baltimore Colts, Chicago Bears, Detroit Lions, Green Bay Packers, New York Yanks, Los Angeles Rams, and the San Francisco Forty-Niners. NFL football had truly become a national sport.

Dan Rooney Café & Bar on General Robinson Street on
Pittsburgh's North Side, ca. 1910. (COURTESY STEELERS)

In the 1920s Art Rooney Sr. (*standing fourth from right*) organized, played for,
and managed the Hope-Harvey semi-pro football club, the predecessor of the team
he took into the NFL in 1933. (COURTESY STEELERS)

Dan Rooney, age ten, with broken arm
suffered after playing with Steelers
equipment stored in the basement
of the family home.
(COURTESY DAN ROONEY)

Top right: During his high school career at North Catholic, Rooney was named
second-team quarterback on the All-Catholic League Team, behind St. Justin
High School quarterback Johnny Unitas. *Above:* Rooney, right center (no. 33),
with the North Catholic High School team. (COURTESY STEELERS)

Bride and groom,
Patricia and Dan Rooney.
(COURTESY DAN ROONEY)

Dan Rooney's family: Art, Patricia (with John), Pat, Kathleen (holding Joan), Rita, Jim, Dan, and Duffy, 1969. (COURTESY DAN ROONEY)

Dan Rooney with grandparents, Dan and Margaret Rooney, ca. 1955.
(COURTESY STEELERS)

In Ireland, Patricia with her grandmother,
Mary Duffy, who reclines on a "kitchen bed,"
1971. (COURTESY DAN ROONEY)

Patricia and Dan Rooney, ca. 1960.
(COURTESY DAN ROONEY)

The Chief and Dan Rooney, 1962. (COURTESY STEELERS)

The Rooney family: Art Sr. and Kathleen center, with sons Art Jr., Pat, John, Tim, and Dan, and their families. (COURTESY DAN ROONEY)

Owners meeting, ca. 1960.
Seated: George Preston Marshall, unidentified, Joe "Jiggs" Donoghue, Bert Bell, Edwin Anderson, and Art Rooney Sr. *Standing:* George Halas, Tex Schramm, Ted Collins, Charles "Stormy" Bidwill, Victor Morabito, Walter Wolfner, Jack Mara, and Don Kellett. (COURTESY STEELERS)

Co-owner of the Steelers and later NFL commissioner, Bert Bell. (COURTESY STEELERS)

Steelers players and coaches with friends, ca. 1960.
Standing: George Halas, John Michelosen, Commissioner Pete Rozelle,
Art Rooney Sr., Buddy Parker, Father Silas (Dan Rooney). Holding Art Rooney
are Johnny "Blood" McNally and Bill Dudley. (COURTESY STEELERS)

Rooney brothers Art Jr., Pat, Tim, John, and Dan huddle with the Chief
at the Steelers office at Three Rivers Stadium, 1975. (COURTESY STEELERS)

Art Rooney Sr. kicks off, as Dan Rooney holds, at the groundbreaking ceremony for Three Rivers Stadium. (COURTESY STEELERS)

Chairman Art Rooney Sr., President Dan Rooney, and Vice President Art Rooney Jr. at Three Rivers Stadium, 1975. (COURTESY STEELERS)

Bell's greatest contribution to the NFL was his belief that the teams had to be competitive. He often said, "On any given Sunday, any team in our league can beat any other team." He knew instinctively that the fans weren't going to stand for one team dominating other teams for years on end. The fans would lose interest. The lesson of the Cleveland Browns dominating the AAFC—they had dropped only four games in four years—was not lost on Bell or the NFL owners.

The answer, Bell saw, was the draft. He had realized this even while co-owner of the Pittsburgh Steelers. Now he could do something about it. Bell pushed for the draft system we know today. Teams with the worst records got the first picks of eligible college players. The neediest teams got the cream of the crop and could rebuild their franchises with fresh talent. In the mid-1930s when Bell (then owner of the Philadelphia Eagles) first suggested the draft system now in use, the owners thought giving the best player in the country to the worst team was crazy. Winning teams participated in the draft as well, but got the lower picks. The draft was the catalyst for the development of the modern scouting system. Teams needed good intelligence in order to make wise selections. A winning team no longer depended on coaches alone.

Scouts—those men out in the field talking to college coaches, compiling statistics, and meeting players—became increasingly important. Draft picks became a valuable commodity and could be traded just as players were traded. The team-building strategy going on in the front office became as important as the coach's strategy in the locker room and on the field.

This change came slowly to the Steelers. I was there, helping select draft picks, and I can tell you we didn't always make good choices. In 1956 we drafted a guy named Gary Glick with our bonus pick. Each year since 1937 one team would get a bonus pick. With it you got the very first pick of the draft—theoretically the best college player in the country. Once the team got its bonus pick, it dropped out of the lottery.

By 1956 there were only three teams left in this lottery: the Green Bay Packers, the Chicago Cardinals, and the Steelers. In April, at the Bellevue Stratford Hotel in Philadelphia, with an eager press corps hovering around, Bert Bell placed three pieces of paper, one marked in pencil with an X and the letters B-O-N-U-S, into a gray felt fedora. I stood right next to him and saw where he placed the three slips. When it came time to draw, he looked at me and said, "Danny, you pick first." Of course, I nabbed the bonus pick. Bert wasn't cheating. Maybe he didn't realize I was paying such close attention, but in any case, I wasn't about to let a gift like this pass us by. The Steelers needed all the help we could get.

But did we take advantage of this golden opportunity? No! A few weeks earlier, Kiesling had gotten a letter from the coach at Colorado A&M in Fort Collins, telling us that he had a player, a defensive back named Gary Glick, who he considered a great talent. Kies was a big defensive guy, and he decided we needed Glick more than anybody since Whizzer White.

From the time the coach's letter arrived, I argued with Kies until I was blue in the face. "The guy's okay. But we don't need to take him as our *bonus* pick. He's a sleeper. Nobody knows a thing about him. In fact, *we* don't know a thing about him. We don't have film, nobody's seen him, all we've got is a letter from a coach we never heard of. We'll take him, if you want, but we don't need to take him with our bonus pick. We can pick him up in the third round."

Kies could not be moved. With the wild-eyed passion of a treasure hunter who's just found the pot of gold, he yelled back, "No, this guy is good and everybody is going to know about him. Everybody will want him!"

I couldn't believe it, so we went to my father. We both made our cases. My father said, "You have to let Kies take the guy he wants."

"But, this is crazy," I said. My father just shook his head. He always used to do that. That's how he was with my brother Tim about Johnny Unitas.

We went ahead and used our bonus pick on Gary Glick, passing over future Hall of Famer Lenny Moore and quarterback Earl Morrall. Pittsburgh sports reporters scratched their heads over the Steelers' draft strategy. Bob Drum wondered, "Who is this Harry Stick?"

Weeks later Mary Regan, Patricia's sister and the Steelers' secretary, told me the film had come in from the starry-eyed coach in Colorado. I took it up to the projection room on the eighth floor of the Union Trust Building in downtown Pittsburgh. Fran Fogarty, Coach Kiesling, and I huddled around the projector to watch Gary Glick, the number-one draft pick in the NFL. Our hearts sank. We saw a wind-swept stadium with open seats, no benches for the players to sit on, dogs running across the field. Glick and the Colorado team were okay, a half-decent team. When the film flapped to an end, we went down to see Dad in his office on the first floor. We didn't say anything, but he could read our faces.

"So he didn't look very good, did he?"

There was nothing for us to say. Let me add, however, Glick was a good player. He made our team and played safety, 1956–1959, and remains the only defensive back in NFL history to be drafted number one overall.

Even though I was proven right about our bonus pick, it would be years before the Steelers would figure out the NFL draft and use it to build a championship team. We had a lot to learn.

It may have been the same old Steelers, but it wasn't the same old NFL. Bert Bell had seen to that. Bell recognized that America's growing love affair with television would impact the game in every way.

Not only would teams be earning record profits thanks to television rights, but the game's live audience would be bigger than ever thanks to Bell's astute management of the blackout rule.

In 1949 the league's television rights amounted to less than $100,000, but by the end of the 1950s those same rights were worth millions. Nearly every American home had a television set as the 1960s began. Bell worried that the medium could kill football, as it had crippled minor league baseball and boxing, as spectator sports. Why would a football fan buy a ticket to a game and sit out in the cold when he could see the same game in the comfort of his living room? Bert's solution was to black out all home games in a seventy-five-mile radius from the stadium to ensure the seats would be filled every Sunday.

This led the U.S. Justice Department to investigate whether the NFL's policy violated antitrust laws. It took two years to determine the legality of home-game blackouts, but on November 12, 1953, U.S. District Court Judge Allan K. Grim handed down a decision in Philadelphia allowing the league to impose television blackouts. Baseball continued without a blackout policy, steadily losing television market share and gate receipts, while football earned more of both.

Bell was the right guy at the right time. The son of a Pennsylvania attorney general, he was a credible witness in court. He knew how to work members of Congress, and he kept owners united on the blackout policy and other contentious issues.

I remember at league meetings how Bert would always get his way, even if he had to resort to crying. Michael MacCambridge, in his fine book *America's Game*, recounts a wonderful story told by Baltimore Colt's owner Carroll Rosenbloom:

When [Bell] wanted to get something done and he wasn't getting his way, Bert would sit there and slowly take out his false teeth and lay 'em on the table. His face would pinch up and he would look sooooo old, so tired, and he would start to cry. He was a great crier.

George Preston Marshall would be walking up and down, screaming and exhorting everybody, and finally they would see that Bert was crying and somebody would say, 'For [Goodness] sakes, George, siddown, you're annoying Bert.'

I remember such scenes. You never felt you had been bullied into a decision. He built consensus, and there was this "we got to stick together, boys" atmosphere that got things done, even with such strong-willed men as George Marshall, George Halas, Paul Brown, Wellington Mara, Dan Reeves, and Curly Lambeau, and, of course, my father.

The idea of a players' union was one of the toughest issues. And, believe me, the players had some legitimate gripes. They wanted, for example, a second pair of shoes (if you look at the Steelers locker room today, each player must have thirty pairs, with shoe manufacturers tripping over themselves to give them more). My father, being from Pittsburgh—a strong union town—supported the idea of a players' union and the value of collective bargaining. He knew that withholding this right wasn't fair and would only antagonize the players. The issue found its way to Congress, where several key legislators championed the cause and pressured the league to accept a players' union. Bert testified before a congressional committee, stating publicly that the league would recognize the union. But the owners hadn't agreed to it, and my father knew it would be a hard sell. Halas and Marshall were dead set against it. Rosenbloom was on the fence. By the 1956 fall league meeting, Bert needed nine of the twelve owners to vote in favor if the resolution was to pass.

Easier said than done.

My father thought we had the votes, but when we walked into the league meeting room (I remember because I was still in my early twenties, and just starting to regularly attend league meetings) I saw George Marshall with his arm over Carroll Rosenbloom's shoulder. George Halas was with them.

"Uh-oh, we've got troubles," my father said.

When the union resolution was advanced, Marshall slammed his fist on the table and shouted, "You can't do that! We can't give in!"

With that, my father stood up, and reasoned, "Listen, if we want any credibility, we have to recognize this union because Bert Bell has told Congress we would. If we don't do it now, then there'll be all kinds of trouble, and the pressure will be terrible. Congress will be after us every chance it gets."

"What are you talking about?" Marshall asked. "What are you trying to do? We don't have to recognize the union."

"We *have* to recognize the union," my father repeated. "Bert went before Congress and said that we would recognize it. And if we don't, then he's finished as a commissioner because they'll say he has no clout, no authority, and can't get the big deals done."

By this time we had eight votes in favor. Bell took Rosenbloom aside, and after he had finished working on him, Carroll came over, too. Only Halas and Marshall voted against the union.

This is the first really important issue I faced at an NFL board meeting. My father had put forward the resolution to recognize the players' union, and it was great seeing how Bert and Dad worked together. These old friends had been around and knew how to get things done.

Dad sent me to represent the Steelers at the first union meeting. He said it would be a good learning experience for me. Each team sent a player representative. Our players sent their teammate Charlie Bradshaw, who was later president of the union (he was replaced by Jack Butler as the Steelers' player representative). The players not only wanted a second pair of shoes, they wanted to get paid for preseason games.

These were reasonable requests and the NFL did the right thing by recognizing the union and agreeing to needed reforms. Looking back on this meeting, held in 1956, I realize now how important—

and historic—it was. For the first time, owners and players from each team sat around the same table to air grievances, discuss issues, and make the NFL a stronger organization. The owners and the players realized there had to be give-and-take if the league were to be successful. We understood for the first time that we were all in this together. It's a much different world today. The Players Union is well established; it's a professional, well-run organization, and the owners take seriously the issues and recommendations it brings forward, doing their best to cooperate on matters of policy.

I was twenty-four years old then, and I can't help but think that I'm the last of the NFL executives who attended that first meeting—all the others are gone.

Bell understood the importance of protecting the league's image. He strictly enforced rules against gambling. Some people may think this odd, but my father supported him and was, in fact, his strongest ally. Betting on sports, especially where a conflict of interest might exist, went against my father's grain. He knew gambling by players, owners, and insiders could ruin the NFL just as it had almost ruined baseball. With Bert, he worked diligently to ban it. Bell came down hard on known gamblers with fines and suspensions. If a player knew of illegal gambling but didn't report it, he'd be suspended, too.

Bell believed the game had to be kept clean and fair. During televised games, he made certain that network cameras would not focus on fights between players. Gratuitous violence had no place in professional football, and no player should have his career ended by a cheap shot or unnecessary roughness.

Bert was a big phone man, he was always on the phone, encouraging, cajoling—and even coercing, if necessary—owners, coaches, and players. He knew the game. He was a real football man and wouldn't allow anything that might hurt the game.

In the 1950s on-field officials did not travel outside their own regions. On the West Coast, West Coast officials ruled. Likewise in the East. Many sports fans suspected the officials were biased in favor of their regional teams.

In a game played on the West Coast in 1955, we were leading 26-24 with less than thirty seconds remaining in the game. My old high school buddy, Richie McCabe, a defensive back, was called for unnecessary roughness. Richie had placed his hand and knee on a downed player. He barely touched the guy, but the Los Angeles–based referee called a fifteen-yard penalty, which stopped the clock and gave the Rams time enough to bring on their field goal unit and win the game. Kies went berserk. LA Coliseum security guards had their hands full keeping Kiesling from tearing the officials apart with his bare hands. I'd never seen him so angry.

Following the game, the Steelers lodged a formal complaint, and the very next season the NFL began randomly assigning officials outside their home regions. This may seem a small thing, but it went a long way to making the game more fair and credible. It's remarkable the Steelers were the ones to blow the whistle on the refs because, in fact, more officials came from Western Pennsylvania than any other part of the country. Just as with players and coaches, our region with its football tradition produced more talent than any other place. You'd have thought we would have enjoyed a built-in advantage in the case of the officials, but it was more important to us to have a fairly called game. I should say here most officials agreed with this change. They wanted fair games, too.

The Steelers of the 1950s and 1960s weren't as bad as their record indicated. We had plenty of talented players and an abundance of genuine characters. In fact, odd characters seemed drawn to the Pittsburgh team ever since my father began the Hope-Harveys, then the

Pittsburgh Pirates, and now the Steelers. In the 1930s Johnny Blood, whose antics entertained the fans, his teammates, and sportswriters, ruled the Pittsburgh gridiron. His real name was John McNally, an outstanding college player who had to change his name in order to moonlight with professional teams. He adopted the name "Blood" after seeing the Rudolph Valentino film *Blood and Sand*. Johnny Blood's free spirit could not be bridled. He caroused, even stole motorcycles if the occasion required it. My father took a chance with Johnny, first as a player, then as a coach. Though he would find his way to the Hall of Fame, during his time in Pittsburgh his performance on the playing field paled in comparison to his performance off the field.

For raw talent, the only player of the era I saw who could hold a candle to Johnny Blood was Bobby Layne. Bobby came to the Steelers in 1958 after quarterbacking the Detroit Lions to two NFL championships. He was the most competitive player I ever knew. The day he first arrived in Pittsburgh, I picked him up at the airport and drove him to our training camp. He questioned me the whole way, wanting to know everything about the players, the coaches, and the city. From the time his foot hit the ground on the field at South Park, Bobby Layne was in charge. He was that kind of guy, always in command.

Within weeks he brought the team together. The players were close, both on and off the field. He'd hang out with them, eat with them, play cards with them, and drink with them. We began to think he might be spending too much time with them, and the drinking got to be a problem. He could carouse all night and be up for the game the next day, but his teammates couldn't.

Layne could do anything. I remember once we played the Giants and he threw only ten passes the whole game, but three of them were for touchdowns. He could run the ball, too. He was smart—one of the smartest quarterbacks we ever had—and he did whatever it took to win.

My dad loved Bobby. He had a soft spot for genuine characters. When it came time to renegotiate his contract, Bobby sat across from my father's big desk.

Dad asked, "What's it going to take to keep you here in Pittsburgh?"

Bobby replied, "Whatever you think I'm worth."

"Well, we have to have a contract."

"Do you have one for me to sign?"

"Yeah, but it's not filled out."

"That's okay, hand it over."

With that, Bobby neatly signed "Robert Layne" at the bottom of the blank contract. "You fill in the rest," he said, "I trust you." Then he walked out of the room.

Bobby was shrewd. The way he handled the situation put a lot of pressure on my father to be fair and, of course, Dad wrote in a bigger salary number than Bobby would have asked for. Bobby was unconventional, and I can think of only a few players who would negotiate this way today.

If anyone could rein in a free spirit like Bobby Layne, it was Coach Raymond "Buddy" Parker. Parker remains one of the winningest coaches in Steelers history. His winning percentage is topped only by Chuck Noll, Bill Cowher, and Jock Sutherland. Parker was a strict disciplinarian and ruled by intimidation. He always told me, "It's mistakes that beat you!" and that's the reason he always preferred veteran players to rookies. He hated rookies and would trade away our draft picks in order to sign old pros. One year we didn't have a pick until the eighth round. It drove me nuts.

In Parker's defense I have to say that in those days we had a lot of veteran talent to choose from. There were just twelve teams in the NFL, and the colleges turned out more good players than the league needed. That's why you'd see rookies like Johnny Unitas get cut. Parker believed if you go with the veteran you'll win today; go with a rookie and you *might* win tomorrow. Parker wasn't alone in this thinking; other experienced coaches also took advantage of the glut of veteran talent.

When he first took over the team from Kiesling in 1957, he wanted to signal to the players that he was now the boss. Kiesling encouraged him in this, warning Parker that he needed to take a strong hand or risk losing the team. Buddy decided to cut talented running back Lynn Chandnois, just to prove no one was indispensable. Even Parker, however, regretted this hasty decision after viewing Chandnois' performance in game film.

But Parker never looked back. He could be a tyrant, especially when he was drinking. Not that he drank often; only after games and whenever he had to make a speech. His axe could fall on luckless players on the bus or plane while coming home from a game. He once cut six players before the fans had even cleared the stadium after a preseason loss to Cleveland. It got so bad, guys would hide after a loss just to stay out of his way, for fear he'd cut them on sight. I worried about Parker's style and wondered how long my father would put up with it.

It always bothers me when I hear people talk about the "same old Steelers" and the "terrible" teams of the 1940s, 1950s, and 1960s. Going back to the postwar years through the 1960s we had half-decent teams. On a given Sunday the Steelers were good enough to win—you just didn't know which Sunday it might be. But one thing you could count on, whoever we played would come out of the game bruised and battered and remember Pittsburgh as a tough, hard-hitting team.

The Pittsburgh legend began to grow, and we had our share of outstanding players, including a number of Hall of Famers.

We had great defensive players in those early days. Guys like Ernie Stautner, a bruising defensive tackle and nine-time Pro Bowler, could drink alongside Bobby Layne and play like the Pro Bowler he was the next day. He flattened running backs like a steamroller. Ernie wound up in the Hall of Fame, and was considered by teammates and opponents alike to be the toughest guy in the league. He's the only Steelers player, ever, to have his jersey, number 70, officially retired.

Eugene "Big Daddy" Lipscomb, a six-foot-seven, 295-pounder, was an aggressive and fearless tackle. He could play with the best and beat them. Lipscomb played hard and lived large. The police believed Eugene died of a heroin overdose. If it really was drugs, then I'm certain it was his first time—any of our trainers would tell you he was afraid of needles and wouldn't go near them. After the autopsy, the coroner found no needle marks or any evidence of habitual drug use. I always thought highly of him and grieved with all of Pittsburgh at his funeral. Had he lived he would have been a Hall of Famer for sure.

Cornerback Jack Butler went to the Pro Bowl eight times. He was smart and could really cover the field. Butler was very popular with the players, so well-liked, in fact, they wanted him as their player representative when the players' association (later the NFLPA) first organized. This is a guy who belongs in the Pro Football Hall of Fame, and it's a crying shame the selectors won't give him the nod simply because they feel there are too many Steelers honored already.

Everyone in the country remembers the famous 1964 *Life* magazine photograph of Y. A. Tittle taken by *Pittsburgh Post-Gazette* photographer Morris Berman at Pitt Stadium. Tittle, the great New York Giants' quarterback, is on his knees, helmet off, blood trickling down the side of his face, looking dazed and beaten. But few remember who delivered the punishing blow that put him there. It was six-foot-six, 270-pound Steelers defensive end John Baker, a mountain of a man that Tittle never forgot.

We had good offensive players, as well.

Tight end Elbie Nickel, a six-foot-one, 200-pounder, was a great blocker and receiver. He is immortalized in a stitched tapestry sewn by Sally Anderson and presented to the Steelers upon the completion of Three Rivers Stadium in 1970. Today it hangs in our South Side training facility. The Xs and Os quilted into this wall hanging depict the most famous play in Steelers history—that is until the Immaculate Reception in 1972. It shows the play action pass from Jim Finks to Nickel that helped beat the Philadelphia Eagles in 1954. The last time the Steelers had played the Eagles, the Philadelphia front line hammered Finks. They broke his jaw so badly it had to be wired shut. Our equipment man had to rig a special face mask for him—not like the ones players wear today, but a bumperlike affair that made him look like the Tin Man in *The Wizard of Oz*.

So this was a grudge match, and we really wanted to win. All Pittsburgh wanted us to win, and forty-two thousand fans filled the stands at Forbes Field, the biggest crowd ever to watch a game in that stadium. We led, 3-0 at halftime. In the second half, we had the ball on our 40-yard line, 4th down, 1 yard to go. The Eagles expected we'd run the ball. Coach Kiesling figured we'd run the ball. But in the huddle, Nickel said, "Finks, I think I can beat this guy deep." Finks looked at him, nodded, and called the play. On the snap, Finks dropped back two steps and faked the handoff to Jim "Popcorn" Brandt. As the Eagle line crowded the line of scrimmage and closed in on Brandt, Nickel slipped behind their secondary, while Finks faded into the pocket. Just when the Eagles figured out Brandt didn't have the ball, Finks aired it long to Nickel, who was streaking down the right sideline. No one ever laid a hand on him. He ran in for the touchdown to give us a 10-0 lead. We went on to win the game 17-7. You never heard such wild cheering, not until 1972.

Dick Hoak, the Penn State MVP, had a career with the Steelers spanning forty-five years as a running back, backfield coach, and running back coach. Because Hoak was never the biggest or fastest back, he carefully studied other players and learned techniques that allowed him to take advantage of any opponent or situation. He had a knack for teaching others and became the longest-serving coach in Steelers history.

John Henry Johnson was a veteran player at the end of his career when we got him. This explosive Hall of Fame power back gave the club two 1,000-yard seasons, and would have been one of the all-time great Steelers if we'd gotten him right out of college.

Not all the Steelers lived up to their potential. Tom Tracy was one of the best running backs of the era when he played at 195 pounds. Problem was: he couldn't keep the weight off. He'd go out on the town with Bobby Layne and Big Daddy Lipscomb and Stautner and he'd pack on the pounds and balloon up to 225. He couldn't keep his speed and could have been great if he had kept his weight down.

And some players were famous for their unsung contributions day in and day out, game after game, like six-foot-one, 240-pound center Ray "Ranger" Mansfield, who played in 154 consecutive games, at that time a team record.

———————

As the Steelers legend grew, we began to pay more attention to uniforms, logos, and what the fans thought of us. In the 1950s our helmets were gold, with player numbers painted on either side. We really didn't have a team logo, other than a little steelworker caricature that sometimes appeared on our letterhead.

But in 1962 we were having a really good season. A representative from Republic Steel came to see me at our offices at the Roosevelt Hotel. He showed me artwork developed by US Steel in 1958 and later adopted as the official mark of the steel industry. His portfolio included drawings of what he called "hypocycloids"—curvy four-pointed diamond shapes—colorful yellow, red, and blue symbols representing how steel "lightens your work, brightens your leisure and widens your world." He wanted to know if we'd like to put them on our helmets—we were the Steelers after all. I kind of liked the crisp, bright, modern design, but I wasn't so sure how it would look on our old gold helmets. So I told equipment manager Jack Hart to put the logo on one side only, until we decided whether we'd stick with it.

The Steelers finished the 1962 season with a 9-5 record, the best in franchise history to date. We finished second in the Eastern Conference and qualified for the Playoff Bowl. I wanted to do something special, so we changed the color of the helmets from gold to black. This helped highlight the new logo. Hart asked, "Should I put it on both sides?" I said, "No. We got here with the logo only on the right side, so let's keep it that way."

This is the way the legendary Steelers logo was born. People ask me all the time, "Why didn't you put it on both sides?" I usually tell them, "Just because you're asking!" It's a curiosity. People wonder why. That's reason enough not to change it.

From the time I started in the Steelers front office, I had been responsible for designing game programs and the team's media guide. In those days we didn't have an art department; we did whatever needed to be done. Ed Kiely was our one-man PR department. My wife, Patricia, worked as our secretary until she was replaced by her sister, Mary Regan, who worked directly for my father, and was with him for nearly forty years.

In 1959 we hired Maurice "Mossy" Murphy to bring the franchise into the mainstream of NFL entertainment. My father and I recognized we were in the football business, but there was an entertainment side of the game we couldn't ignore. I remember sitting in George Preston Marshall's office on a rainy day just before the Steelers took the field against the Redskins. Marshall's band director came marching into the office, red-faced and upset.

"Mr. Marshall, should we wear our new feathered headdresses? It's raining cats and dogs out there!" Without missing a beat, Marshall shot back, "We're in the entertainment business! You put those feathers on and get out there!"

So one hundred marching band members slogged across the field, soggy feathers matted to their tubas, but the show went on as the delighted fans sang "Hail to the Redskins." Marshall understood the value of entertainment. The Steelers would have to learn to be competitive in this arena as well.

Mossy Murphy came straight from Duquesne University, where he had successfully entertained fans and led the student body cheering section. He didn't look anything like a cheerleader. Standing five-foot–nine and weighing well over two hundred pounds, he had a larger-than-life personality and a creative spark that our team sorely needed.

He would try anything. He'd ride around the field on an undersized motor scooter, making certain the halftime performances were choreographed just so. Watching him putt around on that tiny scooter, gesturing, giving orders like a field marshal, left the fans and the team howling with laughter. He brought in professional or high school bands for every home game. The latter innovation was an especially good strategy, since the families and friends of the high school band members helped fill the stands.

He organized elaborate halftime shows. One Sunday it might be a jazz theme, the next we'd fight the Civil War. He always came up with something unusual. He set up a big muzzle-loading cannon in the end zone and torched it off whenever we scored a touchdown. One time he almost blasted receiver Buddy Dial as he crossed the goal line and ran into Mossy's line of fire. Dial's ad-libbed theatrical death scene made the highlight films for many years after.

We didn't need a mascot in those days; we had Mossy. He seemed to be everywhere. When a Pittsburgh politician, Prothonotary David Lee Roberts, annoyed fans by blocking their view—he had season tickets just behind the players' bench at Pitt Stadium—Mossy decided to play a prank on him.

Knowing he loved the limelight, Mossy said to me, "Let's have some fun with Roberts." He jumped on his scooter, rode over to the bench, and with his walkie-talkie in hand, hailed the official, saying, "Mr. Roberts, I'm from CBS. This game is being televised. Would you mind if we interviewed you?"

"Oh, yes, of course!"

Mossy held the walkie-talkie as if it were a microphone and began a lengthy interview, touching on topics ranging from football to politics. Roberts was a huge fan. Waxing eloquent about the Steelers game plan and basking in all the attention, he didn't notice he was speaking into a walkie-talkie instead of a microphone.

Then Mossy said, "Mr. Roberts, turn around and wave to the cameras in the press box."

Of course, there weren't any cameras trained on the Prothonotary, but again he didn't notice. Then I came up and interrupted the interview. "Thank you, Mr. Roberts, we have to cut to a commercial now." Then we led him to an out-of-the-way VIP seat. It was a riot and all we could do to keep from laughing out loud. Mossy could always be counted on to come up with shenanigans like this.

But sometimes he pushed the envelope too far. I remember the time he hired a beautiful baton twirler, decked out in a very tight gold lamé outfit. She's twirling, she's spinning, she's gyrating.

I buzzed Mossy on the walkie-talkie and said, "Listen, you're going to get us both canned if you don't cover her up!" The next thing I see is Mossy's scooter putt-putting across the field, blue smoke trailing behind, straight for the golden girl. He jumps off the scooter and covers her with his raincoat. The poor girl is draped in Mossy's tent of a coat, baton in hand, not knowing what to do. Finally, with coat dragging, she high-steps off the field, much to the crowd's disappointment. It had been quite a show, but I knew such a performance wouldn't sit well with Dad. There had to be limits on how far we'd go for the sake of entertainment.

People often ask me why the Steelers don't have cheerleaders like other teams in the league. The truth is we did have cheerleaders once, in fact, the first in the NFL. In 1961 Mossy recruited a whole squad of girls from Robert Morris College. He dressed them up in pleated gold vests, short skirts, and natty caps. Equipped with black-and-gold pompoms, they performed the kinds of cheers you'd see at high school and college games across the country. They were nice young women, but we felt they unnecessarily distracted players and fans. Television cameras liked them, but we take our football seriously in Pittsburgh. We just didn't need them. By 1969 the Steelerettes were history, and today the Steelers are one of the few NFL franchises without exotic dancing girls on the sidelines.

As the league changed, so did the team. Pittsburgh was changing, too. The smoky city of my youth was undergoing a transformation, a renaissance of sorts. In 1948 the industrial smoke had turned deadly. Just a few miles up the Monongahela River from downtown Pittsburgh, a cloud of smog smothered the small mill town of Donora. Fans at the high school football stadium couldn't see the players on the field. By afternoon you couldn't see your hand in front of your face. The next day eleven people were dead and scores more rushed to area hospitals.

This tragedy prompted local officials and steel industry executives to get serious about air pollution. For the next decade Pittsburgh led the nation in reducing emissions from mills and coal-powered plants of all kinds, and pioneered federal legislation that today allows all Americans to breathe easier. As smoke-control ordinances took effect, Pittsburghers washed decades of soot and grime from the stone facades of municipal buildings, libraries, museums, and churches, uncovering hidden beauty.

In 1958, as Pittsburgh renewed itself, the city celebrated its bicentennial. It had been two hundred years since George Washington and

General John Forbes arrived at the Point and found the smoldering ruins of Fort Duquesne, the French stronghold designed to keep the Three Rivers from the British. Forbes and Washington named the new British settlement "Pittsburgh" in honor of parliamentary leader William Pitt.

Now city leaders pulled out all the stops and hosted a yearlong celebration. They cleared the Point of industrial waste—rusty railroad tracks, empty warehouses, and abandoned mills—to create a beautiful urban park. They erected a festival city, a world's fair, and invited dozens of celebrities, from Gene Kelly and Perry Como to *Gunsmoke*'s James Arness, to join in the festivities. Parades and oratory entertained crowds of people who flocked to the reborn city. State and local dignitaries laid the cornerstone for the civic arena—no small feat considering the round building had no corners. It was the first retractable domed arena in the world, known locally as the "Igloo" (where the Penguins won the Stanley Cup in 1991 and 1992).

Unfortunately, the process of urban renewal impacted the rich history and culture of Pittsburgh's Hill District. Since the 1920s this African-American community had produced amazing talent: Clarence "Pinetop" Smith pioneered boogie-woogie, jazz legends Mary Lou Williams, Billy Strayhorn, and Billy Eckstine played the Crawford Grille, and Kenny Clark originated bebop. The stories of this neighborhood are immortalized in Pulitzer Prize–winning playwright August Wilson's Pittsburgh Series, a ten-play collection that captures the vitality and spirit of the Hill District's golden age.

The Pennsylvania Department of Transportation bored the Ft. Pitt Tunnel through Mt. Washington at the confluence of the Three Rivers. With the opening of this tunnel in 1960, the world discovered Pittsburgh in all its glory, as if a curtain had been raised on a stage. Pulitzer Prize–winning historian and native son David McCullough says, "Pittsburgh is the only city in America that makes an entrance." And he's right. You come through that tunnel and see skyscrapers of glass and steel and aluminum crowded onto the Golden Triangle, where the rivers converge. Towboats push coal barges, and cars and trains cross black-and-gold-painted bridges, the soothing green of the hills and parks contrasting with the hard urban landscape. I feel proud every time I drive into the city.

The sporting world also focused its attention on the city in 1960, when the Pittsburgh Pirates defeated the defending world champion New York Yankees in the seventh game of the World Series. Bill Mazeroski's ninth inning walk-off homerun electrified the nation and made Pittsburghers believe anything was possible. I remember the city went wild—horns honking, church bells ringing, streetcars clanging. In the streets strangers hugged and danced and sang. It was a public celebration on a scale I hadn't seen since World War II and wouldn't see again until the Steelers won their first Super Bowl.

The decade of the 1960s ushered in a new era for the NFL as well. On October 11, 1959, cross-state rivals, the Eagles and Steelers, faced each other in Philadelphia. Commissioner Bert Bell, who once owned a stake in both teams, sat in the cheap seats with the fans—he never liked special treatment or VIP boxes. With two minutes to go in the fourth quarter, the Eagles ahead 28-24, Bell suffered a massive heart attack. At the age of sixty-four, the most influential commissioner in NFL history up to that time was dead. Although a closely guarded secret, some of his close friends knew Bert was planning to resign as commissioner in order to reacquire the Philadelphia Eagles and return to the ranks of NFL owners. He always felt like one of the boys, and he was a real football guy, never entirely happy with the burden of responsibility that came with being the league's chief executive. His passing took us all by surprise and left a big leadership hole in the emerging NFL.

In January 1960 the owners met at the Kenilworth Hotel in Miami to select a new commissioner. Behind the scenes, owners jockeyed for position, lining up their candidates before the meeting convened. Two men, Austin Gunsel and Marshall Leahy, quickly emerged as front runners. By and large, the eastern owners, including George Halas and George Marshall, backed Gunsel, Bert Bell's former assistant, thinking he was someone they could control. The westerners, like Dan Reeves (Los Angeles) and Tony Morabito (San Francisco), wanted Leahy, a San Francisco lawyer and the league's chief outside legal counsel. Some people say the easterners didn't want a commissioner who lived on the West Coast. But I know for a fact that wasn't the case. The two Georges didn't care where Leahy lived—they just didn't like the guy. As I said, they wanted someone they could control.

The balloting seemed to go on forever. The winning candidate needed a two-thirds majority, or nine votes. Those owners supporting Leahy thought they'd made a deal with George Halas. If they got eight votes, he would provide the ninth. They thought they had the election in the bag.

"What do you think about this?" my father asked me.

"Let's vote for Leahy and see what happens," I said.

So my father voted for Leahy. But Halas didn't deliver his vote. The other owners slapped their foreheads and pounded the table. "But you promised us your vote."

George wouldn't give in. "No, I just can't do it," he said. He wanted to expand the league and feared losing the support of either the West Coast or East Coast faction if he backed one candidate or the other. He remained stubbornly indecisive.

"But you promised," they pleaded.

"I can't do it," he answered, "I'm not going to do it."

My father saw George's plight. "Then I'm not voting for Leahy, either," he said, and joined Halas in his holdout.

Dad told the owners, "We need another candidate."

Then out of thin air they started pulling out names. I was there when they suggested my father be the commissioner. But he was too smart for that.

"I'm not running for commissioner," he emphatically stated. "Do you think I was born yesterday?"

Next they proposed Detroit Lions president Edwin Anderson, who sat right next to me. When they put his name up, he thought he was going to get the job, but only two or three votes went his way.

The balloting went on. Round 20, Round 21, Round 22. If Bert himself had been there, by this time he would have taken out his teeth and started crying. When the discussions grew tedious, Bert Bell Jr., who worked in the league office, and I retreated to a palm-tree-shaded shuffleboard court outside the hotel. At first we played for a dollar a game, then for a dollar a shot. It turned out I was pretty good at shuffleboard, though it hardly counts as a sport in my book. I started playing with only a couple of bucks, but by the end of the day my wallet was a good deal fatter.

When we returned to the smoky meeting room, Dan Reeves put forward the name of the thirty-three-year-old general manager of the Los Angeles Rams, Pete Rozelle. The nomination took us by surprise, and no one in the room was more surprised than Pete. He attended the meeting just as I did, at the request of the team owner.

Reeves said, "He's young, but he's very bright, and he's very good."

Dad leaned over to me and asked, "Who is this guy? Do you know him?"

"Yeah, I know him," I said. "He's a good guy. I think he can do the job."

Pete and I were nearly the same age and had worked together on NFL marketing issues. We had spent some time together, and I found him to be bright, articulate, and most important, honest.

"He's all right," I said to my father. "He's someone we can get along with." So my father told Reeves and the others that we'd back Rozelle if he were nominated.

The owners asked Rozelle to leave the room, and while he was killing time in the washroom we elected him without much debate on the twenty-third ballot. My father helped break the logjam. He didn't speak often at league meetings, so when he did, the other guys listened.

The press called Pete the "boy commissioner." He was six years my senior and in some ways seemed like an older brother. After the meeting, we had a good talk. I asked if I could do anything for him, if he needed anything. Although he didn't need much help from me then, as the years passed we formed not only a close working relationship but a friendship that spanned the rest of his career (1960–89) and until his untimely death in 1996. Pete Rozelle was a man of honor, and more than any other commissioner, he is responsible for the NFL we know today.

———————

But the Rozelle era got off to a rough start. At the Warwick Hotel in New York—the very first meeting following his election—the agenda called for Pete to lay out for the owners his plans for the league, and especially our future relationship with television networks. Even at this early date, the owners recognized television was the key to future profits, so a lot was riding on the commissioner's leadership. George Marshall, however, had his own self-serving television agenda, one that would allow him to cut deals without league interference. He was definitely not on the same wavelength as Rozelle. Marshall told us he didn't think the kid was up to the challenge—and he set out to prove it.

When Pete called the meeting to order, Marshall was absent. Just as we dispensed with the preliminaries, the door opened and in strode

Marshall in his pajamas, robe, and slippers. I tell you, it was bizarre, though no one said a word. With a flourish he plunked himself down in a chair at the end of the table, right next to Rozelle.

When Pete began his formal presentation, George interrupted him: "That's not right!" Pete continued. George interrupted a second time: "You're wrong there!"

Without emotion, Pete turned to his rude antagonist. "Mr. Marshall, would you give me the opportunity to complete my remarks?"

"Go ahead, be my guest," George replied with a wave of his hand, then stared at Pete, never moving, not taking notes, as the commissioner finished his report.

When Rozelle concluded, George stood and attacked every point, one by one. To emphasize his argument, he wagged his finger in Rozelle's face. There he was, ridiculous in his bathrobe and slippers, and the owners listening to him as though this was nothing out of the ordinary. But it was extraordinary, even for Marshall. He was deliberately attempting to unnerve and intimidate our young new leader. As goofy as Marshall looked and behaved that day, it would have been a mistake to underestimate him. He had a mind like a steel trap and a personality like a pit bull. George really did a number on Pete. Some men would have broken down under such pressure, but Pete never flinched. By the end of the meeting, everyone knew Rozelle was going to make it as commissioner.

I knew television would be a contentious issue. The twelve teams had all cut their separate deals with the networks. The Colts and the Steelers went with NBC. Marshall had an independent network called Washington South. Cleveland also had its own independent network, sponsored by a beer company, stretching from Texas to the eastern states. The majority of the teams went with CBS, but each had negotiated a different fee schedule, from $75,000 (Green Bay) to $175,000 (New York). The big market clubs, like New York and

Chicago, refused to share their revenues with the smaller market clubs, like Green Bay and Pittsburgh.

It seemed obvious to Rozelle, my father, and me that a package deal—an exclusive contract with one network—would generate more money for the league. It would also allow the smaller clubs to share in the profits and thereby remain financially solvent and competitive on the field. Halas, Marshall, the Maras, and Dan Reeves of the Los Angeles Rams resisted the idea of putting together a biddable package.

At Pete's election the year before, I had a chance to talk to Dan Reeves at the Seaview Hotel in Miami. Reeves said, "If there's going to be a package deal, then the big markets should get more money. There's a couple of ways we can do this."

"There's only one way we can do this," I replied, "and that's to divide the money evenly."

He said, "You'll never get the votes to pass that—it's just not going to happen!"

And I shot back, "Then you'll never be on TV and there won't be any television in this league!"

"What are you talking about?"

I said, "When you come to Pittsburgh to play, we won't put you on—the game won't go back to Los Angeles. We have every right in the world to do this."

"Then you won't get any money," Reeves pointed out.

"Then neither will you! You won't get a dime, and you've got more to lose."

Reeves found this humorous and used to call me "Dirty Dan" over his shoulder. Later, I learned, he told some of the other owners, "That Rooney kid is the toughest guy I've ever met." I was twenty-eight at the time, and though I wasn't a kid, these men still called me "Danny." They were my elders—my father's age or older—but they did respect me, even if they didn't call me "Mr. Rooney."

But a week later, in the elevator of the Roosevelt hotel in Pittsburgh, a player behind me said, "Pardon me, Mr. Rooney," and I turned to see if my father was in the car. He wasn't. The player was addressing me. That made an impression on me. At one of our sessions, Vince Lombardi turned to my father and said, "Danny's talking a lot, isn't he?" Dad smiled. Both of them recognized the young Turks—Rozelle and I—were willing to speak up when necessary.

About this same time, we started calling my father the "Chief." I've talked to my brothers about this and none of us can remember precisely when this occurred, but we all agree that the twins, John and Pat, were responsible for coming up with the name. Most likely it was Pat; he was always inventing playful nicknames.

People think the title "Chief" was inspired by the 1950s *Superman* television series, which featured Clark Kent's editor, Perry White, a silver-haired, cigar chomping, no-nonsense guy, whose decisions were always final. It makes sense, but it just isn't so. The twins simply used the name "Chief" to describe the top guy, the ultimate authority. It's possible that subconsciously Superman's "Chief" entered their minds, but it was not a direct reference.

At first only family members referred to Dad as the Chief, but never to his face. One of my earliest memories of Pat using "Chief" was when he and my father had a disagreement over soccer. Pat and John thought it would be a good idea to get into the soccer business, and we did for a time in the mid-1960s. But Dad couldn't see its appeal. "What do you mean, you can't use your hands? That game will never catch on in Pittsburgh!" Pat, under his breath, said to me, "The Chief has made his decision: no soccer."

Over time the name caught on—it was a perfect fit. And by the late 1960s you heard "Chief" spoken in family circles, locker rooms, and even among sportswriters. Today, my father is known as the Chief around the world. But before the name was commonly used in the Steelers organization, people referred to him as the "Prez."

———————

Back to the NFL and television. I was present when we discussed television at the 1961 league meeting. Rozelle led the charge. He had spent much of the past year developing a television plan that would guide the future of the NFL. He showed how the league had already used the medium to better advantage than any other sport, but without a comprehensive plan football could lose its edge. He enlisted Vince Lombardi and my father to convince the Mara brothers that a package deal was in the league's best interest. Wellington and his brother Jack remained unconvinced. Our side wouldn't budge either.

The discussions grew heated. At one point, Jack turned to my father and said, "How can you do this and call yourself a Catholic?"

Instantly, Dad flared, "Don't you ever question my religion!"

I thought I was going to have to jump between them. Dad knew how to fight, and Jack Mara wouldn't have had a chance. My father was a pretty easygoing guy most of the time, but there were a few things that set him off. This was one of them. They calmed down, but I never again heard Jack bring up religion in a league meeting.

At Dad's urging, we finally agreed the league would put together a biddable package and contract with a single network. The revenues would be shared by all teams equally. In addition, the owners authorized the commissioner to negotiate the contract on our behalf. We also agreed to continue the existing home blackout policy. Plus, every road game would be broadcast back to its own home market.

This represented a great step forward for the NFL. Unfortunately, U.S. District Court Judge Allan K. Grim disagreed. He ruled the NFL's package deal violated federal antitrust laws. This forced the league to go political. Rozelle was up to the challenge, and mobilized the owners to lobby their congressmen and even President Kennedy. In addition, the league satisfied concerns raised by the NCAA by agreeing not to broadcast NFL games on a network on Saturdays during the college season.

On September 30, 1961, Kennedy signed the Sports Broadcasting Bill, which gave professional football a limited exemption from antitrust laws. Within three months, Rozelle signed CBS as the NFL's first exclusive national television contractor. The league would get $4.65 million each year for two years.

We were pretty proud of this deal and the one three years later, which netted the fourteen NFL teams $14.1 million a year for two years from CBS. Then we learned the AFL owners had negotiated an even more lucrative TV contract.

My father pointed out to me at the time, "You will rue this day!" and I asked him why. He said, "Everyone will be telling you how to run the league, asking for money. You will have agents, the television networks, and Congress trying to get involved."

Something had to be done. It was time to negotiate in earnest a merger between the two leagues.

During this period I wasn't focused just on television contracts and possible mergers. By 1962 our family had grown considerably. Patricia and I tried to get away with the kids in the summer, even if only to nearby Ligonier or Shamrock Farms, Dad's horse farm in Winfield, Maryland. That year, we decided to organize a family vacation that combined recreation and educational opportunities. Of course, looking back, I probably went a little overboard. The centennial of the Civil War (1961–65) captured my interest, and I began reading Bruce Catton's award-winning series of books. Then I got out the road maps and charted a thousand-mile road trip. The kids—Art, Kathleen, Rita, and Pat—all had reading or, in the case of the younger ones, coloring assignments (state flags, uniforms, state seals, etc.). Baby Dan was too small to go, so we left him home with Grandma Regan. We took Patricia's younger sister Rita along to help ride herd and packed everyone into our station wagon.

First stop: Harpers Ferry, West Virginia, where John Brown and his antislavery raiders captured the U.S. Arsenal in 1859. The opening shots of the Civil War were fired here (although historians might contend the first shots were fired at Ft. Sumter in 1861), and we took refuge from the rain in the same firehouse that had sheltered Brown and his men from U.S. troops, who were led, strangely enough, by Robert E. Lee and J.E.B. Stuart. On we marched to the Antietam Battlefield, then to Washington, D.C., where we saw every site from the Washington Monument to the Cathedral of the Immaculate Conception, where Father Dan was ordained. The rain came down hard as we drove off to Manassas and the Bull Run Battlefield, where young Artie was awed by the gigantic equestrian statue of "Stonewall" Jackson. "Look, there stands Jackson like a stone wall," he read on the bronze plaque at the base.

"Hey, Dad, why did Colonel [Bernard] Bee say Jackson stood like a stone wall?" he asked. "Was it because he was too scared to move?"

I said, "No, it was that he and his men were too brave to run."

For the rest of the trip we heard "Look! There stands Jackson like a stone wall!"

At Fredericksburg, Chancellorsville, Spotsylvania, Richmond, and Petersburg the statues and cannons became a blur. Jackson followed us, it seemed, always holding his ground. On we went, through fearsome summer storms (it must have rained every day) on a side trip to the 1600s and 1700s, Jamestown and Williamsburg, where the kids marched with redcoats down the Duke of Gloucester Street to the music of fifes and drums.

Off we went to Virginia Beach, where it stopped raining long enough for us to wade in the surf. That evening Artie learned to swim in the Hilton Hotel pool and made a big splash with his "cannonballs" from the diving board. Back in the station wagon again we headed home by way of Gettysburg for one last charge. By this time we had exhausted our supply of Civil War songs, coloring books, puzzles, car games (counting cows, license plates, car colors), and good humor. It had been a memorable journey, the first of many family expeditions.

I attended the 1963 dedication of the Pro Football Hall of Fame in Canton, Ohio. I remember thinking at the time that Pittsburgh had as much right as Canton to be the home of the Hall of Fame, since pro football began in Pittsburgh in 1892. But the Canton people had a legitimate claim, since the NFL was born there in 1920 at the Hupmobile dealership. In any event, the Canton people did a bang-up job.

It must have been tough deciding who would make the cut for that first class. The selectors made it a point to honor the men who helped found the league: Bert Bell, Joe Carr, George Halas, Curly Lambeau, Tim Mara, George Preston Marshall, and, of course, Jim Thorpe, the league's first president. In addition, the selectors recognized some of the early greats of the game: Sammy Baugh, Dutch Clark, Red Grange, Mel Hein, Pete Henry, Cal Hubbard, Don Hutson, Johnny Blood, Bronko Nagurski, and Ernie Nevers. In 1964 my father proudly accepted the honor of his selection in the second class of inductees, alongside Jimmy Conzelman, Ed Healey, Clarke Hinkle, Link Lyman, Mike Michalske, and Brute Trafton. I can remember few honors he treasured more than his induction into the Pro Football Hall of Fame.

On November 21, 1963, the U.S. Fourth Court of Appeals decided in favor of the NFL in a $10 million antitrust suit, filed by the American Football League. This new league, founded by Lamar Hunt, meant to compete with the NFL head to head. The news of this victory was sweet. But the following day, Friday, November 22, as Dad and I sipped coffee in the restaurant of the Roosevelt Hotel in Pittsburgh, someone shouted out, "The president's been shot!" We ran to our office and turned on the television, to learn John F. Kennedy had been gunned down in Dallas. We stayed glued to the TV set all day, caught up by the tragic events unfolding before our eyes. By nightfall, the tolling church bells echoed throughout the city. The next morning, the flags at half staff confirmed the death of the president. Steeped in Catholic tradition and strongly Democratic, Pittsburgh mourned.

I was still in shock when I received a call from Pete Rozelle late Friday, asking what I thought about playing football on Sunday as usual. I thought the assassination of the president demanded we cancel all games and told him so. We had a good talk and Pete agreed to think about it before making a final decision. Pete had called me instead of my father, not only because I was in charge of the day-to-day activities of the team, but because we had become very good friends. We always seemed to think alike.

Over the next two days, Pete and I talked almost hourly. Both of us received a flood of calls from family, friends, politicians, and business leaders. Of course, I talked to my father. He knew the Catholic community was especially shaken by the assassination.

Bud Rieland, my best man and longtime friend, called and said, "You're not really considering playing the game on Sunday, are you?"

While I tested the pulse of the community, Pete consulted the president's press secretary, Pierre Salinger. I knew they were good friends and years before had been classmates at the University of San Francisco.

When Pete called me he said, "Pierre says we should go ahead with the games. Jack Kennedy would have wanted it that way." Rozelle had discussed with Pierre the fact that no games had been scheduled in Dallas or Washington, D.C., that Sunday, which made the decision to go ahead with the games a little easier. Pete thought Salinger was right. Playing football on Sunday might have a positive effect on the country and signal to the world that America could still function during this time of tragedy and crisis. Remember, this was at the height of the Cold War. We didn't know whether the assassination was part of a Soviet-backed conspiracy or the work of a madman. Still, I didn't agree with the decision to play on Sunday, and I told Pete it was a mistake.

The back-and-forth calls continued until, finally, early Saturday morning, Pete called and told me the games would go on. I told him, "Okay, Pete, I disagree, but I'll support you."

Hours later Rozelle issued the following statement: "It has been traditional in sports for athletes to perform in times of great personal tragedy. Football was Mr. Kennedy's game. He thrived on competition." The games were played but not televised.

Pete later told me it was the wrong decision, one of the few he regretted making during his term as commissioner. But no one could have anticipated what came next. That Sunday, just two hours before kickoff, I was on the stadium roof at Forbes Field with a transistor radio pressed to my ear. Newscasters reported from Dallas that Jack Ruby had shot Lee Harvey Oswald, Kennedy's assassin. The Chicago Bears had already taken the field to warm up when I called security to alert them of this newest development. We determined to go ahead with the game and not make any announcements until all the facts were in. Following the national anthem, the somber crowd hushed for a minute of silent prayer and the game went on.

When we played at Forbes Field, I always watched the game from the roof, because here I could get the best view and follow the action as it moved downfield. Mike Ditka, a Western Pennsylvania boy who had starred at Aliquippa High School and later at the University of Pittsburgh, had a terrific game for the Bears. The Bears would go on to win the NFL championship that year, but the Steelers fought them to a 17-17 tie. My mind was on the news reports from Dallas coming through my little transistor radio, and calls from our security team. We really didn't know what to expect that day. Fortunately, there were no incidents.

While I paced the roof, my father stayed in the press box. He had given strict instructions for the Steelerettes to stay seated on the bench and not lead any cheers. It was a very cold day, and by halftime a light snow began to fall. Dad took pity on the shivering girls and asked an equipment man to run to the locker room and get jackets for them. Soon they were decked out in oversized Steelers jackets, now warm but invisible to the crowd.

Rozelle and the league received a great deal of criticism for the decision to go on with the games, especially since the rival AFL had cancelled its games. When I reflect on this terrible time, it helps put football in perspective. There are more important things than playing football every Sunday, and we have to make decisions based on what's right. The NFL learned this lesson; we all learned this lesson in 1963. When Commissioner Paul Tagliabue called me following the terrorist attacks on September 11, 2001, there was little question we would postpone all the games scheduled that week.

The year 1963 tested the NFL in other ways, as well. Gambling represents one of the greatest threats to professional sports. Rozelle recognized this. Early in his administration he launched an investigation of players, coaches, and even owners to ensure that the NFL was squeaky clean. He hired former FBI agents to uncover any trace of gambling within the league. Then early in the year came shocking news. Two of the NFL's greatest stars, Paul Hornung, the Green Bay Packers MVP running back, and Alex Karras, the Detroit Lions All-Pro defensive tackle, had bet on games—including games involving their own teams. The national news media broke the story and Rozelle knew he had to get to the bottom of the rumors. If they were true, he'd have to make an example of these superstars. The reputation of the league depended upon swift and decisive action.

My father and I backed him all the way and so did most of the other owners, although Carroll Rosenbloom, co-owner of the Baltimore Colts, was under league investigation himself. The evidence against Hornung and Karras was overwhelming. With the approval of the owners, Rozelle suspended both players, levied heavy fines, and sent a warning to the league that gambling would not be tolerated. He posted signs in every locker room, reminding players and coaches of the NFL's no-tolerance policy. Pete's toughness on this issue reflected my father's feelings exactly, and set a standard in the NFL that guides the league.

Both Hornung and Karras would return to their teams after missing one full season. But four years later, Karras made the front pages again. In August 1967 he fanned the burning competition between the NFL and AFL into open flame and threatened the fragile partnership brokered by Rozelle in 1966. The Detroit Lions traveled to Denver to play the Broncos in a preseason game. No AFL team had ever beaten an NFL team. In January, the NFL Green Bay Packers had defeated the AFL Kansas City Chiefs in the first Super Bowl. The Packers' domination of the Chiefs confirmed what many sportswriters thought: the NFL was a much better league and it would be years before the AFL would be competitive. Karras was so confident of victory over the Broncos that he announced on national television, "If Denver wins I'll walk home."

I also believed the NFL to be the superior league, but I knew the AFL had latched on to a lot of talent, and several teams had the potential to be competitive with our teams. I didn't think Karras shooting his mouth off like that was appropriate. It wouldn't help the delicate merger process, and I didn't feel Karras was the ideal spokesman for our league, considering his gambling troubles.

So what do you think happens? Denver wins, the first AFL team to beat an NFL team, ever, and the chant "Walk, Karras, walk!" could be heard in every NFL stadium.

This incident is only a small indication of the intensity of the rivalry that had been brewing since the founding of the AFL in 1960. The AFL comprised eight teams: Boston Patriots (later the New England Patriots in 1971), Los Angeles Chargers (later San Diego Chargers in 1961), Denver Broncos, New York Titans (later the New York Jets in April 1963), Houston Oilers, Buffalo Bills, Dallas Texans (later Kansas City Chiefs in 1963), and Oakland Raiders.

The genius behind the new league was Lamar Hunt, owner of the Dallas Texans, who had tried and failed to acquire an NFL franchise. Locked out of our league, he founded his own. The AFL was well financed and well organized, with its owners willing to go after the best talent in the country and pay top dollar. AFL coaches and scouts scoured the country looking for the best college players.

The NFL was so worried about losing top college talent, especially quarterbacks, that we implemented a "hand-holders" program. This odd scheme worked like this: we used experienced former players, coaches, and college associates to establish "relationships" with top-ranked players and make sure they didn't sign an AFL contract. The hand-holders got to know their charges and helped them in any way they could without violating NCAA and amateur rules. Above all, the hand-holders needed to keep the college kids away from the AFL agents who worked hard to lure them away.

The Steelers had set their sights on a kid named Aaron Brown, a big defensive lineman from the University of Minnesota. We assigned Buddy Young to take Brown under his wing. Only five foot four, Buddy was a stand-out African-American running back, known as the "Bronze Bullet," and had played for several AAFC and NFL teams. He put Aaron up in a hotel but made the mistake of getting a room on the first floor. The AFL guys sneaked him out through a back window, and Brown was halfway to Kansas City before we knew what happened. Brown went on to have a successful career with the Chiefs and, later, with the Green Bay Packers. Buddy was a good hand-holder, and he went on to become one of the first black executives in the NFL.

The bidding war was ruining us. The AFL teams seemed to have money to burn. Take Joe Namath, who signed with the New York Jets in 1965 for the unheard salary of $427,000. Namath quarterbacked his high school team in Beaver Falls, near Pittsburgh, before going on to break records at Alabama for Bear Bryant's Crimson Tide. He was brash, he was bold, a phenomenal talent, and everyone wanted him. The AFL guys simply outbid us.

Nothing like this had happened in the NFL since my father had signed Whizzer White in 1938 for $15,800, a salary three times the going rate. Just as then, Namath's contract shattered the salary barrier and the NFL-AFL rivalry entered a new phase.

In 1966 Al Davis, coach and general manager of the AFL's Oakland Raiders, took over as AFL commissioner. Lamar Hunt knew exactly what he was doing. He needed a tough guy at the bargaining table. Davis had already attracted attention with his in-your-face style, hard-nosed football, and aggressive pursuit of NFL-bound college players. He wanted nothing to do with the NFL, and would fight it tooth and nail, city by city. And he wanted the merger to come on his terms. Now he was AFL commissioner.

To complicate matters, in the spring of 1966 the New York Giants signed soccer-style kicker Pete Gogolak away from the AFL's Buffalo Bills. This shattered the six-year unwritten agreement that neither league would raid the other's veteran players. Davis encouraged retaliation by raiding NFL quarterbacks. At the very moment the war between the leagues seemed about to explode, Rozelle met with Tex Schramm and Lamar Hunt.

Tex was president of the Dallas Cowboys, an expansion team that entered the NFL in 1960. Tex had given Rozelle his big break years earlier when he hired him shortly after the war as the director of publicity for the Los Angeles Rams. They were close friends, and Pete believed Tex was the guy to negotiate with the AFL. Pete asked him to meet in secret with Hunt, the kingpin of the AFL, because he didn't want Davis to undermine the negotiations.

Then on June 8, 1966, in a surprising joint statement, the AFL and NFL announced they had reached a merger agreement. It would be a gradual transition. Both leagues would remain separate until 1970, when the two leagues would combine to form the new National Football League with two conferences—the American Football Conference (AFC) and the National Football Conference (NFC). Until the final merger in 1970, play between the leagues would be limited to preseason games and a "Super Bowl" between the AFL and NFL champions at the end of each season. The provisions of the merger included two-network TV coverage (NBC-AFC and CBS-NFC) and the addition of four franchises. No franchises would move from their present cities. Most important, a common draft, beginning in 1967, would eliminate the bidding war.

No doubt, Davis felt betrayed, not only by the merger itself but by the way he had been deliberately cut out of the negotiations. The AFL owners had obviously used him when they needed a tough guy in order to gain a better bargaining position. Then they left him twisting in the wind. By the terms of the agreement, Davis would be out of a job in four years and, in the meantime, he would have to play second fiddle to the NFL commissioner.

I got to know Al Davis well in the late 1960s. He didn't take the Rozelle appointment well; maybe he thought he should have gotten the job. He quit after only three months as AFL commissioner to return to Oakland, where he emerged as part owner and general manager of the Raiders. From the start, Al and I were usually on different sides. He deliberately tried to confuse issues so he could gain an advantage. Everyone realized the merger was inevitable, that in four years we'd be one league, but Davis still played by the old rules, treating other NFL teams as the enemy.

———

Unless you were there, you can't imagine the excitement generated by those first Super Bowls. The name itself fit the game, though it came about in a very unusual way. In 1966, as we talked about a "world championship" game, some owners referred to it as the "World Series of football," but of course that was a name already associated with Major League Baseball. I remember when Lamar Hunt first used the term "Super Bowl," a name inspired by the Wham-O Super Ball then popular with kids.

We were sitting around a table talking about championship games when someone asked, "Wait, which championship are you talking about, the league championships or the world championship?"

Hunt said, "I'm talking about the Super Bowl."

Informally, everyone began referring to the world championship as the Super Bowl, expecting at some later date to give it a more appropriate name. But the media, the public, and even the players and coaches latched on to "Super," and it stuck. Not everyone thought this the best name. I remember Stormy Bidwill kidded about everything being "super."

The first World Championship, later to be called Super Bowl I, matched Vince Lombardi's Green Bay Packers against Lamar Hunt's Kansas City Chiefs. When the teams arrived at the Coliseum in Los Angeles on game day, they found an army of sportswriters and television crews already encamped. Lombardi bristled when reporters acted as if the outcome of the game had already been determined, that the AFL Chiefs had no chance against the superior NFL Packers. "If you guys already know who won, why should we bother playing at all? I think those guys want to prove they're as good as we are.

Let's play the game and find out, if you gentlemen of the press don't mind." There was a lot of pressure on Vince to win this game, not just for the Packers but for all of us in the NFL. We believed our league the superior one, but we had to prove it. Losing was not an option.

No one felt the tension more than the players. It was as bad as I've ever seen it. In the locker room and in the tunnel before the game, guys on both sides were shaking with nerves, some of them throwing up. The kickoff released seven years of pent-up excitement. To everyone's surprise, at the half the game was tight, with the Packers leading only 14-10. When the halftime show began we were pretty worried. I worried the NFL might lose; Pete worried the leagues wouldn't be competitive. But so far it had been a great game. In the second half Lombardi's Packers calmed down and hit their stride, decisively winning 35-10. In the elevator after the game, Pete was all smiles. We'd passed a milestone in the history of the NFL, and it looked like the merger would work after all.

Super Bowl II found Lombardi's Packers pitted against Al Davis's Oakland Raiders. There was no love lost between them, and the game got personal. Davis is the kind of guy you either loved or hated. I wanted the Packers to destroy the Raiders—and they did.

Then came Super Bowl III at the Orange Bowl in Miami. The New York Jets dominated the Baltimore Colts, winning 16-7. Broadway Joe Namath put on a show that shocked the sports world. He passed for over 200 yards and made good on his pre-game prediction, "We're gonna win the game. I guarantee it." The cocky Namath, the very symbol of the AFL, was named MVP in the showcase game of the merged leagues.

The old guard of the NFL took it hard. Soon after the game, at the Kenilworth Hotel in Miami, I had dinner with Wellington Mara, Art Modell, Tex Schramm, and Vince Lombardi. They were furious, almost ready to throw Carroll Rosenbloom out the window. The Colts had embarrassed themselves and let the league down. Lombardi criticized the Baltimore coaching staff, listing the could'ves and should'ves that would have won the game. There was no excuse—Coach Don Shula and his assistant Chuck Noll were both top guys. But Earl Morrall's quarterbacking had been disastrous, and the Colts only scored in the fourth quarter when the injured Johnny Unitas came off the bench to rally the team and drive downfield for a touchdown.

I was as much an NFL guy as the rest of them. I thought the Colts played a bad game—they were the better team—and Namath and the Jets had gotten lucky. But I agreed with Pete Rozelle. The loss to the Jets wasn't all bad. It showed the public the two leagues could be competitive, that there was balance.

Merging the two leagues was not a simple matter. The devil was in the details. There would be two conferences, but how would we align the divisions? The AFL now had ten teams, and the NFL had sixteen. After much debate, we agreed that three teams from the NFL would move over to the AFL to balance the conferences. But which teams? The AFL wanted the Steelers, Colts, and Browns because these established NFL teams would be good for the new conference's image. But we would be placed in separate divisions, which would disrupt the traditional rivalries between the three clubs and antagonize our fans. I was totally against this.

Early in 1969, as the final merger date approached, I began to think that we'd never get the deal done. I didn't want the Pittsburgh Steelers to be one of the three teams to move over to the AFL. We weren't a second-rate team that could just be ripped out of the NFL. We had tradition, we had a strong fan base, and we had our regional rivals. We weren't pawns that could be moved at the whim of the league. What would our fans think? We'd look like chumps, like the league's whipping boy.

The combined owners met in New York at the league's Park Avenue offices. Rozelle announced that no one was going home until the conference and division alignments were set. Division champions of each conference, of course, would make the postseason playoffs. The conference champions would match up in the Super Bowl, so every team wanted to be in a division that offered the best combination of geography, financial advantages, and strong regional rivalries. To sweeten the pot, Rozelle announced that the three NFL teams willing to make the shift would receive a $3 million bonus, paid by the owners of the other teams.

I still opposed shifting the Steelers to the AFC, but Dad was beginning to warm up to the idea. "Hey, it's a lot easier to receive $3 million than to pay it." After a long, hard day of negotiating, Dad and I, along with Wellington Mara, went to see our old friend Art Modell, owner of the Cleveland Browns. Art had been rushed to Doctors Hospital with a bleeding ulcer. I told him of the divisional stalemate and explained that none of the NFL teams wanted to move. The AFL guys specifically wanted the Steelers because of our tradition and reputation, which they believed would give greater credibility to the new conference.

As we stood around his bed, Modell looked up and said, "Boys, I'm ready to break this logjam. If the Steelers agree to move, I'll move Cleveland."

We'd been fighting the AFL for a decade and I wasn't about to join the enemy. It had been a war of sorts, and it wasn't easy for me to go over to the other side just like that. "Wait!" I said. "We're not going to join the American Football Conference!"

Dad put his hand on my shoulder and said, "Danny, hold on. Let's think about this."

After we left the hospital, I continued to work on Dad as Wellington listened. I restated my reasons for not joining the AFC and thought I had convinced him that we were better off staying with the NFC.

"Let someone else make the move," I said as I paced the room, trying to keep my emotions in check.

Wellington stepped in my path. "Pacing isn't going to help. Don't get too excited about this. You don't know where it's going. This may work out for you."

Dad and I had dinner that night, but I didn't say much. I thought I had him convinced. After dinner we returned to the league offices, but before joining the other owners, who were sacked out in chairs and talking in small groups in the hallways, we walked into Pete's office. Pete looked me in the eye and handed me a tiny slip of paper, not much bigger than a Chinese cookie fortune. It read: "CLEV, PITT, HOU, CINCY."

Then and there I knew the Steelers would be moving to the AFC. Pete had come up with the perfect mix of traditional rivals, big-market cities, and he added the appeal of Houston with its brand-new Astrodome.

Dad asked me, "What is that?"

I handed him the piece of paper. "Here's our new division."

My father took the slip of paper, then said, "That's right." As we walked down to the meeting room, he whispered, "If you hadn't been so stubborn, we wouldn't have gotten such a great division."

Pete announced the new alignment to the bleary-eyed NFC owners seated around the table in the "Fish Room," so named for the stuffed swordfish (Rozelle was a great fisherman) that dominated the wall. They all seemed relieved.

Then Rozelle led my father and me, as well as representatives of the Cleveland Browns and Baltimore Colts—the other two NFL swing teams—down the hall to the Red Room, where the AFC owners had gathered. Pete announced the three NFL teams that had agreed to move. Then he introduced me. I said we would move over to the AFC and announced our new division alignment: Pittsburgh, Cleveland, Cincinnati, and Houston.

As soon as the words were out of my mouth, Al Davis shouted, "No! We have to debate, then vote on the divisions as we go along!"

"This alignment is set. It's untouchable," I said.

Davis shot back, "No, it isn't!"

"Listen, this division is set. I don't care what you do as far as the other divisions, but this division is set. If you don't think so, we're out of here right now!"

Sid Gillman of the San Diego Chargers rose. "Danny," he said, "don't pay any attention to him. Your division is set, our division is set—it's good, and that's the way it's going to be."

Then we all sat down and began working on the other details of the AFL.

But Davis walked out.

Outside the Red Room, I heard a commotion. Vince Lombardi had somehow heard of my argument with Davis. In the hallway Vince grabbed Al by the collar, lifted him up, and pressed him against the wall—hard. "If you're going to cause these people trouble," he warned, "you'll be run out of here. You're getting the best teams. Dan Rooney came a long way for this, so settle down or we'll throw you out. We don't need you!"

Lombardi wasn't fooling around and Davis knew it. Al returned to the Red Room visibly shaken and sat down quietly. He said nothing more about the Steelers' divisional alignment. How could he? It was the best for everyone.

Right after the meeting I made some important calls.

First, I called Chuck Noll, the Steelers head coach I'd just brought on board a few months earlier. "It's a good move," he said. Chuck had been in the AFL and had coached on the West Coast with San Diego and Los Angeles. He knew a lot about the AFL teams and thought the new Steelers team he was building would be strong.

Next I called Patricia. She always had her own opinions about football. Sometimes she agreed with me, sometimes she didn't. This time she said it was fine with her, so long as I thought it was the way to go. "But," she added, "you'd better call Artie!"

Our son was away at school in Cleveland at Gilmore Academy. He had been an outstanding quarterback there and loved football. I left this call for last—I knew it would be my toughest.

Pat Livingston of the *Pittsburgh Press* was my next call. Livingston was the city's top sportswriter and I knew he'd be a key guy in shaping fan opinion. Pat reacted negatively: "You're selling out!"

"Wait a second," I said, "hear me out. This move will be good for the Steelers. It'll give us a new start." After I explained the new schedule he said, "Hey, that does sound pretty good. Okay, I'm for it!" And that's the way he wrote it the next day.

Next up, Roy Jefferson, the Steelers player representative. "Roy," I said, "what do you think?"

"Sounds great, Mr. Rooney, you know what's best. The team will support you."

Now came my call to Artie. You think Pat Livingston was hard on me? Artie let me have it with both barrels. "This is terrible! You quit! You sold us down the river! We've been fighting these guys for nine years and now you're with them?"

"Calm down," I said, knowing exactly how he felt; I had felt the same way myself just a few hours earlier. "You've got to understand, this compromise actually puts us in better position than we are now. Playing the Oilers in the Astrodome will be great for TV. Cincinnati and Cleveland are our natural rivals. The fans will love it."

I could tell Artie was upset, and I flashed back to that day in 1941 when my father called to tell me he wasn't selling the Steelers to Lex Thompson. I realized that Artie cared as much about the Steelers as I did. History was repeating itself. In time, both of us came to understand that the merger was the best thing that ever happened to the Steelers and the NFL.

Then I checked in with my brother Art. After four years at St. Vincent College, where he was a good offensive tackle, Art had gone to New York to become an actor. Madame Dahakonavich, his teacher, encouraged him and told him he could have a career in the theater. But he returned to Pittsburgh, loafed with the Steelers scouts, and discovered that football was more his style. Art saw the benefits of joining the AFC almost immediately. Then I called Jack McGinley, who quickly came on board.

———

The NFL had come of age, and the Steelers would begin fresh in a new conference. By the time of the merger in 1970, my father had already entrusted the daily operations of the Steelers to me. Now the organization needed a strong head coach and a plan for the future. That coach and plan came in the person of Charles Henry Noll.

CHAPTER 5

SUPER STEELERS

Hɪʀɪɴɢ Cʜᴜᴄᴋ Nᴏʟʟ was the best decision we ever made for the Steelers. You can trace the origin of the Super Steelers of the 1970s to the moment I called Chuck following the Jets victory over the Colts in Super Bowl III, January 12, 1969. To become world champions, we needed a coach with the right combination of vision, intelligence, and leadership: someone who could teach us how to win. Over the past ten years, we'd had three coaches, and while all of them had some talent, none of them brought together in one package everything we needed.

We thought we had a winner in Buddy Parker when he took over the team in 1957. He'd won two NFL championships as coach of the Detroit Lions. He was a real football guy, an excellent tactician, and by 1964 already the winningest coach in the Steelers' thirty-two-year history.

But Parker could be unpredictable on and off the field. He hated rules and regulations, and he fought authority, from Bell and Rozelle to my father and me. He refused to play rookies because they made mistakes. His players both respected and feared him. Parker could not earn their loyalty because he traded them at the drop of a hat. In fact, he traded away the team's future with his mismanagement of the draft. For these reasons, his players never developed the closeness that is essential in a championship team.

After our poor 5-9 showing in the 1964 season, I'd warned Parker not to cut or trade without my approval. But during the 1965 preseason, he continued his erratic cutting and trading. I could not have made our policy more clear, but Parker wouldn't listen. He wasn't about to take orders from an owner, let alone the son of an owner only half his age. In the past, he'd gone around me in order to get the answers he wanted from my father. But things had to change—I was running the daily operations of the team. Immediately following a preseason game at Brown University in Rhode Island, Buddy called to tell me he planned to trade defensive end Ben McGee (McGee went on to become a two-time Pro Bowler for the Steelers).

I said, "Don't do anything tonight. Let's talk about it in the morning."

Buddy shot back, "You don't understand. I've made up my mind— I'm gonna do it. And if you don't like it, I'll resign."

"I think you better reconsider that, too. Let's sleep on it."

But Parker was insistent—it was a power play. He wanted to prove that he had control. I felt the time had come to stand my ground.

He kept pushing. "I'm the coach," he said, "you can't tell me what to do."

"I told you to check with me first before making a trade, but you say you won't. I can't allow that."

"I can't work like this. Maybe it's better if I leave."

"I'm sorry, then, Buddy. I'm going to have to accept your resignation. But it's late. We'll meet in the morning."

That night Dad and I discussed the situation. He said, "Maybe you should think about it. I hope you know what you're doing—don't make a mistake."

Was I making the right decision? We were two weeks away from our regular season opener against Green Bay. But I knew in my heart the team needed to rebuild with fresh talent—we'd never do it with Buddy at the helm.

The next morning, Buddy saw I wouldn't back down, and I accepted his resignation. The next day, after talking about it with the Chief, I notified Mike Nixon, our assistant coach, that he'd be running the team this season. Nixon was a Western Pennsylvania guy and a University of Pittsburgh graduate who had played and coached under Jock Sutherland. Mike had gone on to coach at Notre Dame and with the Washington Redskins. He was no slouch, but I knew he wasn't the man to take the Steelers in a new direction. But as an interim head coach, with only days to go before the first game of the season, I figured we had little choice but to keep him on. We'd review his position at the end of the season.

Nixon was a disappointment, and we had one of our worst seasons in years, 2-12. We needed a new coach, and this time we weren't going to hire just anyone. The process would be thorough and thoughtful. I scoured the country in search of coaching talent, professional and collegiate, and came up with five good prospects. I called Bill Austin, assistant coach for Los Angeles, who had once served as assistant coach under Vince Lombardi during the Packers' glory years. I asked him to come to Pittsburgh for an interview. Austin had played seven years for the New York Giants before going to Green Bay.

Bill interviewed well. He seemed like a guy we could get along with, so my father called Vince to get the inside story. Lombardi thought the world of him, and said he'd make a terrific head coach.

That was enough for Dad. "Let's hire him!"

"Wait!" I said. "This is only our first interview. Let's take a look at the other guys."

"If Vince says he okay, let's take him!"

That's the way my father operated. If he could, he'd hire a friend. If he couldn't, a recommendation from a friend was often good enough.

And so we hired Bill Austin. Sure, I was running the team, but the Chief was the boss. When he stepped in to make decisions like this, I sometimes joked with him: "What are you doing, pulling out your stock certificate on me?" We'd laugh about it, but his decision was final.

I was trying to bring the Steelers into the modern era, and I knew the right coach was the key. In this case, the hiring process had been disrupted. It was a single interview; the Steelers deserved better.

The Chief liked to loaf with the coaches and talk football and everything else under the sun. When making a decision about anything, my father had a tendency to give equal weight to all opinions. His world was a perfect democracy—one man, one vote. For instance, some guy who just happened to be in the room—his driver, the groundskeeper, a custodian, a North Side crony, or his accountant—would offer advice, and Dad would listen. If there were five people present, there'd be five votes. I used to say to him, "That doesn't work. This guy is a good guy, but he doesn't know anything about what were talking about." When it came to football, this tendency to listen to just anyone drove me crazy.

Dad didn't take football as seriously as I did. His passion was baseball. Everything revolved around baseball. Whenever we went on long drives, he would fiddle with the radio dial constantly trying to tune in a baseball game. It didn't matter what team—any game would do. He'd settle for static on a baseball station rather than listen to a crystal-clear football game. The Chief was a great boxer and a good football player, but baseball was his game. When push came to shove, baseball always won out.

During Austin's three-year coaching career with the team, both the Steelers and the Pirates contracted with KDKA Radio to broadcast games. My father was fine with this arrangement, but I couldn't stand it, because the Pirates would push us off the air whenever the teams were scheduled to play at the same time. When that happened, the Steelers would be forced to an FM or a short-range, 5,000-watt station. I remember once the Pirates had to play a makeup game on a Sunday at the same time our game was scheduled. KDKA called me and said they wanted to bump the Pirates and air the Steelers game.

I told them, "Great! We've been waiting years for this!"

But then Jim Herron, the Pirates' business manager, called Dad and put the pressure on. Now, Dad's office was next to mine, and I remember arguing with him about it.

He said, "You can't interfere with the baseball game."

"But this means the Steelers have arrived. KDKA wants to get the better ratings. We've got more fans than baseball!"

"You can't do it. It's baseball."

He told me I just didn't understand, and he was right. I could never understand his unswerving devotion to baseball. In his mind, it would always be America's game.

In the three seasons Austin coached the Steelers, the team went 11-28-3. He modeled his coaching after the legendary Lombardi, but Austin was no Lombardi. He could execute Lombardi's instructions, but as head coach of the Steelers, he was over his head and didn't have the creative spark that outstanding coaches have. He put great stock in the Knute Rockne–style locker room pep talk—"Win this one for Mr. Rooney" or "Win this one for Pittsburgh"—but he never inspired the team. Andy Russell once told me that some of our players on those Steelers teams who had been in Green Bay when Austin was an assistant there remembered the rah-rah speeches he gave in Pittsburgh were the same—verbatim—as the ones Lombardi gave the Packers in Green Bay.

Austin had a knack for reading defenses and could occasionally exploit weakness and come up with big offensive plays. He was tough, and believed in hard-hitting, basic football. And because his background was as an offensive line coach, our line did show some improvement. But he beat the players up in practice. Many of them were out of shape, especially since Austin did not advocate weight-training, arguing in favor of intense drills. He believed an athlete could "play himself into shape"—but he had to play all-out in practice in order to effectively simulate real game conditions. This took its toll on the players, who began to dread practices. Injuries mounted.

I remember the day Austin lost the team. It was a hot, humid afternoon at St. Vincent during summer camp. Austin didn't feel the players were giving their all. He didn't like the team's performance or its attitude. In a misguided effort to regain control, he pushed every man to his limit. He demanded they play the whole scrimmage with the intensity of a goal-line drill—all-out, full speed, as if it were a real game.

This scrimmage resulted in a number of serious injuries, not to mention minor bruises and sprains. Among the wounded were some key players. Linebacker Bill Saul wrecked his knee and his career. Defensive tackle Ken Kortas's sprained ankle nearly knocked him out of the opening game and slowed him down for the rest of the season. Jim "Cannonball" Butler's damaged knee sidelined him for most of the season and severely handicapped the Steelers' running game. Defensive back Paul Martha made a hit that split his helmet down the middle like a cracked nut, leaving him with a concussion and a serious cut over his right eye.

That's when Austin lost the team. The players no longer had confidence in their coach. Austin responded the only way he knew. He threw tantrums and publicly berated players. The team's discipline deteriorated on and off the field. Drinking by some of the players became a problem.

Bill Austin is the only coach I felt I had to yell at. On Mondays, after games, we'd be in the Roosevelt Hotel or the deli next door, and I'd say to him, "You have to run the ball!" or "What was your thinking when you passed deep on second down!"

This kind of second-guessing wasn't me, but I knew I had to do something to get us back on track. We lost not because we didn't have good players. Remember, we had guys like linebacker Andy Russell, running back Rocky Bleier, guard Sam Davis, defensive back Paul Martha, and punter Bobby Walden.

Austin had lost the team, and I knew I had to make a change. By the end of the 1968 season, I had already begun the search for a new coach. I didn't tell Austin, but he must have seen the handwriting on the wall. With the season's 2-11-1 record, he should have.

The day after the last game of the season, I planned to meet with Austin to tell him we couldn't use him anymore. But before I left for the office, Patricia informed me that it was time to take her to the hospital for the birth of our ninth child. We arrived at the Mercy emergency room entrance, where Dr. Datillo greeted us. By now he was an old friend—he had delivered Duffy, John, and Jim—and we had great confidence in him. This was going to be a busy day. Doctor Datillo said, "Don't worry. You've got plenty of time to go to the office and take care of business. In the meantime, Patricia and I will take care of things here."

At the office, Austin was waiting for me.

"I'm sorry Bill, it just isn't working out," I said. "Thank you for coming to Pittsburgh and for your three years with the Steelers, but we're going in another direction." He seemed to know what was coming and was very gracious.

We talked for a while, and I felt comfortable enough with him that I called a press conference for the afternoon. I invited Bill to the conference and gave him an opportunity to speak after I announced there'd be a coaching change. It all went well, and Bill and I parted on good terms.

Just as the reporters rushed off to file their reports, my secretary, Rene Seavy, came in and said the doctor was on the line. "Dan, you have a beautiful, little girl."

I drove over to the hospital to see Patricia and baby Joan. Everything had gone fine. Looking into Joanie's face for the first time reminded me what's important in life. At times football consumed me, but the miracle of our nine children—Art, Pat, Kathleen, Rita, Dan, Duffy, John, Jim, and Joan—mattered more to me than anything. Family, Faith, Football—those are my priorities. As future events would unfold, I'd have to work to keep things in perspective.

———

On Monday, January 13, 1969, the day after Super Bowl III, Chuck Noll and I met for the first time. We talked for more than two hours. Noll's general knowledge of football and his specific knowledge of the Steelers' strengths, weaknesses, and potential struck me as extraordinary. I mean, it's the day after the Super Bowl, with all the attendant hype, hoopla, and pressure, and he's telling me details about our offense and defense I would have thought only our own coaches would know. He pointed out that the Steelers had traded away their future. He thought the way to build a championship team was through the draft. Get young, raw talent, then teach the fundamentals of the game. Above all, he counseled patience. He knew it would take some time to rebuild the team and instill in the players a winning attitude. It was clear from this very first meeting that Noll was not about building a good team—he wanted nothing less than a Super Bowl championship team.

Chuck and I hit it off from the start. Why wouldn't we? We were both thirty-five years old. He'd grown up in Cleveland, a working-class city much like Pittsburgh, and attended Benedictine High, a Catholic school, where he played football as a running back and defensive lineman. At the University of Dayton, he made an impression as an undersized guard and linebacker. The coaches matched him up against bigger players, forcing him to learn techniques that would offset the size difference. He had to play smart.

In 1953 Paul Brown recruited him. He played seven seasons with the Cleveland Browns as an offensive guard and linebacker. Brown respected Noll's knowledge of the game and once said Chuck could have called the plays as well as the quarterback—or maybe the coach. I think that's right. While Chuck was playing for the Browns, he also attended Cleveland Marshall Law School at night. He told me the reason he chose football over law was because he didn't really like the constant confrontation and arguments that come with being a lawyer. I'm sure there are a lot of NFL officials from his time as a head coach who would laugh if they heard that. Then, in 1960, when the American Football League got started, Sid Gillman lured him to the West Coast to coach for the Chargers.

His good reputation as a defensive coach attracted the attention of Don Shula, who brought him to Baltimore as the Colts' defensive backfield coach. By the end of his three-year run in Baltimore, Noll had taken charge of the entire defense. During his years as coach for the Chargers and Colts, Noll had learned how to win.

No question about it. Noll impressed me, but this time I was determined to go through a thoughtful and systematic hiring process. When I told my father about my interview with Noll, he said, "Sounds pretty good. Keep him on the list."

We interviewed Joe Paterno. In three years as head coach at Penn State, Joe's Nittany Lions racked up an impressive 24-7-1 record. He topped off his 1968, 11-0 season with an Orange Bowl victory over Kansas. The forty-year-old Paterno was a coach's coach and an outstanding teacher. Joe and his wife Sue were good friends of mine before he was the head coach at Penn State. Joe and I attended coaches' conventions and loafed together when we could. When he came to Pittsburgh recruiting for the Nittany Lions, I would tell him about the kids from North Catholic. Of course I saw him when he would speak at banquets in Pittsburgh and elsewhere. He talked to me when he got offers to coach in the NFL, and I always gave him the best advice I could. After the first interview, we were interested, but it became clear Joe was committed to Penn State. So we turned to the other candidates on our short list, interviewed them, and circled back around to Noll.

The second time I met with Chuck, the Chief sat in. He saw right away Chuck was a good man. He had character and integrity. Though he wasn't from Pittsburgh, he appreciated the city and understood the people. My father and I both picked up on his intensity and his passion for winning. He was our kind of guy.

Though we didn't agree on every issue, I admired his honesty and willingness to stand up for what he believed. We wanted someone who shared our philosophy, but not a yes-man. We needed a coach who could take the team, mold it, and make it his own.

By the third meeting, we were convinced Noll was our man. For this last interview, he brought his wife and son to Pittsburgh. Marianne and Chris stayed at our house. While Marianne and Patricia talked about school and housing, Chris and our kids played in the backyard of our Mt. Lebanon home. We knew Chuck had interviewed with other teams, Buffalo and Boston, but all of us seemed to know that Pittsburgh was the right fit.

On January 27, 1969, we announced Chuck Noll as the Steelers head coach and introduced him to the Pittsburgh press corps. The reporters noted that Noll was the fourteenth head coach in the Steelers' thirty-six-year history. One writer asked him why he thought he was the guy who could end all the years of losing football teams in

Pittsburgh. I loved Chuck's answer. He looked the reporter right in the eye and said, "Losing has nothing to do with geography." We'd had a new coach every two or three years. If Noll was the guy we thought he was, we'd put a stop to this revolving door.

———————

Chuck hadn't even unpacked his bags when the 1969 draft began on January 29, 1969. For the last three years he had personally scouted Joe Greene, a six-foot-four, 275-pound defensive tackle at North Texas State. Chuck saw something special in Greene: He refused to lose. In his three-year career at North Texas, he had lost only five games and acquired the nickname "Mean Joe," though Greene himself hated it. Initially, Chuck was drawn to Joe's ferocious play, but looking deeper, he saw a natural athlete who had the potential to be a team leader. Noll believed a man had to be a great player on the field before he could become a team leader. A leader didn't just talk a good game—he played a good game. In Noll's mind, Greene would be the Steelers' number-one draft pick.

The Steelers' scouting corps, however, had been looking at quarterback Terry Hanratty. Terry was a Western Pennsylvania boy from Butler and a Notre Dame All-American. In 1966, he had led the Irish to a national championship.

My brother Art came to the Steelers in 1964, and by 1969 he headed our scouting corps. In the mid-1960s, Buddy Parker came up with the idea for a scouting combine. Under Parker's direction former Steelers cornerback and later scout, Jack Butler, established the multiteam scouting collaborative known as LESTO (Lions, Eagles, Steelers Talent Organization). I talked to Jack almost every night and reviewed with him the operations of the combine. When the Chicago Bears later joined, it became BLESTO. The combine allowed member clubs to scout college talent across the nation, while sharing the expense four ways. BLESTO scouts tested and scored players, providing measurable information—weight, height, speed, strength, and productivity—as well as intangibles like intensity and attitude. This system vastly improved our ability to scout and make good draft decisions. It was a far cry from the days of Ray Byrne's letters, newspaper clippings, and three-by-five cards.

Under Butler's leadership, BLESTO became one of the best scouting collaboratives in football. For fifty years, he did a great job and trained most of the good scouts in the NFL.

Noll took into account BLESTO information, but relied heavily on his own knowledge and keen sights. He knew exactly what players he needed. First, he would build his defense. He always said, "In order to win a game, you have to first not lose it." Chuck picked Joe Greene—not Hanratty—in the first round.

He didn't even have business cards yet, and already he had made one of the most important draft selections in Steelers history. He would build the team on Joe Greene's broad shoulders. Hanratty came to us in the second round. Bill Nunn advised Chuck and Art to draft defensive lineman L.C. Greenwood, who with Joe Greene would make up half the famed "Steel Curtain" of the 1970s.

It was a good start.

Now Noll had to win the team. He had to get them together and make them think and act as one. They had to care about winning—and they had to care about one another. He knew he couldn't build a championship team without that kind of closeness. This was easier said than done. From the very first there was trouble. Joe Greene, our Steelers number-one draft pick, held out in a salary dispute and reported to summer camp at Latrobe a day late.

He wasn't happy about being drafted by Pittsburgh. He felt the Steelers were losers and admitted, "When I came into the league, you could have given me a choice of all the professional teams in existence at that time and I would have picked the Pittsburgh Steelers last. It wasn't a very good football team, it lost a lot of ballgames. I didn't celebrate the day I got drafted."

To make matters worse, the Pittsburgh press wasn't kind to Greene—"Joe Who?" the Pittsburgh headlines read. As big and mean as he looked, Joe was a sensitive guy. The mean-spirited headlines hurt his pride, and when he finally reported to camp after all the other players, we feared his negative attitude might infect the entire team. But, in fact, it was just the opposite. Joe's intensity and his desire to win marked him as a leader from the very start.

At his first practice, Noll called an "Oklahoma Drill," a scrimmage which pitted one offensive lineman against one defensive lineman. The job for the offense was to open a hole for the running back, while the goal for the defense was to shed the blocker and make the tackle—full speed, full contact. Our veteran linemen—Sam Davis, Ray Mansfield, Bruce Van Dyke—were waiting for him, eager to show the rookie what professional football was all about. But Joe put on a defensive tour de force, a clinic on how the game should be played. He literally threw our offensive linemen aside and clobbered our backs. This one-man wrecking crew shook up our players and made them realize they would have to kick it into high gear if they were to compete with this "rookie."

Andy Russell told me he felt this practice was a turning point in the history of the franchise. He said the old vets thought, "Who does this guy think he is?" He and the other veterans were very cynical, just as the media was. How good could he be? Russell and I talked about the Oklahoma Drill and how difficult it is for a defensive player. Andy said, "The offensive guy knows the count, and to make the tackle you have to be strong enough to get rid of that blocker quickly to have any chance at getting a clean shot at the running back. Ray Mansfield was first, and Joe threw him away like he was a paper doll and crushed the back. I was standing there with some other guys, and we just looked at each other. This kid was backing up his mouth. That was the start, and from that day Joe Greene set a tone and an attitude on the practice field and in games that losing is completely unacceptable."

If his teammates weren't playing up to their potential, Greene would get in their faces and tell them so. This was exactly what Noll wanted. He aimed to take Pittsburgh to the Super Bowl, and he dished out some pretty tough talk of his own. At his very first meeting with the players, he announced that many of them weren't good enough to make the team. Those who did would have to prove themselves. The players soon divided in their opinion of Noll. Some of them were impressed, others were just scared.

And rightly so. Chuck told me we could make some trades and quick fixes to win a game or two, but to get to the Super Bowl, we needed to start from scratch, to build for the long haul. The veterans—those few worth keeping—would have to relearn the basics of blocking and tackling. What he looked for in a rookie was athleticism: raw talent that he could shape. He'd rather have rookie athletes than experienced players, for the veterans had to unlearn bad habits. He required veterans to learn a proper three-point stance, the placement of their feet and hands—inches mattered—and how to read and exploit an opponent's look or move.

Russell, one of the veterans who did make the cut, told me later, "[Chuck] had not hired a linebacker coach that year. So he was not only the head coach, but the linebacker coach. He drove me crazy through the next few weeks because he really believed in technique. He got down to, 'I want your right foot two inches outside of your opponent's foot. I want you to reach with your right hand.' It became very mechanical. For a while, I felt like I was losing my own personal style. I thought I'd done okay . . . He was really into detail. He taught that success is in the details. It's not about the rah-rah and macho. It doesn't have anything to do with that stuff. It has a lot to do with details. A lot of those details come from understanding the opponent and anticipating what the opponent will do."

Even though he was already a Pro Bowler, Andy agreed that Chuck Noll made him a better player. Chuck had a way of bringing out the best in our players.

Noll imposed strict discipline on the camp. He would have rules, and they would be obeyed. He enforced curfews—if a player came in late, he got fined. That's what happened to our star receiver, Roy Jefferson. In 1968 Jefferson was our best offensive player, a receiver who had over a thousand yards and scored eleven touchdowns, a major accomplishment considering that team wasn't very good and there were only fourteen games on the schedule back then. In 1969 we played a preseason game in Montreal against the New York Giants, and Jefferson missed a curfew. This was Noll's first season, and when he found out Jefferson had come in late, Chuck called me and asked if I was going to back him when he disciplined one of the best players on the team. I told Chuck, "You know I'm going to back you."

So we called Jefferson and had him come to Chuck's room for a meeting. Chuck told him, "You missed curfew, so we're sending you home." Jefferson tried to talk his way out of it, but when that didn't work, he turned to me and said, "Dan, this is going to make me look like a bad guy." But I told Roy we had to have discipline on the team—Chuck Noll was in charge, and he had my complete support. Well, there were a couple of other incidents with Roy in 1969, and even though he posted another 1,000-yard receiving season and scored nine more touchdowns and made the Pro Bowl again, we traded him to Baltimore for a fourth-round draft choice. If it seems the Colts pulled one over on us, we used that fourth-round draft pick to get Dwight White, who became part of the Steel Curtain and started at defensive end on four Super Bowl teams.

The players came to respect Chuck's authority because they respected his knowledge of the game—and his plan for success. Everyone understood what he expected of them, whether at a practice drill, the classroom, or in the weight room. He instilled in the team a winning attitude and made the players believe in themselves, not through phony pep-talks or red-faced harangues, but through a system of intense preparation, rigorous study, and team closeness. When it all came together, the team would play better than the sum of its parts.

To the fans Chuck's first season looked like a disaster. The Steelers went 1-13. In the second game of the season, the Philadelphia Eagles beat us 41-27. In this game, we started to come back in the fourth quarter. On third down and short, maybe two yards to go, we didn't make it. We went for it on fourth down and again didn't make it. In a fit of frustration, Joe Greene picked up the ball and threw it into the stands. This got him thrown out of the game, and most people in the league thought he was a smart-aleck. But when I saw him do that, I knew we had a good man. This guy wanted to win and wouldn't tolerate failure.

Despite losing the next twelve games, Noll didn't lose the team. I noticed it, and so did my father. It was an amazing thing to see. The players understood that building the team would take time. They could see progress, even if the fans and sportswriters didn't.

Everything depended on the draft. Noll's practiced eye and insight, coupled with BLESTO intelligence and great scouting from Art, Bill Nunn, and Dick Haley, brought outstanding talent to the Steelers.

Nunn, the sports editor for the *Pittsburgh Courier*, one of the country's largest African-American newspapers, joined the Steelers' scouting staff full time in 1969 when Noll took over the team. Focusing his attention on black colleges in the South, like Grambling and Prairie View and Florida A&M, he discovered amazing talent. For years he had covered and reported on black college players overlooked by NFL scouts and sportswriters for America's major newspapers.

The Steelers had black players going back to the very first season in 1933, but we didn't systematically scout or recruit them. Like all the other pro teams, we tended to scout the big universities, which at that time were predominantly white, so we seldom saw black players.

In 1967 I'd been reading Bill Nunn's column in the *Courier* and was especially interested in his annual Black College All-America Team. Why didn't we know about these guys? A reporter at the *Courier*, Rick Roberts, used to hang around our offices at the Roosevelt Hotel, so I asked him why Bill Nunn never came around. Roberts went back and told Nunn what I said, and Nunn told him to tell me that I didn't have to worry about Bill Nunn coming down to the Steelers offices, because he didn't like the way the Steelers did business. So I called the *Courier* and asked Bill if he would come talk to me. He hesitated at first, then agreed to meet.

"How come we never see you down here?" I asked.

"There have been many times when I felt getting into the press box and different things, that because I was the black newspaper, I wasn't particularly welcome," Nunn said. "Plus, I turn out an All-America football team every year, and nobody from the Steelers has ever contacted me. I heard from the Los Angeles Rams about 'Deacon' Dan Towler, and I even heard from the New York Giants about Roosevelt Brown. To tell you the truth, nobody from the Steelers ever called me. I don't think you'll ever be a winner."

"Well, why don't you join us, scout for us?"

"I've got a job," he replied.

"Work for us half time, then," I said. "Look at the games, take notes on the players, and send us reports—tell us what you think."

I think Nunn was surprised I even called him. He may have thought we were deliberately excluding black players, but the truth was we didn't know them or how good they were.

I can't tell you how important Bill Nunn was to our organization. His father, Bill Nunn Sr., was editor-in-chief of the *Courier*. He sent his son to college at West Virginia State, where he excelled at basketball, so much so that the Harlem Globetrotters wanted him. The NBA wasn't integrated in the late 1940s, but some NBA teams looked at him as well, thinking he might be the one to break that color barrier. As it turned out, another Pittsburgher, Chuck Cooper of Duquesne, had that honor. Bill decided not to pursue a career in basketball but instead went to work with his father at the *Pittsburgh Courier.*

When Bill came to the Steelers, he gave us an edge other teams didn't have. Joe Gilliam, John Stallworth, Mel Blount, Ernie Holmes, Chuck Hinton, Ben McGee, Donnie Shell, Jack McClairen, Willie McClung, and Frank Lewis—all appeared on Bill's black All-America team. He had a great eye for talent and scouted the Big 10 schools as well. From the beginning, Nunn was more than a scout. He was a trusted advisor to Noll, Art, and to me, and a confidant to the players. Working in our front office, he became the first African-American executive on any NFL club.

As we worked together we got to know each other very well. We became friends. One of the greatest compliments I've ever received came from Nunn. He told Joe Gordon, our communications director, "I don't think Dan sees color. And I don't say that about a lot of people." Bill Nunn made a real difference for generations of African-American athletes. He provided opportunities in the NFL, opening doors for black coaches and front office employees. For him to say someone didn't see color really carried a lot of weight.

With Nunn, Art, Chuck, and director of player personnel Dick Haley focused on the draft, the Steelers scored big in the years from 1970 to 1972. We had the overall number-one draft pick in 1970. With it we took Terry Bradshaw from Louisiana Tech. Our scouts believed a talent like Bradshaw would come around only once in a decade.

In round three, we took Mel Blount, a great defensive back from Southern University. Nunn and Noll disagreed whether Blount was a safety or cornerback. Nunn worried the six-foot–four Blount might not be quick enough to cover deep. But poring over game film, Noll correctly predicted Blount could use his size to bump speedy wide receivers at the line, disrupt their patterns, and cover them deep.

As Noll built the Steelers with the addition of Bradshaw and Blount in 1970, I worked at opening Three Rivers Stadium. The Steelers had never had a home of their own. Most recently, we had played at aging Forbes Field and competed with the University of Pittsburgh Panthers for the use of Pitt Stadium. During the season we practiced in the dilapidated facilities of South Park. Owned by Allegheny County, South Park was better suited for stock shows and county fairs. The "locker room" didn't have any lockers—just hooks for uniforms and equipment. Most of the showers didn't work, the players had to run cross-country for lack of a track (during the Buddy Parker and Bill Austin years some of the veterans never ran at all but loafed in the woods, only joining the rookies when they reached the tree line), and the whole place reeked of decay. It was pretty hard to feel like a winner in these conditions.

Since 1965 both the Pirates and Steelers had worked with city and county officials to build a new stadium with state-of-the-art facilities. I never told the city we'd move the team if we didn't get a stadium the equal of other NFL teams, but I know the fans and others worried about it. My father and I never considered taking the team out of Pittsburgh. In many ways, we always felt the team belonged to the people of Pittsburgh, and we held it in trust for them.

But figuring out what the city would contribute and putting together the financing package was a big job. Fortunately, good will prevailed on all sides. We agreed on a North Side site for the new combination football-baseball stadium. In fact, we located it right where old Exposition Park once stood, where professional football began and where my father had played as a youth.

I worked with the designers to develop the architectural program for Three Rivers Stadium. In its final design, it looked like a big layer cake, perfectly round. The seating capacity of 50,000 was much greater than Forbes Field (35,000) and about equal to Pitt Stadium (55,000), with three tiers of grandstands. Three Rivers' synthetic grass (Tartan Turf), giant electronic scoreboard, and elegant indoor restaurant (the Allegheny Club) contrasted starkly with the muddy infield, manual scoreboard, and hotdog vendors and peanut gallery at Forbes Field.

With Three Rivers Stadium we finally had a facility we could be proud of. The stadium had to work for both baseball and football, so there were many compromises. All in all, I think we did a pretty good job. One day, before opening, I took my father on a tour. He wanted to see the location of our boxes, so I took him to the second tier. Our box overlooked the 50-yard line, perfect to watch a football game.

He complained, "This is a terrible place!"

I said, "Why? It's the best place to be."

"No," he answered, "I can't see the baseball. You put me behind home plate!"

As I said, Dad always was a baseball man.

———

We opened the stadium for football on September 20, 1970, with the help of 45,538 cheering Steelers fans. Our jubilation was dampened somewhat by the 19-7 loss to the Houston Oilers. The Steelers broke their sixteen-game losing streak with a 23-10 win over the Buffalo Bills on October 11—our first victory in the new stadium. Later that season, on November 2, we played our first regular season *Monday Night Football* game at Three Rivers Stadium, beating the Cincinnati Bengals, 21-10. ABC televised the game with Howard Cosell, Don Meredith, and Keith Jackson calling the action.

The new facility could be accessed by bus, car, and boat. The large parking lots—thirty-five acres—surrounding the stadium proved ideal for tailgating parties, which quickly became a Steelers tradition. At first, we used whatever promotions we could to help fill seats; giveaways and fireworks always boosted attendance. I felt good when the ticket office reported our first sellout crowd, 50,353, for our game against the New York Jets on November 8, 1970. The standing-room-only crowd went wild when we beat Namath and company, 21-17.

The 1971 draft proved to be one of our best. With it we acquired the nucleus of the Super Bowl championship teams that would soon follow.

Receiver Frank Lewis of Grambling came in the first round.

Penn State linebacker Jack Ham in the second.

In the fourth round we tapped East Texas State defensive end Dwight White and offensive guard Gerry "Moon" Mullins of Southern Cal.

Round five brought Larry Brown, a tight end from the University of Kansas.

Craig Hanneman, a guard from Oregon State, was our sixth-round pick.

Ernie Holmes, a defensive tackle from Texas Southern, came in the eighth round.

We nabbed safeties Mike Wagner, from Western Illinois, in the eleventh round and Glen Edwards, from Florida A&M, as a free agent.

We fought Cleveland for the lead of the AFC Central Division for most of the 1971 season. Toward the end of the year we were both tied with 5-5 records. Then our lack of experience caught up with us, and we lost three of our last four games. It was a disappointing end to the season, but we had been in the run for a championship for the first time in many years.

We felt 1972 would be our year. Our number-one draft pick, Franco Harris, the outstanding Penn State running back, filled a key position and made an impact on the team almost immediately. Some say my brother Art and Chuck disagreed over who our number-one pick should be. Noll always energized these conversations and debates by throwing in a name that would create controversy and force everyone to take a stand. He did this with running back Robert Newhouse, who had been scouted by Bill Nunn and was a guy Nunn thought fit our style better. But I can tell you that we all ultimately agreed on Franco. There was never any question he'd be our number-one pick. And Franco won Nunn over the first time he put on a Steelers uniform. "The thing that impressed me about Franco," said Nunn, "was that coming out of Penn State, he wasn't the number-one back, but he showed a willingness to work. That first day at practice, he ran everything to the goal line, and he had those quick feet."

Joe Gilliam, one of the first African-American quarterbacks to be drafted in the NFL, came to us from Tennessee State. Other draft picks helped bolster the already formidable "Steel Curtain," a term coined just a few months before in a Pittsburgh radio contest. Even with Greene, Greenwood, Holmes, and White, Noll continued to seek defensive depth.

Al Davis's Oakland Raiders came to Three Rivers to open the 1972 season. Al had built a tough team, but linebacker Henry Davis blocked a punt, and Bradshaw ran for two touchdowns and passed for another in a 34-28 win. Then we traveled to Cincinnati, for a disappointing 15-10 loss. On the road again at St. Louis, we defeated the Cardinals, 25-19. Then on to Dallas, where the Cowboys squeezed past us, 17-13. Following our loss to the Cowboys we went on a five-game winning streak, starting with Houston, 24-7. The Steel Curtain nearly shut down New England, 33-3. Our offense powered past Buffalo, 38-21, then back home to play Cincinnati, where we avenged our earlier loss, 40-17. Against Kansas City, our defense held the Chiefs to only one score and we beat them, 16-7, a big win for us—they had been Super Bowl champions two years before. In a last-minute nail-biter,

Cleveland defeated us, 26-24. We would not be defeated again for the rest of the season, and two of those wins proved to be important building blocks for the new Steelers.

The November 26 game against Minnesota brought a lot of national sportswriters to town, and these guys weren't used to seeing the Steelers win important games this late in the season. Beating the Vikings was similar to defeating the Chiefs. Minnesota had won three straight division championships and played in Super Bowl IV. Dave Anderson of the *New York Times* wrote this from the Three Rivers Stadium press box that day:

> The weather never seems to change much here this time of year. It's usually cloudy and gloomy . . . Art Rooney never seems to change much, either . . . But his Pittsburgh Steelers have changed. They used to find a way to lose. But today, they found a way to win a big game from the Minnesota Vikings, and if they find a way to a win over the Cleveland Browns here next Sunday, they may go on to win their first division title in the 40-year history of the franchise. In other National Football League cities, a division title is a stepping-stone to the playoffs. Here, it's a milestone.

We did beat the Browns that next Sunday, but that didn't clinch the AFC Central Division title. To do that we had to go to Houston and beat an Oilers team that would finish 1-13 that season. It sounds like a piece of cake, but it wasn't. L.C. Greenwood and starting guard Sam Davis were out with injuries. Two more starting offensive linemen, Jon Kolb and Gerry Mullins, had bad cases of the flu, and Mullins only made it into the third quarter. Another starting guard, Bruce Van Dyke, pulled a calf muscle in the first quarter and was done for the day. Ron Shanklin, our leading receiver, suffered an injury in the first quarter and was done for the day. Jim Clack injured an ankle and was done. Craig Hanneman, Greenwood's backup, aggravated a knee injury and was done for the day. Terry Bradshaw dislocated a finger in the second quarter and left the game, never to return. Dwight White injured a knee, and Steve Furness, a backup defensive lineman, sprained an ankle. Larry Brown, usually our tight end, had to play flanker.

In this situation a great player steps up, and that's exactly what Joe Greene did on December 10, 1972, in the Astrodome. Greene had five sacks, blocked a short field goal, recovered one fumble, and forced another that set up two field goals for us. So in what turned out to be a 9-3 win that kept our hopes alive, Joe Greene personally accounted for nine of the game's twelve points.

That win put us in a position where all we had to do to win the AFC Central Division was to travel to San Diego and beat the Chargers. We did that, 24-2, and we won the first division championship in Steelers history. We thought we were unstoppable. When we took the field against the Oakland Raiders at Three Rivers Stadium on December 23, 1972, we felt like a Super Bowl team. We had assembled a team like no other in Steelers history.

The Steelers hadn't played in a meaningful postseason game since 1947, when we lost to the Philadelphia Eagles in a game to decide the Eastern Division championship. In 1962 we had played in what the NFL then called the Playoff Bowl, really nothing but a consolation game for the two teams that finished second in their divisions. But now we were going into the 1972 playoffs as the AFC Central Division champions against Davis's AFC West champion Oakland Raiders.

Game time was 12:30. Usually I picked up my father an hour or two before kickoff, but today I wanted to get there early, so I drove directly to Three Rivers, while someone else picked up the Chief. I arrived at about 10 a.m. and began making the rounds, talking to groundskeepers, game officials and referees, league representatives, and even the scoreboard people. I also looked for Mossy Murphy, Bill

Day, and Joe Gordon to check on the afternoon's entertainment. Everything seemed a go, and Steelers fans were already streaming into the stands.

Offense	Defense
RB, Rocky Bleier	S, Ralph Anderson
QB, Terry Bradshaw	CB, Mel Blount
TE, Larry Brown	LB, Ed Bradley
C, Jim Clack	LB, Henry Davis
G, Sam Davis	CB, John Dockery
RB, Steve Davis	S, Glen Edwards
RB, John Fuqua	DT, Joe Greene
OT, Gordon Gravelle	DE, L.C. Greenwood
QB, Terry Hanratty	LB, Jack Ham
RB, Franco Harris	DT, Craig Hanneman
OT, Mel Holmes	DT, Ernie Holmes
OT, Jon Kolb	DT, Ben McGee
C, Ray Mansfield	CB, John Rowser
TE, John McMakin	LB, Andy Russell
G, Gerry Mullins	LB, Brian Stenger
WR, Barry Pearson	S, Mike Wagner
RB, Preston Pearson	LB, George Webster
WR, Ron Shanklin	DE, Dwight White
G, Bruce Van Dyke	
WR, Al Young	

Punter-Kicker
K, Roy Gerela
P, Bob Walden

I saw Al Davis on the sidelines as the Raiders began their warm-up routine. Al always liked to talk to the best players on the other team during pre-game. He'd say things like, "Hey, Blount, you would look good in silver and black." Or, "Franco, the weather in Oakland is better than this." He was always looking for ways to distract an opponent. I wanted to be sure he left our players alone—especially for a big game like this—so I walked over to say hello. We exchanged pleasantries, nothing of substance. It had been three years since the difficult realignment talks in 1969. Since then, when we saw each other at games and league meetings, we were always cordial. But I can't say we were friends. We shook hands, chatted a while about league matters, and then I went up to the press box.

The Three Rivers' press box was long and narrow. This day, it was packed with newsmen. The public address announcer and television and radio broadcasters worked in smaller boxes. The camera operators positioned themselves on a stand higher in the stadium, above all the people, and another stand in the end zone.

The Chief arrived at the stadium about 11 a.m. We met in our offices, which were located on the ground floor. My son Art was with him, along with a couple of Steelers staff, who worked security with their two-way radios.

Patricia, the girls, and some of our younger boys sat in an outside box. My daughter Kathleen was the most vocal. She would yell and scream at the officials—and the coaches. "They don't know what they're doing," she'd shout, and she was usually right. The McGinleys and some of my brothers were in a box nearby, and Marianne Noll sat about four boxes down, with young Chris. These boxes were not elaborate affairs. They had concrete floors and were exposed to the open air.

The day was cold, not freezing, but cold and gray. Franco's Italian Army got the fans warmed up with chants and cheers. It was amazing how quickly this twenty-two-year-old rookie had captured the hearts of the Pittsburgh fans. African American, Italian American, Irish American . . . it didn't matter. In the fourteen-game regular season he had rushed for over a thousand yards, an incredible accomplishment for a rookie. When he first came to camp we weren't sure he was aggressive enough. But on game day he not only found the holes, he knew which way to bounce and run for daylight. You can't teach that kind of thing. And when he had to, he put his head down and plowed through defenders. Franco was not only a special football player but a special person. I found him to be an exceptional individual off the field as well as on. He was quiet and thoughtful, he didn't stay out late drinking with the veterans, and I could see he had the qualities of a leader.

The Raiders won the coin toss. At exactly 12:30 we kicked off. Both defenses played tough and neither offense could move the ball. At halftime the game was scoreless. In the third quarter, our kicker Roy Gerela booted an 18-yard field goal for the first points of the game. In the fourth quarter, Gerela kicked a 29-yarder, putting the Steelers up 6-0. Despite the low score, I thought we were dominating the Raiders. In the third quarter, Raiders' quarterback Ken Stabler came in for Daryle Lamonica, who had thrown two interceptions and been sacked four times. But Stabler didn't move the Raiders any better than Lamonica had—until he read a blitz and took advantage of it. With less than two minutes on the clock, he turned the corner on defensive end Craig Hanneman and scampered 30 yards down the left side for the go-ahead touchdown.

Bradshaw came back and advanced the ball to our 40-yard line. The Raiders really tightened up. One, two, three plays—we were getting nowhere. We called a timeout on fourth down. So it's fourth-and-10, we have the ball on our 40-yard line, last play, no question. In our box no one said a thing. The clock on the scoreboard read 22 seconds. Bradshaw took the snap, scrambled out of the pocket, dodged

Raiders linemen, and threw that ball with everything he had . . . Well, as you know, the rest is history. Franco's Immaculate Reception was a defining moment for the Steelers. We showed the world that this was a team to be reckoned with—no longer lovable losers—a team of destiny.

Even so, the controversy over the Immaculate Reception call began almost immediately. In our locker room, Chuck Noll said, "The officials know what they're doing—they said it hit Tatum, so that's what it did."

When I talked to Frenchy Fuqua in the locker room, Andy Russell had already taken him aside and counseled him not to say anything to the press that might cast doubt on the call. Frenchy contributed to the mystery, saying, "I'm not telling anybody, this will go to the grave with me."

But I agree with Russell: I don't think Frenchy really knew what happened. Tatum clobbered him, and Frenchy didn't know whether the ball, Tatum—or a ton of bricks—hit him.

Myron Cope, who loves to tell stories, claimed to be the only person to see the WTAE film of the hit. He claims the television station secured it in a vault and then lost it. He liked to play it up, same as Frenchy, but both those guys loved media attention.

Al Davis and Raiders coach John Madden were furious with the call. They thought the Raiders had the game in the bag. To this day, I don't think either one has any idea what happened. At the end of the next regular league business meeting in March, Davis told me, "We got robbed." Later still, he told me that if it hadn't been for that game, the Raiders would have gone on to win many Super Bowls and be remembered as the greatest football team ever. I don't know about that. They may have been "greater" than the NFC teams, but they had to get past the black and gold to get to the Super Bowl.

What I do know is that fans, sportswriters, scientists, conspiracy theorists, and even psychics have studied and dissected and diagrammed this one play to death. I believe the ball bounced off Tatum, and Franco made a great catch. But the greatest play in NFL history will forever remain a mystery.

Elated fans mobbed the players before the team even got off the field. Some of the players couldn't get into the tunnel leading to the locker room. I was worried our guys might get hurt, that a fan would trip a player and the crowd might fall on him. But the Pittsburgh people were really, really good as they celebrated our first division title in forty years.

NFL spokesman Val Pinchbeck said to the *Pittsburgh Press*, "Pittsburgh never won anything before so their fans don't know how to act." This stupid comment really upset my father. He hated seeing this kind of thing in print, because it made Pittsburgh—and our fans—look bad. It was a cheap shot. In the next day or two, Dad set the record straight. "The crowds were fine. If you saw the pictures, they weren't looking to cause trouble. They were having a joyous time and congratulating the team. Nobody tried to pull down the goal posts."

After the hubbub of the game died down, our family met for a quiet dinner at Tambellini's Italian restaurant on Seventh Street. The smiling faces at the restaurant told us how proud people were of the Steelers' achievement. But everyone maintained a respectful distance. A nod of the head, a handshake, or a simple "Congratulations"— that's all.

It's hard to explain how much the Steelers meant to the people of Pittsburgh at this time. The old days of steel mills and thriving industry were fast disappearing. As the factories and steel mills closed, tens of thousands of industrial workers found themselves laid off. The region's economy had hit the skids, and Pittsburghers left by the thousands to find work in other parts of the country. We had thought steel would be here forever. It was part of our identity, our character—it was the name of our team. Our self-confidence as a people had been shaken to its core. Pittsburgh's sports teams helped restore some of that old confidence.

The Pirates won the pennant and brought home the World Series trophy in 1971. Now, it was the Steelers' turn to step up and show everyone what Pittsburgh could do.

––––––––––

We all knew beating Miami next week was not a forgone conclusion. But if we beat the Dolphins, we'd have a shot at our first Super Bowl, something our veterans couldn't even imagine a few years ago. Now we were only a game away from professional football's ultimate contest.

The AFC championship game would be played in Pittsburgh. Although they were undefeated, the Dolphins would have to play in our new stadium, on our turf. The home sites in those days were set before the season started, according to a rotation formula. It was our AFC Central Division's turn to host the game. In 1975 the formula would change so that the team with the best record would host the game. Pete Rozelle and NFL officials moved to Pittsburgh and set up an office and press room in the William Penn Hotel.

The world got a pretty good look at Pittsburgh. Even the weather cooperated. The Goodyear Blimp captured on film the Three Rivers with Miami-like weather. On game day, December 31, the thermometer hit seventy-one—warmer that day than Miami.

Three Rivers Stadium and Pittsburgh looked great as the undefeated Dolphins took the field. We scored first after a Bradshaw fumble rolled into the Dolphins' end zone and "Moon" Mullins fell on it. But Terry was badly shaken up on the play (he later told me he didn't know where he was and that the playbook looked like Greek to him) and wouldn't return until near the end of the game. The Dolphins tied the score after a fake punt resulted in a run by kicker Larry

Seiple. Everybody in the stands could see what was happening. As soon as the ball was snapped, our front line turned to form a wedge for our punt returner. But Seiple was on the run already.

We were on our feet shouting, "Turn around! Turn around!"

But no one saw him—Seiple cruised for a 37-yard gain. This set up a 9-yard Earl Morrall touchdown pass to Larry Csonka and the Dolphins had tied us. The fake punt changed the momentum of the game.

In the third quarter, Roy Gerela's field goal gave Pittsburgh a 10-7 lead. But then the Dolphins' Bob Griese, who had been sidelined for the previous ten weeks with a broken leg, came in for Morrall. Right off the bench he threw a 52-yard pass to Paul Warfield, which set up a Jim Kiick touchdown run. Griese led another touchdown drive. Then Noll sent Bradshaw back into the game. He was still shaken, but Bradshaw wanted to play. He threw a touchdown pass, and might have thrown another, but with twenty-two seconds left the Dolphins' Nick Buoniconti intercepted and the game was over. The Dolphins won, 21-17. What a heartbreaker. We thought we were the better team, and the city went into a deep gloom.

That very night, a plane carrying Pirates' great Roberto Clemente, on a humanitarian mission to Managua, Nicaragua, crashed into the ocean. The next day, New Years Day 1973, the city of Pittsburgh mourned.

The 1973 season began with high expectations. Steelers fans bought season tickets in record numbers. In fact, the Steelers have sold out every home game since the Immaculate Reception in 1972. And it wasn't just Pittsburgh that was captivated by the Steelers story. *Sports Illustrated* commissioned award-winning writer Roy Blount Jr. to write a book about our team. While doing the research for *About*

Three Bricks Shy of a Load, Blount embedded himself with the team—he lived, ate, slept, and loafed with the players, in camp and on the road.

Noll didn't like this one bit. Blount would be a fox in the hen house, a threat to Noll's code of secrecy: don't reveal anything—player health, training techniques, football philosophy, or personnel problems—not to other teams, the press, or the fans. Any intelligence might be used by another team to gain an advantage. In this league, coaches believe even a slight edge can mean the difference between winning and losing.

I believed if we were careful and did not speak out of turn, Blount's presence might contribute to the team's closeness. This proved to be the case, as some veteran players later told me.

Feelings for the team ran so high that even pessimistic Pittsburghers allowed themselves to believe this could be the year the Steelers would go all the way to the Super Bowl.

But 1973 would not be our year.

Injuries and inconsistent quarterbacking plagued the team. Frenchy Fuqua injured his shoulder, and Joe Greene was hospitalized with a bad back. Wide receiver Frank Lewis, offensive tackle Gordon Gravelle, and guard/center Jim Clack were all out of action for a part of the season. Even more troubling was the quarterback situation. Bradshaw had proven himself in 1972 but threw too many interceptions. Noll worried Bradshaw wasn't taking his job seriously enough. His inattention drove Chuck crazy. Terry would say, "Just give me the ball and let's go play." Then Bradshaw hurt his shoulder and was out four weeks. Noll turned to Hanratty and Joe Gilliam. Hanratty couldn't shake the stigma of his 1969 rookie season, when the team went 1-13. He was smart and seemed to understand what Noll wanted of him, but he was quickly eclipsed when Bradshaw came to Pittsburgh as the number-one draft pick in 1970. When Hanratty saw he wasn't going to play, he lost his focus and took to clowning around in team meetings. Gilliam, from Tennessee State, came on board in 1972. Intense, focused, almost combative with Noll, he questioned everything.

Who would lead the team? Although Hanratty had a stellar career at Notre Dame—he'd been on the cover of *Sports Illustrated* and *Time*—the players just didn't rally around him. Gilliam, a gifted passer, wanted to throw every play, much to Noll's frustration. Bradshaw had tremendous talent. If he could mature and avoid making mistakes, the players would support him. While Noll tried to figure out which quarterback should have the job, Greene saw the potential in the athletic and affable Bradshaw. Greene's influence with the other players cannot be overestimated. He had emerged as a team leader, and when he took Bradshaw under his wing it seemed clear to everyone who our quarterback would be.

Outside the Steelers organization there was much speculation. Nothing, outside of the weather, concerned Pittsburghers more than the Steelers quarterback controversy. Heated debate could be overheard on every street corner wherever more than one Steelers fan congregated. The newspapers weighed in. The *Courier* touted Gilliam's strong arm. The *Pittsburgh Press* defended Bradshaw, the "Blond Bomber," against charges that he was really the "Bayou Bumpkin" and too dumb to call plays and lead a team. Other papers lauded Hanratty's intelligence and ability.

The San Diego Chargers had the audacity to ask me whether we might like to trade for Johnny Unitas. Johnny, then forty years old, had been let go by the Colts and signed by the Chargers a year earlier. His arm was long gone and his knees were shot—a sad end to a brilliant career. With no disrespect to Johnny, I told them, "No thanks, we're happy with the guys we have."

Although the Steelers finished with a 10-4 record, we came in second in our division. That qualified us for a wild-card game against the Western Division champion Raiders, who we had beaten earlier in the regular season. In that game—played without Terry Bradshaw—Oakland hammered us statistically, but with toughness and big plays by the defense we found a way to win, 17-9. Mike Wagner recovered a fumble, and Mel Blount, Glen Edwards, and Dwight White combined for four interceptions. But the playoff game was a different story. The Raiders embarrassed us in Oakland, 33-14, and ended our Super Bowl hopes for 1973.

———————

The 1974 draft made history. Since the draft was first instituted in 1936, never has one team drafted so many Hall of Famers. That year the Steelers picked Lynn Swann, Jack Lambert, John Stallworth, and Mike Webster. My brother Art, Bill Nunn, and Dick Haley, along with Chuck Noll, had done their homework. They knew which players they wanted and had developed a strategy to get them. But I'll be the first to admit, a little bit of luck figured in our success.

We took Lynn Swann in the first round, an amazing, acrobatic wide receiver from the University of Southern California. We believed Swann could outrun or outjump any defensive back matched up against him—just the kind of talented individual who could help complete our passing attack. We had the throwers, now we needed the catchers.

Noll wanted John Stallworth for his second-round pick. Bill Nunn had brought back excellent reports on this Alabama A&M wide receiver. But he convinced Noll that we could wait until the fourth round to get him because no other team had scouted him as thoroughly as we had. As was the custom back then, Nunn had traveled with the BLESTO scouts on their swing through the South, but the practice track was wet on the rainy day they timed Stallworth in the 40-yard dash. Nunn's intuition told him there was something special about this young man. The next day Nunn faked a bout of the flu and told the other BLESTO scouts to go on without him. When they left, he didn't waste a minute. He got Stallworth on a dry track, put him through his paces, and got good times on him, much better than those recorded by the BLESTO guys the day before.

Later, when the BLESTO game film of Stallworth arrived at the Steelers office, it somehow got lost and never made it to the other clubs. I can't explain to this day whether this was deliberate or just a fortunate foul-up. We also got a break at the Senior Bowl—the college all-star game that's attended by droves of NFL scouts—when the coaches there played Stallworth at defensive back instead of wide receiver.

Noll was concerned about missing out on Stallworth, but he trusted Nunn's judgment. We'd wait on Stallworth until our next pick in round four (we had traded away our third-round choice to Oakland) and take Jack Lambert as our second-round pick. Lambert appeared too tall and thin to be a linebacker, but our scouts chanced to see him at Kent State. Art watched a practice that had been moved from a muddy field to a gravel parking lot. He saw this guy tackling full speed on the gravel, then calmly picking rock chips out of his knees and elbows as he hustled back to the huddle. He didn't have much meat on his bones but he used everything he had. We got Lambert as the forty-sixth pick of the draft.

Much to Noll's relief, we got Stallworth with one of our two picks in the fourth round—UCLA cornerback Jim Allen was the other— just as Nunn had predicted.

In the fifth round, we got a guy who proved to be the key to our offensive line, Mike Webster, a great, quick center from Wisconsin. He wasn't the biggest center around, but he was impossible to intimidate and knew how to utilize leverage to stop in their tracks guys fifty pounds heavier.

At first, not everyone saw the brilliance of this draft. The *Pittsburgh Post-Gazette* offered this opinion:

The Steelers seemed to have come out of the first five rounds of the draft appreciably strengthened at wide receiver but nowhere else. They didn't get a tight end, and the ones remaining are more suspect than prospect. They didn't get a punter, although none of the nation's best collegiate kickers went in the first five rounds. They didn't get an offensive tackle that might've shored up what could well become a weakness. What they did get was Swann, who seems to be a sure-pop to help; Lambert, who figures to be the number-5 linebacker if he pans out; and three question marks.

I guess sportswriters often know their stuff and sometimes get it right. This time they didn't understand our needs and didn't appreciate our draft strategy. Working together—the coaches and the scouts—we hit the jackpot in 1974.

Just when things seemed to be going well, the 1974 season began to unravel almost before it started. On July 3, 1974, the National Football League Players Association (NFLPA), founded in 1956, called a strike. With a list of fifty-seven grievances, about a quarter of the veteran players across the league refused to report to summer camp. The main issue seemed to be free agency. When a player's contract expired and he wanted to go to another team, the "Rozelle Rule," in effect since 1963, mandated compensation—either in draft picks or cash—to the original club. This made free agency practically meaningless in the NFL. Few, if any, clubs wanted to pick up a veteran who might cost them draft picks. Between 1963 and 1974, only four players successfully moved to other clubs. The players' union wanted the league to allow "free agents" to sign with new teams without compensation to the original club. Most owners objected to doing business this way, fearing it would encourage raiding and ruin the competitive balance of the league, which we had achieved through the draft.

At St. Vincent on the first day of camp, we found a picket line. Bradshaw and other veterans would not cross the line. Our rookies reported and so did some of our older players, who feared missing their opportunity to play in the National Football League. Joe Gilliam was in this latter category.

Now, when I say picket line I don't mean shouting people armed with clubs and bricks. This wasn't the Homestead Strike of 1892. No Pinkertons this time, just a bunch of athletes, some of them with signs, most of them with long hair and mustaches—this was the 1970s after all—loafing, talking, and not at all threatening. I asked the Steelers player representative, Rocky Bleier, to check with the union and see if I might talk to the team. Rocky said it was okay and that he would stand beside me. Together, we'd answer any questions the players might have. I think talking to them did some good.

Certainly, there were no hard feelings on either side. In some ways, it brought our team closer together. Joe Greene took a special interest in Terry Bradshaw during the strike, letting the other players know that as far as he was concerned, strike or no strike, Terry was the team's number-one quarterback. Greene also made sure Terry didn't get caught up in union politics and protected him from the media, which seemed determined to make a controversy out of the Steelers quarterback situation. Greene knew these distractions would hurt not only Terry but the team as well.

The strike continued well into August. On my first visit to the picket line I struck up a conversation with Joe Gilliam, who was about to cross. He said, "Mr. Rooney, I have to cross. It's my only chance to make this team. If I don't cross, I know I'm gone. This is my shot."

I said, "You've got to do what you think is right."

I talked to the other guys about some of the issues. The list kept growing (by the end of the strike it had grown to ninety-three grievances). I wanted them to know I respected their right to organize and negotiate for what they thought was fair. I didn't promise we could agree right now on everything, but I told them we'd make every effort to work things out.

By the time of our first preseason game, we had enough players to field a team. All our talented rookies—Swann, Lambert, Stallworth, Webster, and a free agent named Donnie Shell—were there, as was Joe Gilliam. Gilliam got in a lot of time throwing passes to Swann and Stallworth, and running plays with the first team. Usually, these guys wouldn't have gotten the full attention of the coaching staff, and certainly they wouldn't have gotten in much playing time. Lambert had been making weekly trips from his home in Ohio to Pittsburgh to study films and learn the playbook. He and the other rookies were highly motivated. In a way, the strike gave the rookies—and Gilliam— a real leg up on the players who stayed out. Gilliam had a very good preseason, and played a big role in our perfect 6-0 record. So when we started the season for real, Noll gave him the nod as quarterback, even though Bradshaw and the other veterans had ended their holdout.

On September 15, 1974, we played Baltimore in our season opener. Gilliam led us to a 30-0 victory, completing 17 of 31 passes for 257 yards, including a 54-yard touchdown bomb to Lynn Swann. Noll, of course, allowed his quarterbacks to call their own plays, but he wasn't pleased with Gilliam's reliance on the pass. But who could argue with a 30-0 win? For Noll the real story was the defense. This was the first shutout we'd had since December 1972, and our defense dominated the Colts, sacking the Baltimore quarterbacks six times.

Next we went to Mile High Stadium in Denver and battled the Broncos to a grueling 35-35 overtime tie—the first overtime tie in NFL history, because the league had just instituted the rule to play one 15-minute sudden-death overtime period in any regular season game that was tied after four quarters. The game lasted 3 hours 49 minutes with 160 plays. Unbelievably, Gilliam threw 50 passes, completing 31 for 348 yards and one touchdown.

Our first loss of the season came at the hands of Oakland. They killed us 17-0, our first shutout loss since 1964. Oakland's defense limited Gilliam to 8 completions in 31 attempts. The Raiders intercepted him three times.

Noll grew more and more frustrated with Gilliam's one-dimensional attack. He continued to defy Noll and never established the ground game even though we had Franco and Rocky. He'd call a pass on third and inches—the Raiders knew he'd throw every time and were ready for him.

The next week we played in the Astrodome in Houston. We didn't expect to have trouble with the Oilers, but they intercepted Gilliam twice. Their only score came on a 47-yard scramble on an end around by rookie sensation Billy "White Shoes" Johnson. With the exception of that one lapse, our defense continued to dominate.

We were all wondering about the inconsistency of our offense, and Noll now had real concern about the quarterback position. He gave Gilliam every chance to prove himself, but Joe resisted Chuck's instructions. He wouldn't follow the game plan, wouldn't bring our running backs into the play mix.

At Arrowhead Stadium in Kansas City, we faced the Chiefs and a crowd of over 65,000. Gilliam had a decent game, completing 14 of 37 passes for 214 yards, but we won because of the outstanding play of our defense. Glen Edwards, Jack Ham, and Jack Lambert each picked off two passes, and pressure by the Steel Curtain resulted in three sacks and two fumble recoveries. Final score, 34-24.

The following Sunday, at home in Three Rivers, Gilliam had a terrible day, completing 5 of 18 passes for only 66 yards. Roy Gerela's two field goals proved decisive in our 20-16 victory. The real story was again our defense, which sacked Cleveland's quarterback six times for a loss of 33 yards. Franco Harris began making a difference, running for 81 yards and one touchdown on fourteen carries.

Gilliam just wasn't cutting it. Chuck told me he planned to start

Bradshaw in the next game against Atlanta. The *Post-Gazette* sponsored a public opinion poll, asking who should start at quarterback. The quarterback question became the talk of the town, and I'm afraid some of that talk turned racist. Gilliam received threatening letters.

But I can tell you all the public debate and speculation in the press had no effect on Chuck Noll or his decision to play Bradshaw. Like Chuck, I felt we had given Joe every chance. He had tremendous talent, a pure passer—I'd never seen a stronger arm. He was hard working, intense, and desperately wanted to succeed—that's what made pulling him so tough. He took it hard.

Each of the three quarterbacks had their advocates on the team. Dwight White strongly believed Gilliam had all the tools and had proven himself. Former Steelers running back and Hall of Famer John Henry Johnson backed Terry Hanratty. Joe Greene had bonded with Bradshaw during the players' strike and made it known he thought Terry should lead the team.

Noll played Bradshaw because he thought it time to go with his first-round draft pick. Race was not an issue. Noll believed Terry could get the job done—it was that simple. In hindsight, it's obvious Chuck made the right call.

When we took the field against the Atlanta Falcons at Three Rivers Stadium, the pressure on Bradshaw increased. He hadn't played all season, but he had a terrific team behind him. The Steelers defense sacked Falcon's quarterback Bob Lee seven times, increasing its league-leading total to twenty-eight. Franco Harris set a career high of 141 yards rushing, and Rocky Bleier ran for 78 more.

The Rocky Bleier story is incredible. We drafted him from Notre Dame in 1968, but then he was drafted again, this time by the U.S. Army, and sent to Vietnam in 1969. Wounded in action, he came back to the Steelers in 1970 with a Bronze Star, Purple Heart, and shrapnel in his foot. He had lost weight and his wounds slowed him down. Chuck Noll released him in the final cut that summer.

I'd kept an eye on Rocky, watched him in practice, and talked to the coaches. Dick Hoak, our offensive backfield coach, and others thought highly of him, but no one thought he'd make the team. Before he went to Southeast Asia he'd played well. Now he was giving his all, despite the searing pain in his foot. Our equipment manager, Tony Parisi, came to see me. "Dan, you've got to do something. This kid's suffering. He's got shrapnel in his foot."

I went to the Chief because I knew it would be a big expense to keep Rocky on the payroll. I asked him if he'd be okay with getting Bleier the operation he needed and keeping him on the team. "Go ahead. Do what you think is right."

After clearing it with Chuck (I didn't want him to think I was second-guessing his decision), I called Rocky the next morning and told him we'd like him to consider having another operation—his third—this time performed by our doctors. Instead of placing him on waivers, I said we'd put him on injured reserve. Slowly, through self discipline and hard work, he got himself back into shape. In fact, the best shape in his life. Noll and Hoak couldn't believe it, but he actually improved his speed in the 40-yard dash.

By 1974 he had cracked the starting lineup on merit and come into his own as a powerful blocker and smart running back. Rocky's comeback was an inspiration to many of our players—and to America. I never once regretted our decision to keep him on the team.

Bradshaw really showed what he could do in our November 3 game against the Philadelphia Eagles. We played at Three Rivers Stadium, and Terry directed a 375-yard offense, gaining 48 yards rushing himself. Our defense posted its second shutout of the year. We crushed them, 27-0.

Bradshaw seemed to lose his concentration in our 17-10 loss to

Cincinnati. He completed only a third of his passes, threw one interception, and got badly out-quarterbacked by the Bengals' Ken Anderson. In Bradshaw's defense, Anderson set two records that day—one for completing sixteen consecutive passes, the other for his 90 percent game completion percentage. But Anderson's stellar record didn't matter to Noll. He thought we should have won the game.

On November 17, we played the Browns in Cleveland Stadium before 77,000 screaming Browns fans. With Bradshaw and Gilliam benched, Terry Hanratty started his first game of the season as quarterback. Gerela's 14 points made him the leading scorer and the top kicker in the AFC. Franco rushed for 156 yards. Final score, Pittsburgh 26, Cleveland 16.

Right after Thanksgiving we played the Saints at Tulane Stadium, almost a homecoming for Bradshaw, who Noll brought back as our starting quarterback. We overpowered the Saints 28-7, with Bradshaw throwing two touchdown passes and rushing for 99 yards, including an 18-yard scoring run. He almost equaled Franco's 114 rushing yards. The six sacks by our defense boosted our sack total to a league-leading forty-six, and our players started thinking about a return trip in January to New Orleans, the site of Super Bowl IX. But we were getting ahead of ourselves.

Back to Three Rivers again, in the freezing rain, we lost to Houston, 13-10. Bradshaw left the game in the third quarter with bruised ribs. The Oilers defense racked up four sacks and three interceptions, and shut us out in the second half.

Despite the disappointing showing against Houston, we came back the next week to beat New England at Schaefer Stadium, clinching our second AFC Central Division championship and eliminating New England from a wild-card berth. Bradshaw used his running game to good advantage. Franco chalked up 136 yards rushing, while our tough defense made the Patriots' pay for every one of their 184 yards of offense.

We played our last game of the regular season at home against Cincinnati, avenging our earlier loss to them with a 27-3 victory. Franco went over the 1,000-yard mark and Bradshaw threw two touchdown passes. With two field goals and three conversions, Gerela earned the AFC scoring title with 93 points. Lynn Swann showed his versatility by returning three punts for 112 yards and ending the season with 577 return yards, just short of the team record.

In the first round of the playoffs, at Three Rivers Stadium, we faced O. J. Simpson and the Buffalo Bills. Simpson was the league's premier rusher, and in 1972 gained 189 yards on 22 carries against us, including a 89-yard touchdown run. Since then, our defense had improved, and during the 1974 season our coaches also had devised an alignment called the "Stunt 4-3." The Stunt 4-3 placed Greene directly over the center but in a stance at a 45-degree angle. Sometimes Ernie Holmes lined up that way. If the offensive line tried to double-team Greene, Holmes often found himself with a free path into the backfield. If the offensive line concentrated on Holmes, it counted on one guy to stop Greene's charge. "It started out as a pass technique," explained Noll, "but we found out it really screws up the offensive blocking. It's an aggressive defensive play because our front four isn't sitting and reading the offense. Instead, they're the ones making things happen."

That day, O. J. Simpson and his famous offensive line—called "the Electric Company" because it turned on "the juice"—managed only 49-yards rushing. Bradshaw himself ran for 48 yards that game and passed for over 200. Twenty-six of our points came in the second quarter, when Bradshaw led drives totaling 438 yards. We won 32-14, and moved into the AFC championship game against the Raiders.

Going into this game, we had all heard the reports that Raiders coach John Madden had said he'd already seen the best two teams in the league the previous week, when Oakland defeated the two-time Super Bowl champion Miami Dolphins. Usually cool and calm, Noll couldn't contain himself. He called the team together for a talk. He told the players he didn't see how it was possible for Madden to have already seen the best teams in the league, because the best team was sitting right here in the Steelers locker room. Noll's talk really pumped up the team. Both Franco Harris and Joe Greene told me after that speech, the players felt like they couldn't lose. Chuck was not given to locker-room pep talks—but on that day he instilled in our players a sense of confidence that made them feel invincible.

This turned out to be our first conference championship in forty-two years. Oakland never knew what hit them—we had so many weapons on offense and defense. When it wasn't Franco tearing through their line, it was Rocky. Between them they ran for more than 200 yards. Bradshaw and Lynn Swann were a dangerous combination. And then there was the Steel Curtain. Joe Greene, Fats Holmes, L.C. Greenwood, and Dwight White, backed by Andy Russell, Jack Lambert, and Jack Ham, forced three Ken Stabler interceptions and held the Raiders' ground game to only 29 yards. After our 24-13 victory, Davis and Madden didn't have any public comment about who they now thought were the best teams in the league.

So we went off to New Orleans to play the Minnesota Vikings in Super Bowl IX.

The oddsmakers favored the Vikings. They had been to the Super Bowl twice before, and their quarterback, Fran Tarkenton, was an exceptional field tactician. The papers made much of the contrast between Tarkenton, the veteran, poised professional, and the brash young Bradshaw.

Terry had gone through a really tough year. After two strong seasons, 1972 and 1973, he'd been benched in favor of Joe Gilliam, who had proven himself during the preseason following the players strike. And some fans and sportswriters questioned whether Terry was smart enough to lead the team.

I want to set the record straight on this. Bradshaw is no dummy. He's a very bright guy. Noll trusted him to call his own plays—that's saying a lot. In 1974, after the last regular season game against Cincinnati, Chuck told Terry that from then on he was the Steelers' starting quarterback. He went on to lead us to four Super Bowls. After his playing career, he went on to become a great television commentator and analyst. Terry has authored several successful books and is an excellent public speaker. This guy's got a lot on the ball and should never be underestimated. That business about him being dumb—people wish they could be so dumb.

But Terry is a sensitive guy. The hateful mail he received, the catcalls from the stands, attacks in the media—all hurt him. I remember him saying how much he wanted the people of Pittsburgh to be proud of him. But in his first two or three seasons, he felt terribly alone. That's when Joe Greene really stood by him. Terry had an unusual relationship with Noll. There was a great deal of respect between the two men, but they were so different. Chuck: cool, calculating, focused. Terry: loose, free-spirited, a gunslinger. What a pair. They learned to work with each other, and that's what won us Super Bowls.

He got through the public criticism with his wonderful sense of humor. I remember one day I was sitting in my office at Three Rivers when Terry came running in all out of breath. He yelled, "They stole my golf clubs out of my car!"

I said, "Well, did you lock it, Terry?"

He thought for a moment, then said, "I locked one side of it!"

We both started to laugh, and I said, "Well, maybe they just stole half of the clubs. Go look around!"

Terry and I enjoyed each other, but he and the Chief had almost a father-son relationship. They spent long hours talking. They discussed everything, from football to love and marriage. After Terry's divorce, Dad told him, "You know what you need? You need one of those farmers' daughters to take care of you." Terry allowed that maybe it was so—he'd try harder next time. Sometimes he would go into Dad's office even when the Chief wasn't there. It became his refuge, a place he could go just to get away from it all—and smoke my father's fat cigars.

The Chief presented Terry with a gift horse, a stallion from our horse farm. Terry may not have known it, but this was quite an honor. My father didn't give away fine horses to just anyone.

But when Terry got the feed and boarding bill, Dad called him on it. "You're not paying your bill," he said.

"I thought you gave me the horse!"

"Sure I did, but I didn't say I was going to take care of it forever!"

"What, are you too cheap to pay for it?" Terry said, laughing, and pulled a dollar bill out of his wallet and dropped it in a trophy on the Chief's desk. "Well, that ought to cover it!"

We were all in stitches by the end of this episode. Dad told his trainers to take the horse and put it back in the paddock.

Don't get me wrong. Terry genuinely loved horses—their speed and grace. He once said, "Imagine yourself sitting on top of a great thoroughbred horse. You sit up there and feel that power. That's what it was like, playing quarterback on that team. It was a great ride."

I've seen a lot of quarterbacks in my years with the Steelers and the NFL. The only quarterback I'd rate above Terry Bradshaw is the great Johnny Unitas. Dan Marino is up there high on the list, as is John Elway, but Bradshaw had something special. A tremendous athlete, big and strong, he could pass, he could run, he could even kick when we asked him to. He was smart, called his own plays, and was a team leader in the locker room. He contributed to the closeness of the team, and in critical games his sense of humor helped keep the players loose.

———

The closeness of our young players and their ability to stay loose gave us a great advantage as we went into our first Super Bowl against the veteran Vikings. Both defenses dominated the first half, the only score coming on a safety when Tarkenton recovered his own fumble in the end zone and was downed by Dwight White.

We kicked off to open the second half. The Vikings' Bill Brown fumbled and Marv Kellum recovered for us on the Minnesota 30-yard line. Four plays later, Franco scored from 9 yards out. By the end of the day, Franco had rushed for 158 yards, then a Super Bowl record. Rocky contributed another 65 yards, while the Steelers' defense held Minnesota to only 17 yards on the ground. The Steel Curtain kept Tarkenton on the run all day, allowing only eleven of twenty-six passes to reach their intended receivers. Three passes were intercepted, and four deflected.

Bradshaw finished off the Vikings with a 30-yard pass completion to Larry Brown, setting up another pass to Brown for a touchdown. In this final 66-yard drive, Bradshaw demonstrated real leadership, managing the clock, mixing his plays, and exploiting the weak points in the Viking defense. He showed poise and confidence. The final score, 16-6, told the whole story. Both Bradshaw and the Steelers had arrived.

It seemed everyone in the country wanted the Chief and the Steelers to win the Super Bowl that year—except, of course, the Minnesota people, and Al Davis. Pete Rozelle especially admired my father. Pete often said that handing the Chief the Lombardi Trophy in our very emotional locker room was the highlight of his career as commissioner. My father wanted me to accept it, but I said, "No, this is yours, Dad." And it was his. He had founded the team, kept it in Pittsburgh, stuck it out through the lean times. He was the beloved Chief. He was the legend.

What a party it was in New Orleans. Of our five Super Bowls, this victory is still the sweetest because it was our first. When we returned home, all of Pittsburgh turned out to greet us. The outpouring of affection overwhelmed me and reminded me how important the Steelers were to our community.

Our family celebrated with a trip to Ireland. Dad, especially, enjoyed this visit to the Old Sod. When we got off the plane, the reporters there asked him his views on boxing and baseball. He said, "Aren't you going to ask me about the Super Bowl?"

They said, "What's that?" They had no clue about American football.

"What a relief," Dad replied, "I'm happy you don't know anything about it, because that's all I've been hearing about for weeks."

When we got back to the States, my father came into my office and said, "Dan, I think it's time we call you 'president'—you've been doing the job for years."

"Do you think we need to make an announcement?" I asked.

"No, just put it in the Media Guide and let them read it at the beginning of the season."

Though I'd been running the team for some time, we never worried about titles. Dad never liked to take credit for things. He tried to push me forward into the limelight. But he deserved to shine. He was quite a guy.

When the Media Guide came out in the summer of 1975, Dad appeared as "Chairman of the Board," followed by me as "President," and my brother Art and Jack McGinley each as "Vice President." The newspapers quoted me as saying, "Dad walked into my office and said, 'You're the president!' There wasn't a lot of fanfare involved. It's a title without a raise."

But as far as I was concerned, the most important guy on that page was "Head Coach," Chuck Noll.

CHAPTER 6

STEELERS DYNASTY

THE STEELERS WERE FLYING HIGH in early 1975 after our victory in Super Bowl IX. And rightly so. We had rebuilt the team almost from scratch. In five years we had gone from the basement to the very top of the National Football League. Sometimes people forget the magnitude of this accomplishment. It takes a combination of talented players, coaching, team closeness, and good management. Without any one of these essential ingredients, you don't have a Super Bowl winner. There are some teams in the NFL that have never experienced a Super Bowl. In the 1970s the Steelers won the Super Bowl four times—we won every time we appeared in pro football's ultimate game. Plus, we did it back to back—twice—all within six years. That had never been done before, and no team has done it since.

I hear and read how the Dallas Cowboys—"America's Team"—was. the team of the 1970s because they appeared in five Super Bowls.

Well, we won four Super Bowls and beat those guys both times we played them for the championship. Don't get me wrong. Tex Schramm and Tom Landry fielded some incredibly talented teams in those years, but I'd sure take the Steelers over the Cowboys if I had to pick the team of the decade.

I lived and breathed football during these years, but I somehow found time to do other things. I don't think it's healthy to be totally consumed by any one pursuit. You'll go nuts. For me, I had my family, my faith, and some meaningful outside interests as well.

Chuck Noll not only coached the team but became a friend. He's a Renaissance man—a connoisseur of fine wine and food, an aficionado of classical music (he once guest-conducted the Pittsburgh Symphony Orchestra), and an expert pilot. In 1974 Chuck took me flying in his Beechcraft A35 Bonanza V-tail, and in 1975 I earned a pilot's license.

I'd been interested in flying since I was six years old. That's when our whole family went out to Allegheny County Airport to see my uncle Dan (Father Silas) leave for his mission to China. My father had a pilot's license in his early years, and I remember when he flew from New York to Miami Beach in one of those Yankee Clipper flying boats, the kind that could land in the water. He took off from New York harbor and flew to Florida, splashing down near Miami. A crew towed the plane to a dock, where the passengers disembarked. My mother drove me there to meet him. The plane fascinated me, and I've been interested in flying ever since.

During World War II, my father gave me a "spotter's guide," which pictured silhouettes of military and civilian aircraft. I would scan the sky for hours, watching and identifying every plane I saw. I knew all of the planes made in the United States, how they were used, what they could do, and how fast they were. I remember being at our summer place in Ligonier outside of Pittsburgh, just lying in the grass on a hill above the cemetery, when suddenly a huge bomber returning from a practice mission flew over at treetop level—my first sighting of a B-29. It was massive, and the engine noise practically deafened me. You know how you remember impressions from your youth? Well, this is one of those, and the image remains vivid in my memory.

I read everything I could on flying and the heroes of the skies, like the amazing Chuck Yeager, war ace and test pilot, and Joe White, who flew the X-15. Many of these aviators believed if we could have flown a plane into space, our space program would have progressed more rapidly, safely, and ultimately more successfully. Instead, rockets won out over fixed-wing aircraft. Men like Yeager and White argued for pilot control of spacecraft. They believed the first astronauts shot into space in rockets were the guinea pigs of the scientists at Mission Control; they had no more control over their craft than the monkeys sent before them. I can understand why, when those pilots put their lives on the line, they'd feel that way. But those original astronauts had a lot of guts.

When Chuck Noll decided he wanted a new and larger aircraft, a twin-engine Beechcraft Baron, he asked me if I wanted to buy his Bonanza for what he'd paid for it. It was a good deal, and it got me flying. I worked with a flight instructor and became instrument rated. Since then I have accumulated more than twenty-five hundred flight hours.

When I first got my license, I flew to Washington, Pennsylvania. On this trip, while performing a touch-and-go landing, I advanced the manifold and heard an ominous "pop." The plane lost power, but I could still fly. To maintain altitude, I had to open it up and fly at full power. On the way back to Allegheny County, I constantly watched for a spot to make an emergency landing. But I made it safely back to the airport, where I learned that the rocker arm connecting the camshaft to the valve-stem had broken off. That's why the engine lost

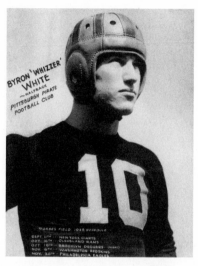

Top left: Johnny "Blood" McNally was considered one of the best running backs in the NFL during his playing days in the 1930s. He served as both a player and coach for the Pittsburgh football Pirates. (COURTESY STEELERS)

Top right: All-American running back Byron "Whizzer" White became the highest paid NFL player when Art Rooney hired him to play for the Pittsburgh Pirates Football Club in 1938. He led the league in rushing that year, then went on to a legal career and eventually the U.S. Supreme Court. (COURTESY STEELERS)

Above: Dr. John Bain "Jock" Sutherland led the Steelers in 1946 and 1947. His advanced coaching principles gave the Steelers a taste of victory. (COURTESY STEELERS)

Raymond "Buddy" Parker was the Steelers' head coach from 1956 to 1964 and led the team to four winning seasons. (COURTESY STEELERS)

Hall of Fame Steelers quarterback Bobby Layne, 1958–1962, was a team leader who played hard on and off the field. ((COURTESY STEELERS)

Hall of Fame tackle (1950–63) Ernie Stautner's "70" is the only number officially retired by the Steelers in a 1964 halftime ceremony at Pitt Stadium. Stautner's opponents and teammates considered him one of the toughest players in the league. He missed just six games during his fourteen-year career. (COURTESY STEELERS)

The Steelers drafted Johnny Unitas in 1955 but released him before the season began. (COURTESY STEELERS)

Walt Kiesling, Hall of Famer and three-time Steelers head coach, spent thirty-four years in the NFL as player, assistant coach, and head coach. His teams earned a reputation for playing rugged, hard-hitting football. (COURTESY STEELERS)

Hall of Famer John Henry Johnson was at the end of his pro career when he played for the Steelers, 1960–65, but he led the team's running attack and still ranks third among all Steelers rushers. (COURTESY STEELERS)

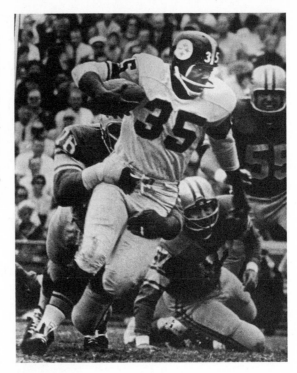

Richie McCabe grew up on Pittsburgh's North Side and later played for the Steelers, 1955, 1957–58. (COURTESY STEELERS)

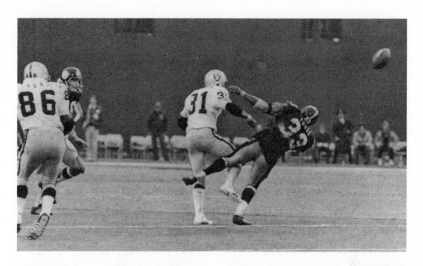

The Immaculate Reception, 1972. Jack Tatum collides with Frenchy Fuqua as the ball ricochets into the air. Following the play, Franco Harris makes a shoestring catch, eludes tacklers, and speeds toward the end zone. (COURTESY STEELERS)

Super Bowl MVPs Franco Harris, Lynn Swann,and Terry Bradshaw, 1980.
(COURTESY STEELERS)

Joe Greene and Jack Lambert in the Three Rivers Stadium locker room after the
victory over Oakland in the 1975 AFC Championship game. (COURTESY STEELERS)

Hall of Fame linebacker Jack Lambert,
1974–84,was known for his vicious
tackling and is recognized as the
premier linebacker of his era.
(COURTESY STEELERS)

Steelers Hall of Fame coach
Chuck Noll.
(COURTESY STEELERS/MIKE FABUS)

The "Steel Curtain": Dwight White, Ernie Holmes, Joe Greene, and L.C. Greenwood.
(COURTESY STEELERS)

Lynn Swann's acrobatic catch, Super Bowl X. (COURTESY STEELERS)

Joe Greene impulsively ran to his unconscious teammate, Lynn Swann, and carried him off the field in the 1975 AFC Championship game.
(COURTESY STEELERS)

compression and power. This was a little hairy for a young and inexperienced pilot, but I kept my cool.

A pilot can't panic. That's why it's important to do your homework, learn the flight systems, review emergency procedures (for engine failure, engine fire, electric fire, alternator failure, etc.), and keep your head.

I've flown to New York on many occasions. One time, as a student pilot flying over the Hudson on a foggy day, I couldn't see the other side of the river. I became a little concerned and checked in with the New York Center air traffic controller. "Am I over the ocean or the river?" I asked.

"You're here," the controller assured me.

"Where's here?"

"You're practically on top of us!"

I made it to the airport okay. For a moment or so I was a little unsure where I was. But that's how you learn.

On another trip to New York, I again had to ask for help. "How do I get to Westchester County Airport?"

The controller gave me directions, but I still couldn't see the landing strip.

Finally, he said, "Hey, just make a right turn, go down to where you see the big bridge, make a left at the bridge, and it'll be right there a few miles out."

I thought he was being funny, but I followed the directions exactly and found the airport.

I guess my most notable flying story occurred on a return flight to Pittsburgh from Latrobe during summer training camp in 2000. The mechanics who had just rebuilt the engine of the Bonanza either did not put the alternator on properly or installed a defective unit. I had no problem flying to Latrobe, but on the way back I ran into trouble. The lights on my instrument panel began to blink off. All electric needles shimmied side to side, then off. The radio went dead. I switched on the standby alternator. Nothing. The red light on the landing gear indicator remained on, but only dimly. The landing gear was almost all the way up but not completely retracted. "Don't panic. Just get this plane back to Allegheny County Airport," I said aloud to myself as I tried to crank the landing gear down manually. I couldn't fly the plane and reach around to the back of the seat on the passenger side to wind the hand crank that would manually extend the gear. I just couldn't do it. I called the tower on my cell phone but got voice mail. This was not good.

I called 911. The operator didn't believe me when I said I was Dan Rooney.

"Dan Rooney? Of the Pittsburgh Steelers? Yeah, right."

It might have been funny if the situation hadn't been so serious. After convincing him who I was, I asked if he would please get in touch with the tower. Without electricity I had no radio—the tower couldn't get back to me directly. So I had to rely on the 911 operator to relay messages for me. I'd tell the operator where I was, and he would talk to the tower. In turn, the controller sent back instructions.

I told them my location as I passed over Rostraver Airport. "Don't land at Rostraver," they said. "Just keep coming in to Allegheny County." That was okay with me, because I was more familiar with the Allegheny County Airport. From my position I could see the U.S. Steel Plant just off the airport's Runway 28.

They told me to continue toward Runway 28 and fly over the tower so they could inspect my gear. I descended to eight hundred feet and passed over the tower. The tower confirmed through my 911 operator that the gear was not down. They called a mechanic to see if he had any ideas. In the meantime, they directed me to burn off as much fuel as I could.

"Listen, when that sun goes down, I'm landing," I said, "and I'm landing in the grass between the runway and the taxiway."

I made about four passes on a west heading, elongating the pattern by going east farther than normal. I don't know how much fuel I burned off, but it couldn't have been much.

On my last pass, the sun sank below the horizon—just as my cell phone's battery died. Now I didn't have any communications at all. I flew over the tower and rocked my wings so they knew I was coming in to land.

I came in at eighty knots, then at the last second nosed up to slow down even more.

I think I made the best landing I'd ever made in my life. It surprised me how far the plane traveled after it touched down and skidded over the ground. I hit the marker for Runway 28, veered left, and came to a stop. Fortunately, the marker didn't hit the wing tanks and there was no fire, but as a precaution all the fire trucks, an ambulance, and every emergency vehicle for miles around were there.

I shut everything down, got out of the plane, and stood on the wing surveying the damage. When the firefighters pulled up with their lights flashing, I figured I'd better get out of the way. They soon saw there was nothing they could do—no fire or dangerous fuel leaks. The EMTs wanted to take me to the hospital in the ambulance.

"Hey, I'm fine. There's no problem," I protested as they took me into the ambulance to make sure I was okay.

They drove me to my hangar, and I called Dr. Yates, my aviation medical examiner, to try to get him to tell the EMTs I didn't need to go to the hospital. He convinced them that if I said I was okay, I was okay.

Then I called home. "Patricia," I said, "I just crash-landed the plane, but I'm all right."

"You did what?" she asked.

"Yeah, the electrical system went out," I explained to her. "They shut the whole airport down while I was flying patterns."

Jerry Richardson, my friend and owner of the Carolina Panthers, started calling me "Crash." If that was the worst of this incident, I could live with it. Besides, "Crash Rooney" had a certain ring to it.

Some members of the family don't like to fly with me because of stories like this. Once our son John flew back home with me from Chuck Noll's place in Fort Meyers, Florida. On that flight we had to keep climbing higher to try to get above the clouds.

"We've got to get down," John said when we were cruising at 12,500 feet, "I'm getting sick."

To go down I had to find a hole in the clouds. "See if you can find an airport down there," I said. He got even more alarmed, and his face whitened. But we descended safely and landed in Raleigh, North Carolina.

After we took on fuel and had something to eat, we took off again. I assured John that it would be smooth flying from here on out. But then, just as we took off, the passenger door popped open. I had to return to the ground to close it and latch it properly. In landing, I hit the nose wheel a little hard. The damage was slight, but John always said this one trip kept him from flying again. John's very bright and is mechanically inclined. He'd make a great pilot but prefers to have his feet firmly on the ground.

Our daughter Rita, an attorney living in Boston, is an excellent pilot. She has a license and her instrument rating. Rita flew a lot when she lived in Pittsburgh. I think my daughter Joan would make a good pilot. My flying skills have come in handy in getting around to league meetings and events, but there's more to it than that.

There's nothing like the sense of freedom that comes with flying. I love soaring over the beautiful Western Pennsylvania countryside, enjoying the sight of the rivers, the forested hills, and coal-patch communities below.

I guess I'm a creature of habit. I have followed the same work schedule for nearly sixty years, whether the team is winning or losing. Six days a week, I go to my office. On the seventh day, if we're playing an away game, I travel with the team. I like everything about my job, the excitement and even the challenges of personnel and league politics. Football and the Steelers have taught me lessons about perseverance, the belief in possibilities, the expansion of boundaries, the kindness of people, and the unpredictability of life. The Steelers have been part of me since the day I was born.

And so has Ireland.

My father, the son of Irish immigrants, talked about Ireland when I was young. He spoke of generation-long wars and economic struggle. Martin Regan, Patricia's father, also told us stories of Ireland when we were courting. Through the Irish songs he sang, we became interested in Irish music. Aunt Alice McNulty could dance some of the Irish jigs, reels, and step dances. To us these songs and dances were strangely Irish, and we were fascinated by what seemed to be a foreign culture. Patricia's mother, Mary Duffy Regan, busy raising a large family and adjusting to a new culture, didn't talk much about Ireland. But she connected with our daughter Kathleen. For hours on end, she told Kathleen the traditional stories she had learned as a girl.

Kathleen loved Irish myths and lore, and participated in St. Patrick's Day events with our Irish-American friends. She wanted to know more and became the first of our children to return to our native land. In the mid-1970s she visited with a girlfriend. They first went to Derrinabrock in County Mayo, the ancestral home of Patricia's Regan relatives. County Mayo is the westernmost of the Irish counties. All of the villages are small and Derrinabrock is no exception. There are a few farms, a church, and one pub. She was enchanted by the thatched-roofed cottages and the deep green of the hills and fields. She studied at Killkenny and learned much about Irish culture.

Later, when our entire family first visited Ireland, the relatives ran from their house, passed me by, and went directly to Kathleen. "Welcome home," they said. It was quite a homecoming.

On our first visit to Ireland, we traveled with Lou Spadia, president of the San Francisco Forty-Niners and his wife, Maggie. The biggest town in the area we visited was Ballaghaderreen in County Roscommon. Ballaghaderreen is large enough to boast a few shops and a school. We searched to find the road to Cloontia in County Mayo, where Patricia's mother grew up, but couldn't find it. So we called back and talked to Patricia's mother in Pittsburgh. She told us where to look, but we still couldn't find Cloontia. Ready to give up, we went into a pub and talked with the girl behind the bar about our problem. "I know some Regans," she said.

She took us to Cloontia and introduced us to a lady whose last name was Gallagher. Patricia's aunt Maggie was married to a Gallagher, and it turned out this woman and Patricia's aunt Maggie Duffy were sisters-in-law. After we told Mrs. Gallagher who Patricia was, she took us to the Duffy's thatched-roof cottage where the family had lived for 150 years. Here, Patricia met her grandmother, Mary Duffy. At first she thought Patricia was her own daughter. Patricia was the first family member from America to return to Ireland since her mother left.

The thatched-roof, two-room, one-window cottage was very dark inside. I opened the window and sat next to it so that the full light came in. It shone on Patricia and her grandmother, who lay in what they called a kitchen bed so she might be near the light and heat of the fireplace. Patricia's grandmother stayed in the bed most of the time. They talked for hours and I took a great photo of the two together. It was a heartwarming and timely reunion. Her grandmother died the following February.

Next we went to see Patricia's uncle Thomas Regan, who had visited the United States and spent time in Pittsburgh in the 1920s. He was the best man in the wedding of Patricia's parents and loved talking about Yanks and his visit to America.

During this first trip in 1971 we got to know Ireland, reconnected with family, and made many new friends. We didn't get back in 1972—the year the Steelers drafted Franco Harris—but we've been returning regularly since then.

It wasn't until we met the charismatic Irishman Tony O'Reilly that the Chief decided he needed to visit the Emerald Isle himself.

In the summer of 1975, following our Super Bowl victory, Tim and I brought Dad with us on his first visit to Ireland. The Rooneys originated in Newry, County Down, a small town about thirty-five miles south of Belfast, Northern Ireland. His father was actually born in Wales, where his grandfather had gone to find work. When asked, "Doesn't that make you Welsh?" he would always say, "If a cat gave birth in an oven, would you call her kittens biscuits? The Rooneys are Irish through and through." My father was proud of his Irish roots, but he was even prouder to be an American.

Tony O'Reilly became an important part of our lives. In 1974 this Irish rugby hero became the second non-Heinz to head the Pittsburgh-based Heinz Company—the ketchup empire. When Tony arrived in Pittsburgh, Merle Gilliand, president of Pittsburgh National Bank (later first CEO of PNC Bank), had a party at his house. "You must meet some of our Irish people," Merle told Tony, and invited Patricia and me.

These are the first words Tony said to me: "I always liked American football. I think I could play. Do you mind if I worked out with the boys?"

Assuming he was talking about running or exercising, I told him a workout could be arranged. When I explained to him what the practice involved, he said, "No, I want to go out and play with the pads and run the plays!"

"Tony, you're thirty-three years old," I said. "You're beyond your playing days. You don't start playing American football at thirty-three, that's when you quit."

Tony never did put on the pads and mix it up with the team, although he was quite an athlete, tall and fast. I think he would have made a better receiver than the running back he thought he could be.

At Merle's party, Tony and I began what would become a long friendship—and the beginning of the Ireland Fund. The Royal College of Surgeons in Ireland had asked Tony to hold a fund-raiser. So Tony proposed to me, "Dan, why don't we honor your father with a banquet?"

I agreed, and we planned a dinner to be held at the Waldorf Astoria in New York at the end of the 1974 football season. As it so happened, this was the season the Steelers won Super Bowl IX. After our victory in January 1975, the dinner took on new importance. Tickets were in demand. In fact, it was a sellout. On the night of the dinner, I looked up and saw the packed ballroom and a standing-room only crowd on every level above.

"This is really big," I said.

Delighted with the turnout, Tony agreed, "Yes, we've raised far more than I ever expected. We can help the Royal College of Surgeons and have enough left over to help three or four more Irish charities."

I told him, "Sure, that's a good idea, but we've got to keep this banquet going, year after year."

The next day we drew up the plans for the annual Ireland Fund dinner. It grew to be the most successful fund-raiser of its kind, although the first couple of years were a little slow. The finances were tight. Tony would always say we had the second Ireland Fund dinner to pay for the first.

At one of our early dinners, a distinguished older man said he would give us a $100,000 donation if we let him speak at the banquet. We needed the money, so we let him talk. He told a long-winded story and bored us to tears. Pete Rozelle, who attended the dinner, said the story wasn't worth the $100,000. To make matters worse, the man had a young wife who nixed the payment the day after the banquet. We received nothing and learned an important lesson about fund-raising and dinner speakers.

Some people wanted to use the Ireland dinner for political purposes. We resisted this. One banquet took place at the same time the world learned of the death of IRA activist Bobby Sands. Sands had died in a British prison following a lengthy hunger strike, and emotions ran high among many Irish people around the world.

Bill McNally, the Ireland Fund's director, got the New York police and Waldorf hotel security to guarantee the safety of the lobby and hall for our high-profile patrons. The situation was tense. I went out and talked to a few of the pickets. McNally agreed to seat Chuck Daly—a former aide to President John F. Kennedy and one of the organizers of this dinner—at a table near the podium in case of any outbursts.

Halfway through dinner, a nun wandered in and made her way to the stage where a band was playing beside the podium. Suddenly, she dashed up the three steps and half ran to the podium. She pulled the mike down to her level and launched into an IRA denunciation of British rule in Ireland. The bandleader ordered his crew to crank up the music. She began shouting in a desperate, shrill voice. This all happened in less than a minute.

Chuck Daly jumped up onto the stage, motioned to the band to stop, and approached her. She was trembling and her eyes were watering. Her shaking hands held a sheaf of notes that looked to me like a telephone book. Chuck put his hand over the mike and spoke to her calmly, "Sister, no one in this hall wants to hurt you. I know how you feel. I'll ask the band to stay quiet if you agree to say only a few more words, and then let us get on with this peaceful dinner where everyone is just trying to help Ireland."

She looked up at him and asked, "Promise?"

"Yes, if you keep it short."

"I will."

She spoke for less than two minutes, then left the hall. It was sad to see her go, but we knew we couldn't solve all of Ireland's political problems. I felt like crying.

Through the years there have been many organizations dedicated to raising money for Ireland. Some of these were charitable and humanitarian, others were not.

Just a few months before his death in 1963, President Kennedy joined with Irish President Eamonn de Valera to form the American Irish Foundation. Its mission fostered connections between Americans of Irish decent and their native country. But many Americans confused this organization with our Ireland Fund. I believed we could have a greater impact if we merged with the American Irish Foundation. One big organization would be more effective than two smaller ones. I asked Tony O'Reilly what he thought of the idea. He agreed wholeheartedly. I called John Brogan, the president of the American Irish Foundation, and asked him if he would be interested in combining our efforts. He was willing to talk.

I arranged to meet him at Westchester County Airport. I flew and he drove. We discussed the proposition at a little lunch table in the airport's dining area and agreed to set up a committee to work out the details. John appointed Billy Vincent, president of the Ireland Fund of Monaco. He, along with Richard Anthony Moore, American ambassador to Ireland, and Brian Burn, who lived in San Francisco, worked diligently to hammer out the details of the merger. I appointed Walter Dumphy, Bill Burke, and Chuck Daly.

Late in 1986, we agreed to meet at the Waldorf in New York to formally discuss the merger. How would we join the treasuries? Billy Vincent was concerned about what we would call the new organization. After much discussion, we decided to call it the American Ireland Fund. The name satisfied the needs and concerns of both organizations—it worked, it really worked.

As in all mergers, there had been some opposition and even heated debate. But in the end, cool heads and compromise prevailed. I met with Tony and our group, and they all agreed we had worked out the best possible solution to a complicated partnership.

On St. Patrick's Day, 1987, in a ceremony at the White House, President Ronald Reagan announced the merger and the creation of the new American Ireland Fund.

Since the beginning, the mission of the fund encompassed peace, culture, and charity. The later addition of educational programs to help young people—North, South, Catholic, Protestant—get involved in business has worked well. The American Ireland Fund has really made a great contribution by helping to bring peace and prosperity to the country. We emphasized programs for children. I've always felt that adults should solve problems, but sometimes you have to start with the children.

At one point, we had difficulty fund-raising and in motivating board members to actively work to achieve our long-range goals and plans. Then came Loretta Brennan Glucksman, who, as chairman, reenergized the board. A third-generation Irish American born in eastern Pennsylvania, she possesses a truly generous heart. She led by example and set a new tone for our fund meetings. Soon she had the organization back on track. The fund has been doing well ever since.

The American Ireland Fund continues to appeal to all Americans for support, but especially to Irish Americans. Today, branches in forty cities around the world—in Ireland, Australia, Canada, France, Germany, Great Britain, New Zealand, Japan, Monaco, China, and the United States—reach a global community of more than seventy million people. One hundred fund-raising activities are attended by some forty thousand people annually. To date, we have raised over $300 million. The Ireland Fund is the largest fund-raising organization for Ireland in the world. It has accomplished much and has made a real difference.

While I've always enjoyed the dinners and events, the American Ireland Fund board meetings have been even more interesting. All the board members are generous of spirit and cooperate in reaching our common goals. We've had many discussions over the years about Ireland, about the purpose and principles of the fund, and we've been careful to keep away from banners and flags and politics. Our board has successfully managed the fund, which today has an endowment of over $100 million.

Since the beginning, the American Ireland Fund board in the United States has worked with an advisory committee in Ireland, which was first chaired by Maurice Hayes, to ensure that contributions and awards go to organizations dedicated to furthering peace. In the early years, critics suggested the money went for guns. It never did. Nor have awards ever supported paramilitary purposes. We've worked hard to make sure the public—and contributors—understand our mission of peace. We've said no to guns and violence from the very start. And I'm proud to say we've never wavered on this principle. Tony O'Reilly guided us to keep those principles. We worked with all people to help bring peace to Ireland.

Around the time of the first banquet, Patricia and I created a special award that became known as the Rooney Prize for Irish Literature. Every year the award is presented to an outstanding Irish-born young writer. Jim Sherwin has chaired the Rooney Prize Committee, which continues to positively influence aspiring authors. The selection committee has steadfastly made excellent choices.

The Rooney family's association with Ireland has been enriched by our work with the Ireland Fund. When we first visited Ireland in 1971, all the kids were young. Since then, our daughter Rita lived in Ireland for four years after she married Larry Conway, who was studying medicine at the Royal College of Surgeons in Dublin. Joan studied for a year at University College in Dublin. The experience inspired her and she returned home a much better student. Our son Art, who studied at the renowned Yeats Summer School, struck up a close friendship with Irish political leader and Nobel Peace Prize laureate John Hume. Today, our children have made it a point to educate their own children about the Rooneys' Irish roots, for which Patricia and I are very grateful.

The months following our Super Bowl IX victory in January 1975 were a special time for the Steelers and our fans. Expectations ran high. But we almost lost the Steel Curtain before the season even began. The newly organized World Football League set its sights on NFL stars. The WFL had already signed Larry Csonka, Jim Kiick, and Paul Warfield, who had helped lead the Miami Dolphins to victories in Super Bowls VII and VIII.

Now the WFL took aim at our front four: Joe Greene, L.C. Greenwood, Ernie Holmes, and Dwight White. Greenwood bought into their salary inducements and signed a contract. Then they went to Joe Greene. But Greene told them, "I'm not going anywhere—I'm a Steeler." They upped their offer, telling Joe he could use the WFL as leverage to get more money when he negotiated his contract with the Steelers. But Joe told them, "I don't do business that way." In the meantime, I had negotiated a new contract with Dwight White, and counseled Ernie Holmes to stay put.

L.C. realized he'd made a mistake and wanted out of the WFL contract. I agreed to go to court and testify on his behalf. Greenwood argued he'd been pressured into signing, and somehow the court accepted our argument.

Preseasons are always a stressful time as players negotiate or extend their contacts. Sometimes players hold out. The whole season depends on the successful resolution of these contracts. It was my job to manage these negotiations and do what was fair for the players and right for the team. All of this is complicated when a rival league, like the WFL, enters the picture. In this case, our players remained loyal to us, and the WFL folded midway through the 1975 season.

As defending champions, we felt we had to play every game during our 1975 season like it was the Super Bowl. Every man on the team believed this. We had to play our best in order to win, because every team in the league was coming after us. Joe Greene said, "Nobody's going to get in our way," and our offense stepped up its play and became as good as the defense. We started the season by shutting out San Diego and went on to finish the year with a 12-2 record. Franco ranked second in the league with 1,246 yards rushing. Swann and Stallworth made significant contributions to the team and allowed Bradshaw to rack up 2,055 yards passing. Our Steel Curtain defense dominated the league, and eight of our eleven starters went to the Pro Bowl—Joe Greene, L.C. Greenwood, Jack Ham, Jack Lambert, Andy Russell, Mel Blount (who led the NFL in interceptions), Glen Edwards, and Mike Wagner.

We knocked off the Baltimore Colts in the division playoff game and then faced the Oakland Raiders at home in Three Rivers Stadium for the AFC championship.

This game on January 4, 1976, became known as the "Ice Bowl" and escalated our rivalry with Oakland to a new level. On the night before the game, the NFL hosted a traditional playoff party. It was held at the Allegheny Club inside the stadium. Looking out the giant picture windows, I began to worry about the weather. Pittsburgh winters can be bitterly cold, especially when the wind sweeps up the Ohio River. Three Rivers was a big concrete bowl, and that evening the frigid wind swirled through the sleet-soaked stadium. I could see the Tartan Turf begin to freeze up as the temperature dropped. I called Dirt DiNardo, the head of our grounds crew, to get a tarp to cover the artificial surface before it turned into an ice rink. Working in the dark, the crew stretched a huge tarp over the field and blew hot air underneath with a powerful heater. But during the night the howling wind lifted the tarp, splitting it down the middle. Water got underneath and ice formed, especially along the sidelines where the heaters couldn't reach.

The Raiders claimed we intentionally tore the tarp so their receivers, who favored down-and-out patterns, would slip and slide on their routes. I still laugh when I recall those Raiders' claims. After all, everyone in the league believed it was the Raiders who intentionally soaked their own home field week after week. They did it to slow down the opponents' fastest running backs and because a wet field favored their slower, heavier fullbacks like Marv Hubbard and Mark van Eeghen. But we didn't have any control over Mother Nature. We didn't sabotage the field as Davis and Madden thought. This just goes to show how intense and irrational the rivalry between the Raiders and the Steelers had become. We played on that same field. Our guys couldn't run on ice any better than theirs could.

Turnovers ruled the game. The windchill turned the sixteen-degree stadium into a twelve-below freezer. With the snow falling and the field iced over, both teams slipped, slid, and fumbled. We suffered eight turnovers, including three Bradshaw interceptions. But they had as many problems as we did. It was a hard-hitting, defensive battle. The outcome wasn't decided until the last play of the game when the clock finally ran out on the Raiders. We prevailed, 16-10.

The brutal conditions of the game stand out in my mind, but even more brutal was the hit Raiders' defensive back George Atkinson delivered to Lynn Swann. The blow knocked Swann unconscious. Almost before the whistle sounded, Joe Greene bolted onto the field, ran over to Lynn's motionless form, and by himself picked him up and carried him off the field. Swann, it turned out, had suffered a serious concussion and spent two days in the hospital. The doctors worried he wouldn't be able to play in the Super Bowl against Dallas two weeks later. Swann himself wondered if he'd ever play again. The doctors warned that another hit like the one he took from Atkinson could leave him permanently disabled. This incident was just the beginning of a growing controversy over unnecessary roughness in the NFL. The week before the Super Bowl, Swann stayed on the sidelines during practice, and Noll listed him as a doubtful starter.

But Swann did return for Super Bowl X. Not only that, he became the game's MVP. On January 18, 1976, at the Orange Bowl in Miami, before more than eighty thousand fans, we faced the Dallas Cowboys in our second straight Super Bowl. A television audience of more than eighty million—the largest in history at that time—watched at home.

The Cowboys' high-tech offense and "flex" defense made them a tough opponent. The flex defense was anchored by Harvey Martin and Ed "Too Tall" Jones. Quarterback Roger Staubach passed for 2,666 yards during the season, and fullback Robert Newhouse led a powerful running attack. Running back Preston Pearson, who we had cut in preseason, rounded out their ground game and was eager to show what he could do against the Steelers.

This Super Bowl was a great match-up—a game for the ages. Though at halftime we trailed 10-7, I thought the most memorable play came in the second quarter when Lynn Swann made a 53-yard circus catch—he seemed to levitate horizontally stretching to catch a tipped pass—an impossible feat that had the Cowboys shaking their heads as they went into the locker room.

The halftime entertainment celebrated America's bicentennial. The popular singing group Up With People performed "200 Years and Just a Baby."

But the party atmosphere of halftime didn't carry over to the intense play on the field. When our kicker Roy Gerela missed a field goal, one he normally would have made, Cowboys safety Cliff Harris patted him on the helmet and thanked him for his help. This taunting of a teammate enraged Jack Lambert, who ran over to Harris, picked him up, and slammed him to the Astroturf. I worried he'd be tossed out of the game, but he wasn't. Instead, his action gave our players a real morale boost just when they needed it. "I don't like the idea of people slapping our kicker or jumping in his face and laughing when he missed a field gold," Lambert told the press after the game. "That stuff you don't need." Chuck Noll obviously agreed, because he told the writers, "Jack Lambert is the defender of all that's right."

We came on strong in the fourth quarter, and a 64-yard bomb from Bradshaw to Swann upped our lead to 21-10. But Terry was knocked out of the game with a concussion on the play. Dallas scored a touchdown to make it 21-17, and then Gerry Mullins recovered an onside kick with 1:48 to play.

With Bradshaw out, we were having trouble running out the clock, and Chuck faced a big decision on a fourth-and-9 at the Cowboys 41-yard line. Punter Bobby Walden had already fumbled one snap, which led to Dallas's first touchdown, and almost had another punt blocked. So Chuck elected to run the football one more time because the Cowboys were out of timeouts. He preferred to take his chances with his defense rather than his special teams. "We had already botched one punt, and they can score a touchdown on a blocked punt," Noll explained after the game. "I had confidence in our defense.

We were giving them the ball with no timeouts, and I figured our defense could do it."

Our defense did it, and the outcome was sealed when Glen Edwards intercepted a Staubach pass in our end zone. The headlines in the *Post-Gazette* told it all: "STEELERS STILL SUPER, CHAMPS WHIP DALLAS IN CLIFFHANGER, 21-17."

Sports Illustrated's cover featured an acrobatic Lynn Swann catch, while the bold print read: "PITTSBURGH DOES IT AGAIN!" The back-to-back victories in Super Bowls IX and X proved to the world that the Steelers weren't a fluke—we were the real deal.

I particularly remember the days leading up to Super Bowl X. The hardest part of winning back-to-back Super Bowls is for a team to maintain its focus. It's easy to get overconfident or distracted by the media hype and the public attention that comes with being a championship team. Noll came to me before the Dallas game and shared his concern that the players seemed to be losing their edge. He wanted them to keep their eye on the prize, to concentrate on what they had to do, individually and as a team, to win. At the same time he wanted them to remain loose and confident.

Chuck called the players around him and told them what he thought would be a good story, but one he thought also contained a message about focus. Here's how he told the story:

"In a game like this you have to be ready. They're going to talk about how we're the champs. You can't get sucked into this hype. You have to concentrate and keep your mind on the game.

"This reminds me of the two Tibetan monks who are walking in the mountains. They come to a swift stream. On the bank they find a damsel in distress. She has her maid with her but doesn't know how to cross without immodestly pulling up her skirts. The monks see her dilemma and agree to help her. The first monk picks her up, wades across the stream, sets her down, and continues on the journey. The monks walk in silence for another mile or so when the second monk says to the first, 'You know, the rules of our order prohibit physical contact with members of the opposite sex.' They continue on until the first monk turns and says, 'That's right, but I put the lady down on the other side of the creek. You're still carrying her.'"

Russell, Ham, and Bleier started to laugh. But Ernie Holmes turned around shaking his head, "What's he *talking* about!"

I spent a good deal of time with Ernie. Everyone called him "Fats," but let me tell you, in his playing days, Holmes was six-foot-two, 265 pounds of muscle. He was a key part of the original Steel Curtain, along with Joe Greene, L.C. Greenwood, and Dwight White. Ernie played with fierce intensity and used his massive forearms to push opponents aside, then push and pull them off balance. When he played well, no one could stop him. Once he shaved his head leaving only an "arrowhead" on the top, facing forward—the only direction he intended to go. This hairdo made all the national sports publications, and the whole team got a kick out of it.

Holmes came to us in 1971 from Texas Southern University in Houston, another of Bill Nunn's finds. Ernie married young and had two sons, but he also developed some serious emotional problems. He would come to me from time to time just to talk. Sometimes he thought people were out to get him and his behavior began to border on paranoia. While driving back from Ohio, after separating from his wife, Ernie worried he'd never see his boys again. On the long drive, for some reason he believed three big trucks were trying to run him off the road. He snapped, pulled a pistol, and started shooting at the trailers. Soon a police helicopter appeared overhead, and he blazed away at that, too. Eventually, he ran off the road and the state police arrested him.

Ernie contacted me, and I assured him I would personally get him the help he needed. The authorities released him into my custody. Ernie pleaded guilty to assault with a deadly weapon and received five years probation. We sent him to Pittsburgh's Western Psychiatric

Hospital, where I visited him regularly. After two months of treatment, he returned to the team and helped us win two Super Bowls. Ernie was a special guy. Regrettably, he was no longer with the team when we made our Super Bowl runs in the late 1970s. But I'm happy to say today he's an ordained minister, and his sons have graduated from college (one is a college professor) and are both fine young men.

Injuries to key players plagued us from the very beginning of the 1976 season. We opened—if you can believe it—in Oakland. Passions ran high on both sides. Remember, Swann had been mugged by George Atkinson in the AFC championship game against the Raiders. That hit was very much on our minds.

From the opening kickoff, we knew it would be a no-holds-barred kind of game. But then, just before the half, George Atkinson struck again. He threw a vicious forearm at the back of Swann's head, knocking him unconscious. I know as well as anyone, hard hits are a part of the game of football, but there's no excuse for cheap shots like that. The play in question was a third-and-5 from the Oakland 44-yard line with 1:24 left in the first half. Terry Bradshaw dumped the ball to Franco Harris down the left sideline. Swann was coming across the field from the right side, completely out of the play, as Franco was running down the left sideline. Atkinson came up from behind and slugged Swann. It seemed like a replay of the shot he had taken from Atkinson the last time we played the Raiders in the AFC championship the year before. With Swann out of the game, we ended up losing by a field goal, 31-28.

Few of us actually saw the hit on Swann at the time it occurred. I was following Franco as he turned a broken play into a big gain. But the next day when I watched the game film with Chuck Noll, we both got angry. Chuck told reporters, "You have a criminal element in all aspects of society. Apparently we have it in the NFL, too." Those words would haunt us for over a year.

We lost four of our first five games, and we hit bottom with a loss to the Browns in Cleveland, a game made infamous by a frightening hit Joe "Turkey" Jones put on Terry Bradshaw. After the whistle, with Bradshaw in his grasp, Jones flipped Terry over his hip and spiked him into the turf headfirst. A lesser man might have suffered a broken neck, and a lesser team might have packed it in for the season. But in that cramped visitors' locker room in Cleveland Stadium, Joe Greene said, "If we have to be in this position all I can tell you is I'd rather be in it with this team, with these people, and particularly with the man running it."

Of course, the man running it was Chuck Noll, and he was able to hold the team together and get it going on what would end up being a nine-game winning streak. This achievement has to be one of the greatest coaching jobs in the history of professional sports.

That streak got us into the playoffs, which opened for us that year in Baltimore against the Colts. That was a wild game. Some crazy pilot decided to pull a stunt and land on the field. He came in low, pulled up, stalled, and crashed in the stands that thankfully had emptied early because we had sent the Colts fans home by rolling up a big lead. No one was hurt, not even the pilot, but that game did produce injuries on the field. Our two running backs, Franco Harris and Rocky Bleier, as well as Gerela, our kicker, suffered injuries that knocked them out of the game. We still won the game, 40-14, but the injuries would take a heavy toll the next week.

During the regular season, our defense had really come together. Bradshaw was out six games, and with the only other quarterback on the roster being rookie Mike Kruczek, our defense had to crank it up a notch. In this instance, words really don't do justice to the way our defense played, so I'm going to rely on some statistics to tell the story. During the nine straight wins that took us from 1-4 to 10-4 by the

end of the regular season, our defense posted five shutouts and allowed a total of 28 points. We had five sacks in the 27-0 win over the
Giants; the defense allowed only seven first downs and had five takeaways in a 23-0 win over San Diego; it was six more takeaways and 34
rushing yards allowed in a 43-0 win over Kansas City; in the 42-0
rout of Tampa Bay, the defense allowed only 11 net yards passing and
eight first downs; and in a 21-0 victory in Houston, the Oilers finished with more punts than first downs, 11-9.

The only thing standing between us and an NFL record three
straight Super Bowl championships in December 1976 was Al Davis's
Oakland Raiders. But the injuries in the Colts game hit us hard. Neither Franco Harris (ribs) nor Rocky Bleier (toe), both of whom had
posted 1,000-yard seasons, suited up for the game, and Frenchy
Fuqua played at less than 100 percent because of a calf injury. Our
only healthy back was Reggie Harrison, and running the ball was the
bread and butter of our offense that season. Again some statistics:
During the nine-game winning streak in the regular season, our offense rushed for more than 200 yards in every game but one—when
we ran for 143 yards against the Houston Oilers at Three Rivers Stadium. That was avenged with 258 yards in the rematch in the Astrodome on the final week of the regular season. During the nine-
game winning streak, the Steelers rushed for 2,101 yards and
averaged 4.5 yards per carry, and we had thirty-three rushing touchdowns on the season, allowing only five.

Without our primary offensive weapons we were at a disadvantage,
but this was another instance when Chuck Noll showed his greatness
as a coach. With only one week to prepare, Noll completely re-
designed our offense into a one-back set—revolutionary for that time
in the NFL. Later Joe Gibbs would use many of these same offensive
principles to win three Super Bowls with the Washington Redskins in
the 1980s and 1990s. But with no real time to install the offense, and

against an opponent as tough as the Raiders, it never had a chance to succeed. We lost that game, 24-7, and the AFC championship.

Yet, even in the atmosphere of this bitter disappointment, our players revealed their heart and character. In the locker room after the game, Jack Lambert said, "I'd play 'em again tomorrow. Just give me a few beers, a couple of hours of sleep, and I'll be out there at 1 p.m. tomorrow."

In my opinion, the defense we fielded in 1976 was the best in the history of the game. Our Steel Curtain defense smothered opponents. In the next two years, the league's Rules Committee recommended and the owners approved changes that would open up the passing game and cut down on injuries. Some of these changes came about as a result of the domination of the Steelers defense. Under the new rules, defenders could still make contact with eligible receivers, but only once. No contact was permissible five yards beyond the line of scrimmage. In addition, the league outlawed the head-slap, which Joe Greene used so effectively.

The Raiders beat the Minnesota Vikings to win Super Bowl XI, Al Davis's first Super Bowl victory. But Davis wasn't one to rest on his laurels. He always looked for the main chance. He believed in keeping his opponents off balance, whether in a tough negotiation at a league meeting or on the playing field. That was his style—just Al being Al.

Remember the words "criminal element"? After Chuck Noll publicly criticized George Atkinson for his cheap shot on Lynn Swann, the press had a field day with Chuck's "criminal element" statement. Pete Rozelle and I both worried about the public perception of violence in the NFL. I told Pete—and I even wrote a letter—his fine of only $1,500 on Atkinson did not send a clear enough message that such flagrant acts of unnecessary violence would not be tolerated. And I thought it was unfair that Pete slapped Noll with a $1,000 fine for speaking his mind on the matter.

With all this going on, I believe Davis saw an opening. He would distract and disrupt the Steelers even before the 1977 season began. I don't think George Atkinson came up with the idea of suing Chuck Noll for $3 million for "slander and defamation of character" all by himself. NFL rules prohibited one team from suing another, but an individual player can take legal action against a team. Of course, I don't know the details of the arrangement, but at the time everyone seemed to suspect Davis supported Atkinson and brought in the best lawyers available. I believe Al bankrolled the whole thing.

Some writers have referred to Al Davis as the "Dark Genius," implying malevolence. I don't know about that. I don't think he's evil. But he's no genius. He's a good football man. I got some insights into the way he thinks from my good friend Richie McCabe. After his playing days with the Steelers, Richie went into coaching, including a brief stint with the Raiders. He wasn't there very long, and when he came back to Pittsburgh I asked him how it went working for Al Davis.

"I can't take him," Richie told me. "I just can't stand it. He'd send a play down and say, 'Run this defense on the third or second down.' I didn't think he knew what he was doing. It wasn't a question of being dumb or not knowing football. Maybe he wasn't paying any attention." Al set the tone for his team. He wanted them to be feared and cultivated in his players a swaggering, almost outlaw image. They were called Raiders and he wanted them to act like Raiders.

The Atkinson lawsuit against Chuck could not have come at a worse time for the Steelers. The trial was scheduled to start in San Francisco in the summer of 1977, just as we opened our training camp in Latrobe. As a defendant in the case, Chuck Noll would be expected to testify, as would a number of our star players, including Andy Russell, Jack Ham, Rocky Bleier, and Terry Bradshaw. The whole thing seemed calculated to foul up our preparations for the 1977 season.

I personally spent four weeks in the MacArthur Suite at the St. Francis Hotel, a long time considering I should have been working on contracts—both Blount and Lambert were holding out—game schedules, and team logistics.

Fortunately, the judge in the case, U.S. District Court Judge Samuel Conti, was a reasonable man. He agreed that Chuck could testify immediately after the opening arguments and then be allowed to return to camp, as long as I was on hand for the entire trial to represent the team's interest. However, the judge also stipulated that Chuck would have to come back near the end of the trial. This schedule would enable him to set up camp and spend at least some time with the team.

We believed we were in the right—that if we honestly presented our case, even a San Francisco jury would do the right thing. But our insurance company advised us to settle out of court with Atkinson for $50,000 to avoid the expense of a lengthy trial. I said, "We're not settling—we're going to win this thing." I felt strongly that Noll had to win in order to be exonerated. We had to think of the league, too. Settling out of court would look like a cover-up.

The insurance company then sent us a lawyer we didn't agree with. So I brought in our own attorney, a very capable Irishman named James Martin MacInnis. MacInnis understood exactly what we needed to do to win the case. He used common sense and sound argument to show the jury why nothing Noll said or did constituted libel.

MacInnis advised us not to challenge any juror during the jury-selection process. We didn't—but the judge did. He asked a prospective juror, a woman, "Do you live in Oakland?"

"Yes I do, Your Honor."

"Are you a Raiders fan?"

"Yes I am. We hold season tickets."

"Do you think it would be fair to have a whole jury composed of people like you?"

"No, Your Honor."

"Thank you. You are excused."

The lead attorney for the plaintiff, Willie Brown, was a very capable lawyer. He later became mayor of San Francisco and speaker in the California Assembly. On the first day of the trial, Chuck Noll took the stand. Now, Chuck is a man of great intelligence. There is an air of importance about him. He doesn't talk a lot, but when he does, people listen. He's a very credible witness—the last thing Brown wanted. In an interview after the trial, Brown described what it was like going head to head with the future Hall of Fame coach, Chuck Noll:

"It is in federal court with a jury. It is a two-week trial. I am in federal court examining Chuck Noll; I've got Chuck Noll on the stand. Chuck Noll is a witness worse than Clarence Thomas. He will answer no questions. He does it with a degree of dignity that you just get angrier, angrier and angrier and angrier. I was going nuts through this hour of examination. I was doing the best job you could do on Chuck Noll, but you really can't shake him. The judge was watching this whole thing with great amusement . . . So I was hammering away, hammering away, and I am getting no place in making the points with Chuck Noll. I finally just kind of looked, gave the judge a glance. The judge asked me if I wanted to take a recess."

Brown regained his composure and changed his strategy. This time he asked Noll, "Do you see any criminals in this courtroom?" Players from both teams filled the room. Noll answered, "No," and Brown walked away feeling he had won the point.

Now the plaintiff's attorney focused on me. Brown wheeled into the courtroom a floor-to-ceiling blowup of the letter I had written to Rozelle, in which I stated my objections to the fines levied against Atkinson (too low) and Noll (too high). That day they called me I wore my white shirt, coat, and tie. In the witness box, I put my hand on the Bible and swore to tell the whole truth.

Brown asked, "Have you ever seen this letter before?"

"Yes."

"What's the nature of it?" he asked, hoping to throw me off by quickly firing questions.

"It's the letter I wrote to the commissioner."

Brown asked, "Did you review the letter with Chuck Noll before you sent it?"

I replied, "No. I don't go over my letters with anyone. If I write a letter, I write the letter."

He asked me if I thought Atkinson should be fined, implying that he didn't do anything more than our guys did. I said, "What do you mean? It was a cheap shot. He gave our guy a concussion and knocked him out of the game!"

MacInnis always seemed to have the trial well in hand. When the plaintiff's lawyer read a newspaper excerpt criticizing our players for unnecessary roughness, MacInnis spoke up and said, "That's an interesting bit of writing. Why don't we read the entire article?" The judge agreed, so MacInnis stood before the jury and read the whole thing aloud. Taken in context, the excerpt described nothing that would damage our case. When MacInnis finished reading, he turned to the jurors and said, "Seems to me, as Shakespeare said, this is 'much ado about nothing.'"

A bunch of our players were called to testify.

Our star witness, it turned out, was Terry Bradshaw. Affable, frank, smiling, Bradshaw played to the courtroom, cracked jokes, and captivated the jury. He was terrific.

After two weeks of testimony and cross-examination, the judge gave the jury members their final instructions and sent them off to deliberate. Four hours later, they returned with a unanimous verdict that Noll was not liable. Chuck was vindicated. After the ordeal, I told a reporter outside the courthouse, "I'm pleased. It has been the most depressing experience of my life, but I'm happy."

It's a good thing we won this case, both for the Steelers and the NFL. Noll's integrity remained intact, as did Pete Rozelle's. Pete had been called to testify and was very concerned about the outcome of the trial. Even more important, the case focused attention on the gratuitous violence represented by Atkinson's blindside clubbing of Lynn Swann. It served notice that such acts would not be condoned. Rozelle ordered the NFL Competition Committee to investigate rule changes that would make the game safer. At the same time, he removed Al Davis from this powerful committee.

―――――――

The NFL faced other issues during this time. No issue received more attention in the mid-1970s than labor relations.

The owners established the NFL Management Council, made up of one member from each of the twenty-eight clubs, to determine the league's labor policy. From this group a six-member Council Executive Committee (CEC) was appointed to negotiate directly with the National Football League Players Association (NFLPA). CEC chairman Wellington Mara appointed me the league's chief labor negotiator in 1976. I had served as chairman of the Expansion Committee in the early 1970s and been successful in bringing the Seattle Seahawks and Tampa Bay Buccaneers into the league. My years of experience in negotiating players' contracts also served me well in this important new appointment.

The league's recognition of the NFLPA in 1956 had greatly improved communications between owners and players. Even so, the NFL suffered a number of player strikes, beginning in the 1960s. The forty-two-day strike in 1974, orchestrated by Edward R. Garvey, executive director of the NFLPA, resolved nothing. The players agreed to end their walkout but their grievances, numbering nearly one hundred, remained unresolved.

Remember, in the 1974 strike the players wanted to eliminate the Rozelle Rule, which put limits on free agency; arbitration of all disputes; elimination of the draft; elimination of the waiver system; and a contract to guarantee salaries. But the strike fizzled when most of the players returned to camp.

Garvey had a staff of eight and an experienced negotiating team. After talks between the league and players broke down, the NFLPA leaders took their fight to the U.S. courts. Once I was appointed chief negotiator for the CEC, I reopened talks with the NFLPA. I was joined by Jim Finks, the former Steelers quarterback and then general manager of the Minnesota Vikings, and Sarge Karch, the CEC's attorney. We met with Garvey and other association representatives repeatedly through the summer and well into the 1976 season. I spent seventy-seven days in New York that year, in addition to meetings in Chicago, Las Vegas, and Miami.

Formal meetings were getting us nowhere, so I began talks with Miami Dolphins All-Pro safety Dick Anderson, the NFLPA president elected by the player representatives from all the teams. These talks were so secret that not even Ed Garvey knew of them. Miami coach Don Shula cooperated in every way and allowed me to talk to Anderson privately, an unusual occurrence given we were in the middle of the football season.

I saw Dick in Buffalo, where the Dolphins played the Bills in a *Monday Night Football* game. We reached an accord, which has since become known as the "Anderson-Rooney Agreement." When Ed Garvey learned what we had been up to, he wasn't happy. He'd been left out of the talks and said our agreement was "illegal." The NFLPA wouldn't accept it. But Anderson and I kept on working.

We again met secretly, this time at Dick's apartment in Miami. In the middle of our discussion the phone rang. No one was supposed to know I was there, but Anderson handed me the phone and said, "It's for you." It was Sig Hyman, the league's outside accountant and chief number-cruncher. Sig said, "You know those figures I gave you? Well, they've changed."

I thought Dick and I had made good progress, and I wanted to keep moving forward, so I told Sig, "It's too late now!" and hung up.

Dick and I continued our talks until we finally hashed out a draft agreement. This became the basis of an agreement both sides could accept, including Ed Garvey, who now entered the discussions, along with Sarge Karch.

During this time, the trust between the players and the league grew, and I got a chance to meet and know Gene Upshaw, the Raiders Pro-Bowl offensive lineman, and other team player representatives. I already knew Paul Martha, a labor arbitrator who had played defensive back for the Steelers. I had worked with him successfully during the construction of Three Rivers Stadium when the Pittsburgh Black Coalition, an organization of African-American business and civil rights leaders, pushed for assurances that black contractors would get construction contracts.

In February 1977, the league ratified a collective bargaining agreement (CBA) with the NFLPA. The five-year agreement was worth $107 million. It allowed for the continuation of the college draft through 1986; included a no-strike, no-suit clause; instituted a forty-three-man active player limit; reduced pension-vesting to four years; increased minimum salaries, as well as preseason and postseason pay; improved insurance and medical benefits; modified player movement and control practices; and reaffirmed the NFL commissioner's authority to discipline players.

With the expiration of the agreement five years later in 1982, the NFLPA authorized another strike. This time the players demanded a percentage of gross revenues for salaries and pensions. They wanted wage scales and compensation tied to seniority. The free agency issue had not been resolved to anyone's satisfaction, and players were concerned about injuries caused by artificial turf. The strike began two games into the regular season and lasted fifty-seven days. Eight games had to be cancelled—the first time anything like this had happened. Because of the shortened season, we devised a sixteen-team playoff tournament to determine who would play in Super Bowl XVII.

As we negotiated with the players during this time, Paul Martha was very helpful in keeping the talks moving. When it seemed things were falling apart, he got it back together. We worked long days and late nights, especially on wages and pensions. I remember one November night I was about ready to call it quits, saying, "We are not giving another dollar." Our meeting broke up, and I went back to my hotel. Only Martha and Garvey knew where I was staying.

About midnight, Paul called. I told him, "I'm leaving. I'm going home in the morning."

Paul urged me not to leave, saying, "It's going to happen. Stay."

And he was right. The logjam broke the next day, and we agreed on a CBA that we could present to the League and the NFLPA.

Paul attended the CEC meeting in New York on November 17, 1982. Chuck Sullivan, the oldest son of Patriots owner Bill Sullivan, then chairman of the committee, may have played up his role in the compromise, but in fact his grandstanding almost killed the agreement when he tried to make last-minute changes to get more than we had already agreed to. Paul Martha stood firm. "We can't change it."

I strongly supported Paul, and told everyone, "We've already been through this—we're not changing anything at this stage of the game. This is the deal we agreed on. Let's vote!" Fortunately, the CEC ignored Sullivan and approved the agreement, which then went on to the league for its approval.

The new CBA would run through 1986, and the NFL draft was extended through 1992. The veteran free-agent system was left unchanged. We agreed to a minimum salary schedule based on seniority;

training camp and postseason pay increased; medical insurance and retirement benefits increased; and a severance pay system was introduced—a first in professional sports.

These were exciting times, and we got a lot accomplished as we built mutual respect and trust. Working together, we formed the Player Club Relations Committee (PCRC). Gene Upshaw and Len Hauss represented the players; Wellington Mara and I spoke for management. We solved problems and made the collective bargaining process work.

It's not hard to know just why we didn't have a more successful season on the field in 1977: distractions. The "criminal element" trial certainly didn't help. Then there were the holdouts by Jack Lambert and Mel Blount; Glen Edwards and Jimmy Allen both left the team briefly during the season in protest of their contract situations; Bradshaw broke his wrist in October and played with a cast for much of the season; and just to top everything off, Chuck Noll slipped on a patch of ice in Cincinnati and broke his arm on the night before a December 10 game against the Bengals that we ended up losing.

We, along with other teams, had to adjust to the rule changes. Noll and the coaching staff liked running the ball, but now with the new rules favoring the passing game, we had to adapt. In the long run the rules changes would help Terry, but this season we couldn't put it all together. Don't get me wrong, in the old days we would have been proud of a 9-5 record. But after two Super Bowl victories, our team and our fans expected more. We knew we had a great football team. We got to the playoffs, but lost in the divisional championship to Denver. The Dallas Cowboys dominated Super Bowl XII, crushing the Broncos, 27-10.

In 1978 everything came together for the Steelers. At one time,

NFL Films rated this team as the greatest in football history. And it's hard to dispute that claim. We had the players on both sides of the ball. Bradshaw won the passing title that year and was named NFL Player of the Year. Harris had another tremendous year—I believe Franco, as much as anyone, was the key to our success. Swann and Stallworth were the best receiving duo in the game. Even with the new rules, our defense continued to dominate.

We had the coaches. Chuck Noll assembled a coaching staff second to none—guys like Rollie Dotsch (defensive line), Dick Hoak (offensive backfield), George Perles (defensive coordinator), and Woody Widenhofer (linebacker and secondary). Chuck said he would build the team with young new talent, and he did. But it was his vision and commitment to excellence that lifted this team to a new level. Joe Greene said, "I've been in locker rooms where you get all kinds of speeches and platitudes—they don't mean a thing. All Chuck said was, 'Play the way you've been coached,' and that's what developed the consistency in that football team."

We had the closeness, one of the essential ingredients in a winning team and perhaps one of the hardest to come by. That's where you need leadership in the locker room and off the field. Joe Greene provided this kind of leadership. It's more than one man, though. It's everyone coming together with a common goal. Players have to care not only about winning but about one another. They coach each other, they look out for one another, they're your best men at weddings and godfathers at baptisms. This closeness permeates the entire organization, from the grounds crew to the players to the coaches to scouts and the front office. We're all in it together.

The management has to recruit the talent and provide the resources to win. It also has to set a tone of honesty, fairness, and integrity, because without these things, there won't be trust.

This is why it came together for us in 1978. We ended the season with a 14-2 record, then defeated the Broncos in the playoffs, 33-10.

We played Houston in the AFC championship game at Three Rivers Stadium in a freezing rain. The Astrodome-coddled Oilers never knew what hit them. Our defense didn't allow them a touchdown and nearly shut them out, 34-5. The game was over for all practical purposes by halftime, when we led, 31-3.

———————

A special coin toss opened Super Bowl XIII—Steelers vs. Cowboys—at the Orange Bowl in Miami, January 21, 1979, a game that would crown the first team to win three Lombardi trophies. And it wasn't just any coin that was tossed. In a tribute to the 1920 founding of the NFL, an antique car transported Bears founder and owner, George Halas, to midfield, where he flipped an 1820 gold piece. I know George appreciated this honor, and no one deserved it more. He was there in Canton when team owners got together with the idea of starting a national football league. Their dream had come true.

The modern NFL was a far cry from that first season when Jim Thorpe was commissioner. As I watched the Steelers take the field, I thought back on the men who founded the NFL and felt privileged to have personally known them. People used to call Halas "Mr. Everything," because he did everything for the Chicago Bears—as player, coach, PR man, and ticket seller. "Papa Bear" was always hawking tickets. He would even sell seats on the visiting team's bench. He did whatever it took to win, from weighing balls before the game to withholding scouting information.

My father and I often argued with George at league meetings. He was always looking for an advantage, but he was a real football man. We used to kid him about "retiring" from coaching every decade. He would put in a coach like Paddy Driscoll, a former player, who would clean house. George would then return to coach and begin the cycle again. In 1967, at age seventy-three, he retired—this time for good. I have the greatest respect for George Halas, and this ceremony was a fitting tribute and a proper way to begin Super Bowl XIII. In 1983, when he died at age eighty-eight, he had been a part of the league for all sixty-three years of its existence.

Dallas won the coin toss for Super Bowl XIII and drove down the field to our 34-yard line, where Drew Pearson fumbled a handoff from Tony Dorsett on an ill-advised gadget play. We recovered on our 47, and seven plays later Bradshaw hit John Stallworth for a 28-yard touchdown. Noll and the defense had done their homework. Poring over game film, we had found a weakness in the Dallas corner-backs and exploited it the first chance we got.

Dallas came right back with a scoring drive of their own, the first time we'd been scored on in the first quarter all season. The Cowboys scored again in the second quarter when Thomas "Hollywood" Henderson locked Bradshaw's arms at his sides, while teammate Mike Hegman ripped it from Terry's grasp and ran in for a touchdown.

Undeterred, on our next drive, Bradshaw fired a pass from our 25-yard line to Stallworth, who broke a tackle and took it in for a touchdown. Before the half ended, the Cowboys went into their two-minute drill. Staubach threw to Drew Pearson, but Mel Blount stepped in and picked it off. With passes to Swann, a run by Harris, and a perfectly timed pass to Rocky Bleier in the end zone, the Steelers pulled ahead, 21-14, as the half ended.

The Steelers bent the highly touted Dallas flex defense nearly to the breaking point. Terry was on fire. He'd outpassed Staubach 229 yards to 61. We held them to a field goal in the third quarter after a wide-open Jackie Smith dropped a Staubach pass in the end zone.

Like most Super Bowls, this game was not without controversy. On a Bradshaw pass to Swann, the Cowboys cornerback Bennie Barnes tripped Lynn before the ball arrived. Both players fell down as the ball bounded away untouched. The back judge didn't make a call. But Fred Swearingen, the field judge, threw a flag and called Barnes for tripping. Coach Tom Landry protested, claiming Swann had interfered with Barnes. Barnes himself shouted, "Swearingen needs glasses, maybe he's from Pittsburgh!" Bradshaw later said, "There was a safety blitz and no pickup and I knew it, so I put the 'Hail Mary' on the ball. It was a good call by the official." Swearingen's call stood. Several plays later, Bradshaw correctly read a Dallas blitz and called a trap play for Franco, who broke over the left side for a touchdown. Terry said, "I was expecting a blitz, so I called for a quick off-tackle trap. You blitz on that play—and Franco will bust it." And he did. We now led, 28-17.

The Cowboys fumbled the kickoff. On the next play, Bradshaw hit Swann in the end zone for an 18-yard touchdown. Gerela's extra point made it 35-17.

I have to tell you, I didn't like the celebration I saw on our bench with six minutes still to play. Our guys were laughing, shaking hands, and slapping each other on the back. I thought a lot could happen in six minutes, especially when you're playing a Super Bowl championship team like the Dallas Cowboys. I could see on their faces they had plenty of fight left. I wasn't surprised when Staubach led an 89-yard touchdown drive. The Cowboys scored again following an onside kick. The score was now 35-31 with twenty-two seconds remaining. The Cowboys lined up for another onside kick, but this time Rocky Bleier fell on it. Terry ran out the clock and we had our third Super Bowl victory. The Steelers were the first team ever to achieve this distinction.

Terry Bradshaw was the MVP of Super Bowl XIII, and deservedly so. You can't imagine the negative press and ribbing Terry took in the two weeks leading up to the game. Bradshaw's performance silenced a lot of critics. He had passed for a record four touchdowns and 318 yards, blowing the top off Bart Starr's old Super Bowl record of 250 yards.

Bradshaw had come into his own, and the Steelers had come of age as well. The next year, we went 12-4 in the regular season, beat Miami in the first round of the playoffs, and defeated Houston once again for the AFC title. On January 20, 1980, we faced the Los Angeles Rams in Pasadena for Super Bowl XIV.

I was worried going into this game. Three of our top assistant coaches—Lionel Taylor, Dan Radakovich, and Bud Carson—had left the Steelers and gone over to the Rams after the 1977 season. They knew our system. They knew everything about us. We'd have to execute perfectly and come up with some new stuff if we were going to win.

It was a close game. We trailed, 13-10, and after the game, Lambert admitted to the press, "At halftime, I was really concerned. I was more than concerned. I was scared. They had all the momentum, and our defense just wasn't playing up to par. It was just a shaky situation. It had been a big-play game, and in those games anything can happen. In the first half, they used a lot of man-in-motion, and it confused us. We finally made some adjustments at halftime."

In the third quarter we went ahead 17-13, when Bradshaw hit Swann with a 47-yard touchdown pass. Rams quarterback Vince Ferragamo connected on a 50-yard pass that moved Los Angeles to the Steelers' 24. On the next play, Lawrence McCutcheon passed to Ron Smith on a halfback option, putting the Rams up 19-17. On the very first possession of the fourth quarter Bradshaw let loose a 73-yard bomb to John Stallworth, and we regained the lead 24-19.

The Rams were driving again, and with 5:35 left in the game they had the ball on our 32-yard line. In another example of a great player making a big play at a critical moment, Lambert dropped deep from his middle linebacker position and cut across a lazy route run by Rams receiver Ron Smith and intercepted Ferragamo's pass. "I was responsible for the deep middle on the play," said Lambert later. "It was a play they like, but they had only run it once before which surprised me. We worked on it in practice the last two weeks, because it had been successful for them all year."

After Lambert's interception, the Chief got up from his seat in our box and started to get ready to go down to the locker room. I asked him, "Where are you going? The game's not over."

He just looked at me and said, "It is now."

He was right. A few plays after Lambert's interception, facing another critical third-down situation, Bradshaw went deep to Stallworth again, this time for 45 yards. Franco Harris sealed the deal on a 1-yard run for a touchdown. The final score: 31-19.

Bradshaw completed fourteen of twenty-one passes for a total of 309 yards and was again voted the game's MVP.

With four Super Bowls in six years, sportswriters and fans now talked about the "Steelers Dynasty." There's no question we were the team of the decade.

But nothing stays the same. The only thing certain in life is change. And so it was with the Steelers, the NFL, and me.

CHAPTER 7

A NEW ERA

THE STEELERS DYNASTY of the 1970s was built around players of extraordinary talent. As I've said, to consistently win in the National Football League, a team must have four things: great coaching, team closeness, good management, and talented players. Of course you need great players. Some teams get them in ones and twos, but in the early 1970s we hit the jackpot. The Pro Football Hall of Fame inducted nine of those athletes, an amazing tribute to the quality of the teams that brought four Lombardi trophies home to Pittsburgh. I have lasting memories of all those players. Though each one of them had unique abilities, all of them shared the desire to be the best, personally and as a team. They were winners—they thrived on the thrill of victory.

Joe Greene could not abide losing. He took it personally. It's what made him great, both as a player and as a team leader. Everyone who came in contact with him felt the heat of the competitive fire that burned within him. No Steeler gave more to his team than Joe Greene. Andy Russell said, "Joe was extremely strong in his attitudes, his opinions, and he wasn't afraid to voice them in the locker room. He was a very positive influence in the locker room."

Bill Nunn saw the Joe Greene who sacrificed himself on the field to make his team better. "Joe Greene was a unique person. He was a mean player; Joe was an intimidator," said Nunn. "He had the quick first-step move, and it kept being effective even when defensive line coach George Perles put him in the Stunt 4-3, which effectively made him a nose tackle who always had to take on the center and get double-teamed. That took a toll on him, because he was getting hit from all angles, but he was making everybody else around him a better player. I think Perles did that to keep blockers off Jack Lambert, to allow Lambert to be free to roam the field, which was his most effective way of playing middle linebacker."

When we played the Houston Oilers at Three Rivers Stadium during our first Super Bowl run in 1974 we had an 8-2 record. We had defeated them earlier in the year and were pretty confident we could do it again. But they beat us, 13-10, and it wasn't that close. They whipped us. The next day, on *Monday Night Football*, Joe Greene watched the Miami Dolphins dismantle the Cincinnati Bengals. He got angry as he watched the Dolphins move the ball like a machine, making no mistakes, no penalties, and doing the things they were coached to do. Joe said, "That's what I want us to be like. I came into our team meeting on Tuesday, and I really didn't like what I was hearing, so I went and cleaned out my locker and walked to my car." He was so upset about losing and playing with guys who didn't seem to care about winning as much as he did that he was ready to walk away from the team—away from football. Fortunately, Lionel Taylor, our receivers coach, himself a Pro Bowl receiver, saw Joe walking out and was able to calm him down. Joe returned to the team. I didn't find out about this until the end of the season, but it didn't surprise me. Joe refused to lose, and he inspired the team with that same intensity, that winning spirit.

We knew what we had in Joe Greene, and so we did things to help him grow and mature as a player and as a person. Over time, Joe went from wishing he hadn't been drafted by the Steelers to appreciating what we all had built together. Joe said, "I probably couldn't have played for a lot of teams. In some ways, I had a personality somewhat similar to Duane Thomas, who was a very talented Cowboys running back in the early 1970s who chafed under the sometimes heavy hand of team management. I told Duane, if we switched places and I was in Dallas and he was in Pittsburgh I'd probably be out of the game and he'd be thriving. The simple fact is that because of Chuck and Dan and Mr. Rooney, they knew they were dealing with kids and they had a way of giving us a helping hand and letting us know it's going to be better. When I had a tantrum and kicked in the door of the equipment room at training camp one summer, all Chuck ever did was he came up to my room and said, 'That'll be $500.' That was it. But I understood, because you can't do that. Through all of my antics, Dan and Chuck kind of felt that my only interest was in winning."

That famous Coca-Cola commercial of a battered and exhausted "Mean Joe" coming through the tunnel after a game wasn't far off the mark. He gave it his all. He never left anything on the field. The example he set helped create the closeness that won us Super Bowls. Joe retired in 1981 and entered the Hall of Fame in 1987, his first year of eligibility.

Jack Ham wrote the book on how to play outside linebacker. Unlike Joe Greene, who wore his emotions on his sleeve, Ham always appeared cool, calculating, and unflappable. He made a science of reading offenses, and he had awesome powers of concentration. But when he got a running back or receiver in his sights, he homed in on him like a guided missile—a stealth missile. And when he hit, there was bound to be an explosion. Bill Nunn always told me he'd hate to get into a fight with him because you'd never see him coming. He was every bit as physical as Joe Greene. Jack earned All-Pro or All-AFC honors in seven consecutive seasons. He played in eight straight Pro Bowls before retiring in 1982. Jack was inducted into the Hall of Fame in 1988, in his first year of eligibility.

Next to Johnny Unitas, I think Terry Bradshaw is the greatest quarterback in history. They called him the "Blond Bomber," and his teammates loved his sense of humor and bravado. The press tormented him with stories about his intelligence. Pittsburgh fans were tough on him—I thought maybe too tough. But he got through all this and became a real team leader. There was no quit in him. When he threw an interception, he came right back gunning. Some sportswriters said he had a problem with Chuck Noll, but he didn't, not really. They were about as different as two people could be, but working together they won four Super Bowls. If you call that having a problem, I'll take it any day. Terry was MVP for Super Bowls XIII and XIV, and NFL MVP in 1978. He finished his career with 27,989 yards passing and 212 touchdowns. He retired in 1983 and entered the Hall of Fame in 1989, also in his first year of eligibility. I continue to make the point of these great players entering the Hall of Fame in their first year of eligibility, because this is one real way to measure the best against the best.

Cornerback Mel Blount was bigger, faster, stronger, and smarter than anyone who played against him. His dominance at his position and his physical style of play caused the NFL to change the rules for pass defense. His fifty-seven interceptions stand as a Steelers record to this day. He played in five Pro Bowls, was named All-Pro four times, and earned the title of NFL defensive MVP in 1975. Like Joe Greene, Mel was a leader and contributed in a big way to the team closeness that won Super Bowls. After he retired in 1983, Mel went on to become director of player relations for the NFL and founded the Mel Blount Youth Home, with a facility in Vidalia, Georgia, and one near Pittsburgh. I was proud and honored to present Mel at the enshrinement ceremony as he entered the Hall of Fame in 1989, his first year of eligibility.

When Franco Harris came to the Steelers in 1972, we started winning. His departure in 1983 marked the end of an era. With 11,950 yards rushing, Franco is the team's all-time rushing leader. I believe his Immaculate Reception is the single greatest play in NFL history. He was a team leader and in his quiet way motivated other players. But Franco impressed me beyond the football field. He's one of the finest, most thoughtful and caring human beings I have ever known. I'll always regret that his career didn't end in Pittsburgh. He played one season for the Seattle Seahawks after we couldn't come to terms on his contract. Looking back on it now, I wish I'd taken money out of my own pocket to seal the deal. The good news is he returned to Pittsburgh after retiring in 1984 and has become an active and important part of our community. He's a successful businessman and serves on a number of nonprofit boards, including the Heinz Endowments and the Senator John Heinz History Center/Western Pennsylvania Sports Museum. He entered the Hall of Fame in 1990, his first year of eligibility.

An exceptional middle linebacker, Jack Lambert was a two-time NFL defensive player of the year, eight-time All Pro, and nine-time Pro Bowler. He led the Steelers in tackles in every season except his last, when a broken toe that just wouldn't heal kept him benched most of the year. Lambert intimidated opponents. He looked like a wild man—who can forget that image of him, his front teeth missing, intensity etched on his face, his feet drumming in anticipation of the snap? But at the same time, he was one of the smartest guys ever to play at that position, and he had a great sense of humor that kept the team loose at critical times and for big games. He was different. His leadership stemmed from his expectation that everybody in the organization—players, coaches, office workers, even me—do their jobs. He wouldn't back down. He'd let you know if you weren't pulling your own weight. He was that kind of a leader. He could get away with this because he had earned the respect of his teammates, the coaches, and me.

One time, later in his career, our new strength coach had decided the players needed to start eating health foods, and so he started replacing things the players enjoyed, like steak and potatoes, and went with more whole grains and nuts and things like that. Well, some of the players had been complaining, and so one day Lambert walks into Chuck Noll's office and puts a paper cup on his desk. Chuck looks at the cup, and sees it's filled with twigs and acorns and stuff he must've scooped off the ground under a tree.

"What's that?" Chuck asked.

Lambert answered with a stone face, "Lunch."

We changed the menu back to the way it was.

It's a shame that the toe injury ended his career in 1984. The Hall of Fame inducted him in 1990, his first year of eligibility. He ended his acceptance speech with this: "If I had to do it all over again, I'd be a professional football player, and you can be sure I'd do it as a Pittsburgh Steeler."

Mike Webster was a model of hard work and consistency. His record shows that he played more seasons, 15, more games, 220, and more consecutive games, 177, than any other Steeler in the history of the franchise. Not large for a center, he was crafty and smart and anchored the offensive line through four Super Bowls. He was a seven-time All Pro and played in nine Pro Bowls. He retired in 1988, and the selectors voted him into the Hall of Fame in 1997. Sadly, he passed away in 2002.

For grace and athleticism, wide receiver Lynn Swann has no peer. He was famous for his acrobatic, leaping receptions. His gravity-defying circus catches in Super Bowl X are still talked about today, and now when a receiver makes a similar play, he'll be described in the press as making a "Swann-like" catch. A first round draft pick, Swann was always at his best in the big games. He earned MVP honors for his performance in Super Bowl X, with four receptions for 161 yards and a touchdown. He never feared going across the middle, though he paid for it with ferocious hits that resulted in numerous concussions. Two of the worst were delivered by George Atkinson. Swann is a highly cultured man. He used his ballet and dance training to enhance his performance as a football player. One sportscaster called him the "Baryshnikov of football." Politically active, Lynn ran for governor of Pennsylvania in 2006. He retired in 1982 with 336 career receptions for 5,462 yards and 51 touchdowns. He was inducted into the Hall of Fame in 2001.

Wide receiver John Stallworth leads the Steelers for most yards, 8,723, and receiving touchdowns, 63. He set Super Bowl records for average yards per catch, 24.4 yards, and for single game average (40.3 in Super Bowl XIV). He was a two-time team MVP. His great speed and leaping ability were matched only by his intelligence. Even before retiring from football in 1987, he founded a very successful engineering and information technology business, Madison Research Corporation. He was enshrined in the Hall of Fame in 2002.

These great players and others—Rocky Bleier, L.C. Greenwood, Ernie Holmes, Andy Russell, Donnie Shell, Mike Wagner, Dwight White—made up the backbone of the Steelers dynasty of the 1970s.

But all good things come to an end. As Chuck Noll always said, "Football is not your life's work," and the career of a professional football player is limited. A human body can only endure so much. Most players can endure it for less than five years. A ten-year career is rare in the NFL. And so the guys we drafted in the 1970s were nearing the end of their careers by the time of our Super Bowl victory in 1980. As Jack Ham put it, "We were old and our best days were behind us."

We thought we had more time to draft and find replacements for our aging players. Terry Bradshaw's elbow had been bothering him, and our doctors knew it. But we didn't know how serious it was, and Terry didn't let on how badly his elbow pained him. Following the 1982 season, he went back home to Louisiana and had a local doctor perform surgery. But the elbow would take time to heal. If we'd understood his true condition, our team orthopedic surgeon would have treated him more aggressively.

With Bradshaw's elbow injury sidelining him, Cliff Stoudt, our backup quarterback since 1977, led the team to a 9-2 record. We then lost the next three games. Chuck Noll called on Bradshaw one last time to help us beat the New York Jets and their powerful "New York Sack Exchange" defense in the next to last game of the regular season, to clinch the division title. Noll expected Terry to protect his arm and run the ball. But he came out gunning, throwing two touchdown passes and sealing the victory, 34-7. It would be Bradshaw's last game. When our young offensive tackle, Tunch Ilkin, asked Terry on the sideline why he was throwing the ball instead of handing off, Bradshaw looked at him and said, "Tunch, I'm a gunslinger, not a mailman." Even injured, Terry Bradshaw had to be true to himself as a player.

We went 10-6 that season but lost to Oakland, 38-10, in the divisional playoffs. Mark Malone was drafted in 1980 to eventually replace Bradshaw. He was another magnificent athlete—maybe too good. In 1981 we had a lot of injuries at wide receiver, and so Chuck asked Mark to help the team out there. Since back-up quarterbacks don't get the opportunity to run many plays in practice during the season, Mark agreed and started working at wide receiver. He caught a 90-yard touchdown pass from Terry that season, but he also injured his knee and was never the same. That's when Cliff Stoudt became our starting quarterback. Stoudt had plenty of talent, but playing in the shadow of Terry Bradshaw—a guy who had been to the Super Bowl four times and come away with four rings—was hard to do.

In 1983 we had a chance to draft Dan Marino. Danny was a Pittsburgh boy. We'd watched him quarterback the Central Catholic team. In his senior year there, *Look* magazine did a story on the three best high school football players in the country. The magazine featured Danny, a young running back from Texas named Eric Dickerson, and a kid from California, John Elway. Pretty select company for a boy from the Oakland neighborhood of Pittsburgh. Danny stayed in Western Pennsylvania and led the University of Pittsburgh Panthers to four straight bowl games. He won the Sugar Bowl in his junior year with a 33-yard touchdown pass on a fourth-and-5 in the final minute of the game. He didn't shine in his senior year, and most scouts weren't looking at him as closely as they were Elway of Stanford, Jim Kelly (another Pittsburgher), from the University of Miami, or Dickerson, from Southern Methodist University.

Being a local boy, Danny Marino stopped by Three Rivers Stadium one day and tossed some passes around to some of our second-string receivers. We looked at each other and said, "Hey, this kid can play."

When the 1983 draft came around, an astute newspaper reporter from the *Pittsburgh Press*, John Clayton (who currently works for ESPN), buttonholed me right outside our draft room. "I'll tell you what you should do with your draft."

"What's that?"

"You should take Danny Marino on your first pick." Remember, we'd been in the playoffs so we were drafting pretty late.

He said again, "You should take Marino as your first pick, then trade Cliff Stoudt for a high second pick. You'll probably get the same guy in the second round that you want in the first because you're drafting twenty-sixth." Now, Noll and the scouts wanted a big defensive tackle from Texas Tech named Gabriel Rivera. Chuck thought he could build a new team around Rivera—just as he built the team of the 1970s around Joe Greene.

I respected Clayton's opinion and thought it was a great idea.

We should have done it. But I made a mistake. When I went to Noll, my brother Art, and Dick Haley, they said, "That's a good idea! How did you come up with that?"

Instead of saying I thought it up myself, I truthfully told them it was John Clayton's idea. With that they threw up their hands and shouted, "Clayton? You gotta be kidding!" And that was the end of it. We could have drafted Marino, and I believe if we had we would have won more Super Bowls in the 1980s. Dan Marino has proven himself to be one of the best quarterbacks of all time. I'd put him right up there after Johnny Unitas and Terry Bradshaw. It's a shame he never won a Super Bowl with the Miami Dolphins.

The year 1982 was one of change for Pittsburgh, the Steelers, and for my family. The American steel industry continued to struggle, and unemployment in Pennsylvania rose to 12 percent, its highest level since the Great Depression of the 1930s. With the economic downturn, workers sought job opportunities wherever they could find them. No longer were Steelers fans confined to Western Pennsylvania. The Steelers Nation now stretched from coast to coast.

The Steelers celebrated our fiftieth anniversary during the 1982 season. We had accomplished so much since my father had founded the franchise fifty years earlier. The original charter was dated July 8, 1933, marking 1982 as our fiftieth season. Joe Greene served as general chairman of the anniversary activities. Special parades, publications, and programs were scheduled throughout the year to call attention to this milestone in football history.

On August 28, at halftime during our preseason game with the Colts, we honored eight members from the original 1933 team—the football Pittsburgh Pirates. On October 8, we set up a "Steelers 50

Seasons" exhibition at the David L. Lawrence Convention Center. This ten-thousand-square-foot show included players' jerseys, game balls, NFL films, photographs, and artwork. The four Lombardi trophies were dramatically mounted on a rotating platform, while strobes bounced light off the glittering silver. The visitors' eyes widened when they saw four diamond-studded Super Bowl rings.

A separate theater showed highlight films from Super Bowls past, and special galleries were dedicated to the Chief and Chuck Noll. Other displays included Man of the Year trophies awarded to Franco and Lynn Swann, Bradshaw's *Sports Illustrated* Man of the Year award, and the eight bronze busts of Steelers inducted to the Hall of Fame— Art Rooney, Bert Bell, Johnny Blood, Cal Hubbard, Bill Dudley, Walt Kiesling, Bobby Layne, and Ernie Stautner. Fans from all over the country paid a dollar apiece to see the exhibit, with the proceeds going to Dapper Dan Charities.

McDonald's and Coca-Cola were the principal sponsors of the anniversary celebration. We distributed more than 1.5 million All-Time Steelers Team ballots at Pittsburgh-area McDonald's and all stores where Coke was sold. More than a hundred thousand fans voted for their favorite players. Memories came flooding back as I reviewed the fans' picks.

More than twenty-six hundred people paid $100 a plate for the Steelers 50 Seasons banquet at the Convention Center on October 9. Some said we should make this a black-tie affair, but I wanted every fan to feel welcome. This extravaganza was really the highlight of the anniversary. It was as much a tribute to my father as it was a celebration of the Steelers' fifty seasons.

But an NFL players' strike threatened to mar the celebration. The NFLPA called for a walkout beginning September 19. Though we had played and won the first two games of the regular season—one over the defending AFC champion Cincinnati Bengals—the fifty-seven-day strike broke our stride and hit right in the middle of our festivities. The next eight games were canceled, and we wouldn't play again until November 21.

Offense

OT-Jon Kolb	Oklahoma 1969
OT-Larry Brown	Kansas 1971
G-Gerry Mullins	USC 1971
G-Sam Davis	Allen (S.C.) 1967
C-Mike Webster	Wisconsin 1974
TE-Elbie Nickel	Cincinnati 1947
QB-Terry Bradshaw	Louisiana Tech 1970
RB-Rocky Bleier	Notre Dame 1968
RB-Franco Harris	Penn State 1972
WR-Lynn Swann	USC 1974
WR-John Stallworth	Alabama A&M 1974
PK-Roy Gerela	New Mexico State 1971

Defense

DE-L.C. Greenwood	Arkansas AM&N 1969
DE-Dwight White	East Texas State 1971
DT-Joe Greene	North Texas State 1969
DT-Ernie Stautner	Boston College 1950
MLB-Jack Lambert	Kent State 1974
OLB-Andy Russell	Missouri 1963
OLB-Jack Ham	Penn State 1971
CB-Mel Blount	Southern 1970
CB-Jack Butler	St. Bonaventure 1951
S-Donnie Shell	South Carolina State 1974
S-Mike Wagner	Western Illinois 1971
P-Pat Brady	Nevada (Reno) 1952

Some people wondered whether we should cancel the dinner, but the fans wanted a celebration. Most of the striking players told me they would come to honor the team and my father, strike or no strike. True to their word, Bradshaw, Franco, Lambert, and the others were there. Only ten of the 1982 team failed to show. And, of course, scores of former players from every decade, including every one of the twenty-four named to the All-Time Steelers Team, came to the banquet.

Franco Harris spoke for the Steelers' offense, saying, "One, two, three, four Super Bowls. We're going after the fifth one—this year. One thing that will never change is Pittsburgh's tradition of hard, rough, tough football."

Andy Russell spoke for the defense. He said to the striking players, "We want to see you come back, but we'll let you make the decision when." People in the audience shouted, "Now! Now!"

The Count Basie Orchestra provided musical entertainment, while rookie running back Walter Abercrombie sang the national anthem. The dinner menu included everything from filet mignon to chocolate cups filled with amaretto mousse.

Howard Cosell emceed the evening, reminding everyone, "This is still the City of Champions. The cheering has stopped for now, but here, in Pittsburgh, the Renaissance City, the cheering will never stop. Being here is one of the greatest moments in my life. I have very deep feelings about this city. This is the City of Champions, not because of the Pirates winning the World Series and not because of the Steelers winning the Super Bowl . . . but when you have Joe Greene and Willie Stargell in the same city in the same era—that's what makes Pittsburgh the City of Champions. When you play Pittsburgh, you play the whole city. Yes, it's still the City of Champions. It has nothing to do with victories. Pittsburgh has a winning character."

Howard was at his best that night. His encyclopedic knowledge of the game and the players amazed me and everyone in the audience. His thoughtful introductions of players hit the mark every time.

"The most productive quarterback in the entire history of the National Football League . . . Terry Bradshaw."

"The most graceful, the most acrobatic wide receiver in football . . . Lynn Swann."

"If there ever was an authentic hero, it's this man . . . Rocky Bleier."

"There are no words and there never will be any to talk about Joe Greene. He was the best there ever was at what he did."

This went on for three and a half hours, but nobody complained or left the hall.

Co-hosts included our game announcers Myron Cope and Jack Fleming, and anniversary chairman, Joe Greene. Joe said, "This is a hard town, an honest town, a tough town. That's what we're all about." Mean Joe got choked up as he looked at the twenty-four members of the All-Time Steelers Team on the dais. He continued, "I like to think of these people as my people, my boys. Yes you are. My coach too. Learned an awful lot about life. I wouldn't trade it for anything—things like Mr. Rooney telling me about the good old days. Loved it. I do. Thank you so much."

Pete Rozelle presented my father with a special award. "You have to love him," Pete said of my father, "he's so honest and down to earth. He has a heart of gold, and that was the Steelers' problem once upon a time. He has a feeling for the tradition of this league, and that's so important in these times."

Pittsburgh mayor Richard Caliguiri commented, "It is easy to get emotional about Art Rooney. He's gone through good times and bad times and enjoyed them both. The Rooneys and the Steelers of the last fifty years are a tremendous source of pride to Pittsburgh."

Other speakers included Supreme Court justice Byron "Whizzer" White, Chuck Noll, Senators Arlen Specter and John Heinz. Senator Heinz said, "I want to thank Art Rooney and the Rooney family for the love and loyalty they have given this city."

My father came to the speaker's stand. He had applauded every one of the players who had been recognized, sometimes with tears in his eyes. Now it was his turn to speak. Even the waiters and bartenders stopped to listen.

"I thought maybe they weren't going to ask me to say something," he said, laughing. Dad went on, "I guess I'm kind of dumb. I didn't even know this was being planned. I wasn't for all of this. I thought we'd bring the old ballplayers in and introduce them to the fans. But this has made me very happy.

"Yesterday, Danny told me there would be very little to say. There would be movies and Howard and Myron Cope and Joe Greene would be here and the players would have something to say. So I figured, good. But I thought I could tell them something about myself that they didn't know. I wanted to say that I was a baseball player and a manager, a football player and a coach, a boxer and a promoter, and a horse player. And I enjoyed every minute of it. Sports have been my life. The present-day ballplayers that came to this affair really made me very happy.

"I spend a good bit of time with our ballplayers, in the training room, in the dressing room, and our offices. I enjoy it. I never had a ballplayer play for me that I didn't think was a star. And I never had a ballplayer play for me that I didn't like.

"I would like to take this opportunity to introduce somebody who the sports world has rarely seen or heard of. But someone who is very important to me, has been a wonderful wife and mother, Mrs. Rooney."

My mother, Kathleen McNulty Rooney, was sitting beside me at a round table directly in front of the dais. She was such a graceful lady, and that night she looked beautiful in her midnight blue lace dress. Around her neck she wore a glittering Super Bowl XIV pendant. As my father introduced her, she smiled shyly and half rose from her seat to wave to the crowd.

Neither my mother nor my father had been privy to the details of the fiftieth anniversary banquet planning. They both enjoyed the evening, seeing old friends and telling stories of the old days. The love that filled the hall that night is almost impossible to describe. But they felt it, and it meant a lot to them both.

On November 28, 1982, a week after the players strike had ended, we played the Seahawks in Seattle. In the middle of the game I received a phone call from Patricia, who was at Allegheny General Hospital in Pittsburgh with my father. My mother had died at the hospital following a heart attack. Patricia gave me the details—my father was too grief-stricken to speak. She told me that my mother had died in our daughter Kathleen's arms. We had named Kathleen after Mom, and they always had a special relationship. As a young woman, Kathleen had been diagnosed with lupus. She would stay with my mother, who would care for her. But in a strange twist of fate, it was Kathleen who cradled my mother in her arms after she suffered her heart attack.

Some weeks before her death Mom had broken her leg. She had a difficult time maneuvering her oversized cast around the house. Under the strain, her heart just gave out. It was hard for me to believe she was gone. She had always been so strong, the glue of the family. She kept us together and always administered love and wisdom and discipline in the right amounts. Imagine what it must have been like for her, raising five athletic and high-spirited boys on Pittsburgh's North Side, as my father worked hard at his various enterprises and built the Steelers from the ground up. We'd been to a lot of funerals, but this one hit us hard, my father, especially. Pete Rozelle, Wellington Mara, Stormy Bidwill, Rankin Smith, Gene Upshaw, and many of our NFL friends attended the funeral service at St. Peter's.

But it was the presence of our nine children—Art, Pat, Kathleen, Rita, Dan, Duffy, John, Jim, Joan—that gave me strength and hope for the future. Like my mother, Patricia had played the greatest role in raising our children. I helped, but she was with them every day. And, also like my mother, she kept all of us—including me—on the right path. Like my father, I often traveled and worked away from home, especially during the football season. I'm happy to say our four boys and five girls grew into fine young men and women. They were baptized and attended Catholic grammar schools and high schools.

Usually, after the football season ended, we took our whole family to Seven Springs in Pennsylvania or to Vail or Beaver Creek, Colorado, to ski. While Patricia watched the younger kids I hit the slopes with the older ones. I found the high mountain snow and clear, dry air invigorating and became quite passionate about skiing—that is, until I broke my leg. After that Patricia tried to slow me down. She urged me to take up cross-country skiing instead of black diamond downhill racing. To humor her, I tried cross-country once, but I just couldn't get into it.

Eventually all of our children would graduate from college—with law degrees, master's degrees, and degrees in special programs—and several would graduate from Catholic colleges, something that Patricia and I had always hoped for. All of them went on to marry and have families of their own. We are proud of each and every one of them.

The day before the Steelers beat New England and won a place in the AFC playoffs, and exactly a month to the day after my mother died, my daughter Pat and her husband Bob presented us with our first grandchild, a beautiful baby girl named Laura. On Christmas Day 1990, my son Art and his wife Greta brought us our first grandson and named him Danny (who in the Rooney tradition has turned out to be a good football player). It seems in this life whenever a door closes another opens.

———————

By 1982 the NFL had evolved into a twenty-eight-team partnership that spanned the nation. Although the league was now big business—

revenues from gate receipts, television, film, ventures, and endorsements totaled in the billions of dollars—it always had been and still was a kind of fraternity. In the early days, the owners were a close-knit group of men who cared about football and looked out for one another. When a man gave his word, he kept it. A handshake was all you needed. Sure, we had our disagreements, but we never threatened another owner or club. The rule against one club suing another is just one example. Of course, we were as competitive as we could be on the field, but no owner would ever deliberately undermine another in a way that might drive him out of business or hurt the league.

But in 1980 the NFL rules of engagement seemed to change. Al Davis determined to move his Oakland Raiders to Los Angeles without league approval and in the process ended up suing the league, even going so far as naming individual owners as defendants. Moving the Raiders to Los Angeles was in itself a direct attack on another owner, in this case Carroll Rosenbloom's widow, Georgia Frontiere (Carroll had drowned in a tragic accident in 1979). By moving to Los Angeles, he directly challenged the Rams' revenue base. Rozelle and the league's attorney, Paul Tagliabue, argued that the move would not only erode the Rams' market but would leave the loyal Oakland fans high and dry without a team. He pointed out that the success of the NFL depended on the fans—those loyal supporters who should never be taken for granted. I supported this view completely. I thought Davis's move was wrong for the NFL, wrong for Los Angeles, and wrong for the fans.

The NFL is a franchise business. You have to understand that the other franchisees are your partners. It's like McDonald's. They wouldn't put one set of golden arches right across the street from another. It wouldn't make any sense. The two restaurants wouldn't make any money, and the resulting war might even threaten the parent organization. That's just what Al Davis's move to the Los Angeles Coliseum amounted to. You try not to get angry about things like this, but the rules are in place for a reason—some people think the rules don't apply to them. Pete and the owners now found themselves pitted against Davis and the Los Angeles Coliseum Commission in an antitrust lawsuit.

The problem really started in 1978 when Carroll Rosenbloom announced he would take his Rams from the Coliseum to Anaheim, thirty-five miles away. The Coliseum then petitioned the league for a new team. When Rozelle didn't deliver, the Coliseum sued, claiming that certain league rules violated federal antitrust laws, because any franchise move required a unanimous vote of the owners. We voted to amend the rules so that any decision on expansion or movement could be made by just a three-fourths vote. Al Davis abstained from this vote, saying, "I reserve my rights." Al later claimed to have said, "I reserve my right to move as I see fit," although none of us remember hearing these last six words.

In January 1980, Davis determined to leave Oakland for Los Angeles and play in the Coliseum. He joined the Coliseum Commission in their suit against the league. We rejected the move twenty-two to zero, with five abstentions. Davis claimed our vote constituted a "business conspiracy" and vowed to fight us. Things were getting ugly—and personal. Davis described Rozelle publicly as a vindictive, power-hungry social climber who spent too much time in court and in Congress, and not enough on being the NFL commissioner.

When he first filed suit, Davis told us in no uncertain terms, "We'll see what happens when this thing gets into punitive damages. You'll see how many guys will back down rather than fight." I told him, "We're committed to go all the way on this thing. Our constitution, our whole league is at stake."

Our dispute with Al Davis even extended into the halls of Congress. Davis, Rozelle, and I were all called on to testify regarding antitrust laws and the moving of sports franchises from one city to another. In September 1982, I testified before a congressional committee: "As one of the twenty-seven club presidents who have been deeply involved in this suit, I can tell you, this committee, that Al Davis' fight is not with the NFL commissioner. It is with league rules to which the Raiders once fully and voluntarily agreed. Mr. Davis' own club has contract commitments to all the other clubs in the NFL, and its partners do not believe that the antitrust laws should be used to permit a successful, well-sponsored team's abandonment of the community where it grew and prospered." Even Tex Schramm, usually an ally, opposed Davis. Most of us felt disputes needed to be resolved within the structure of the league, not in the courts and Congress.

Thanks to an injunction by the City of Oakland, the Raiders continued to play in the Oakland Coliseum until 1982. When the case first went to trial in 1981, it resulted in a hung jury. Retried in March 1982, Davis won the case, and the Raiders began playing in Los Angeles that season.

True to his word, in 1983 Davis and the Coliseum Commission sued the NFL for damages. A jury awarded the Raiders $11.5 million and the Coliseum $33 million. On appeal, however, the court overturned the award to the Raiders, because the higher franchise value the team had in Los Angeles had not been considered. Before a new trial on damages could be held, the league settled out of court for a much smaller amount.

The precedent set by the Raiders' successful move to Los Angeles opened the door for other teams to move. As chairman of the Expansion Committee I generally opposed franchise movement, especially when it didn't seem to be in the interests of the fans or the league. I never thought I'd see the day the Colts would move from Baltimore. The fans there had been among the most loyal in the league. After all, Baltimore is where Johnny Unitas made history. In 1984 Robert Irsay took the Colts franchise to Indianapolis.

I understood Bill Bidwill's move from St. Louis to Phoenix, because at the time it seemed fan support for the Cardinals had dwindled. Years later, the Rams left Anaheim and built a strong franchise in St. Louis. But I was disturbed when I learned that Art Modell would move his Browns from Cleveland. Not only were the Browns the natural rival of the Steelers, one of the best rivalries in sports, but their fans were among the most devoted in the NFL. It was a sad day for Cleveland, a sad day for Pittsburgh, and a sad day for the league when the Browns traded in their orange and brown uniforms for Baltimore Ravens purple.

The 1983 season did not go as we had hoped. Although we went into the playoffs with a 10-6 record, our number-one draft pick, Gabe Rivera, was involved in a terrible automobile crash on October 20. I remember that night well. Patricia and I had gone to the Blarney Stone, a Pittsburgh pub, to hear a world-renowned Irish tenor. Just as the performance was to begin, our waiter pulled me aside to answer a telephone in the hallway. A newspaper reporter informed me that just an hour earlier Gabe had been paralyzed from the chest down and was even now clinging to life. We rushed to the emergency room at Allegheny General Hospital. Pat dropped me off and I started making telephone calls to Gabe's family in Texas, doctors, and our coaches. This tragedy changed the course of Gabe's life. At Texas Tech, he had been known as "Señor Sack." He played only three games in the NFL and had his whole career ahead of him. But after the accident, he never played again and today is confined to a wheelchair. His spirit remains strong, and he's devoted to his wife and two children—and is still an ardent Steelers fan.

We had back-to-back losing seasons in 1985 and 1986. Though 1986 was disappointing, after a 1-6 start we finished strong for a 6-10 season. At the beginning of the season, the Seahawks shut us out, 30-0, in our opener, but most of the remaining games were much closer. We lost five games by less than a touchdown. The real heartbreaker was our loss to the Cleveland Browns in overtime at home—the first time they had ever beaten us at Three Rivers Stadium. Despite the losses, Chuck Noll never lost the team.

The coaches and scouts were a little frustrated. Art and Chuck Noll had had different opinions on the draft ever since Chuck arrived in Pittsburgh. But Chuck had proven himself to be a great coach—a teacher, a perfectionist, dispassionate and methodical, even scientific in his approach. He had shown what he could do and had built the team with draft picks and won Super Bowls.

After our second Super Bowl, Art and Dick Haley came to my office to discuss the role of coaches and scouts in the preparation and selection of the draft choices. It was the ongoing complaint of scouts, especially the heads of personnel, that the coaches had too much say in this process. My position was, the scouts and the coaches, especially the head coach, should all be involved in the discussions about the players who would be drafted. Chuck Noll had made it very clear when we first hired him that he and the coaches expected to be involved with the draft—we all had to be in it together. I knew from experience this was the right way to do it.

All of the great teams of the 1970s were built through the draft, and those drafts were a collaborative effort between scouts and coaches: Bobby Beathard and Joe Gibbs with the Washington Redskins, George Young and Bill Parcells with the New York Giants, Jim Finks and Mike Ditka with the Chicago Bears, Eddie DeBartolo and Bill Walsh of the San Francisco Forty-Niners, Jerry Jones and Jimmy Johnson of the Dallas Cowboys, Scott Pioli and Bill Belichick of the New England Patriots. It could not be all scouts, or all coaches. I learned that in the Parker era. What's more, Chuck had just won two Super Bowls. He was the main reason for our success. We had to stay together.

Art and I disagreed. He and the scouts always felt they should have more control over the draft. I was very firm and said we had to work together. We got through the 1980 draft, and the next November Art and I discussed it again. This time the discussion was more heated. We tried to settle our differences, but couldn't. I could see the separation between the scouts and coaches would only get worse. We couldn't go another year like this. Art and I went to Dad's office and explained the situation. I insisted to Art and Dad that we must listen to Chuck Noll and keep the coaches involved. "This is the way it has to be," I said. Dad understood and agreed. He knew I wouldn't budge on this issue.

Art now heads up our real estate division as Steelers vice president. Our relationship is fine and, in the end, everything worked out well.

The year 1987 remains firmly fixed in my mind. This is the year we lost our daughter Kathleen to lupus. This disease has no cure and primarily affects women in their child-bearing years. Doctors diagnosed Kathleen with the disease shortly after the birth of her daughter Caitlin in 1986. Kathleen was strong of heart, and as a girl always looked out for her younger brothers and sisters. She taught school and made a real difference in the lives of the people she touched. Though the third in birth order of our children, Kathleen blazed the trail back to Ireland. And it was Kathleen who renewed our relationship with our Irish relatives. It seemed almost impossible that this strong, intelligent, caring young woman could be brought down by this debilitating disease. I know she suffered, but she never complained or gave in to self-pity.

On August 29, 1987, we were holding a press conference at the top of the U.S. Steel Building in downtown Pittsburgh to announce the signing of Rod Woodson, our first draft pick. Looking out the window I could see Mercy Hospital in the distance, where Kathleen spent her last hours. Patricia and I were at her side when she died, as were her brothers and sisters. She was only thirty-one years old.

I can't question God's plan. Kathleen's life meant something and she had fulfilled her life's work in the short time she was with us. Kathleen walked without fear and defended others who could not stand up for themselves. She was a devoted Catholic and did God's work. Had she lived, she would have been a major force in our family.

Two years after Kathleen's death, our entire family returned to Ireland to honor her. The people of Cloontia and Patricia's relatives had restored an old church as a community center. A beautiful stone wall stretched from the church to a nearby creek. And near the wall, Tommy Regan and our Irish family members had planted a beech tree in Kathleen's memory. The dedication was an emotional experience for me and our entire family. I return to this lovely and hallowed place whenever I'm in Ireland and think of Kathleen. She will forever remain young and full of life in my memory.

It had been five years since the last collective bargaining contract had been signed with the NFLPA. This time we expected a players' strike. Tex Schramm and Hugh Culverhouse pushed hard for the teams to recruit replacement players in the event the strike occurred. We had found in 1982 many veteran players would have crossed the line if there had been a viable alternative to the strike.

I attended a meeting in Philadelphia with the CEC and the player representatives just before the start of the 1987 season. Hugh Culverhouse of Tampa Bay chaired the meeting. He along with Tex Schramm had made their views known. I knew we were in for a long tough battle—they wanted to beat down the players, not make a deal with them.

Tex made it clear he would not yield to the players' demands—in his words, they were the "cattle" and the owners were the "ranchers."

At one point during the meeting, Gene Upshaw, now director of the NFLPA, looked over to me and turned his palms upward as if to say, "What's going on here?" I just shrugged and shook my head to let him know this was a tough situation and these guys weren't going to back down. I wanted to negotiate this thing in good faith, but Schramm and Culverhouse were adamant. They were ready to lock the players out and go on with the season using retired pros, collegiate has-beens, and NFL wannabes.

We had prepared for the strike, just as the other teams had, and had identified some replacements just in case. When the walkout occurred we scrambled to sign anyone we could get. The Teamsters supported the players and we worried that our replacements would be harassed if they practiced in Pittsburgh. So we moved to Johnstown, sixty miles southeast. Here we were welcomed by the community. Jim Boston, our chief negotiator, set up an office at the Holiday Inn, while our scouts scoured the countryside for talent.

The strike lasted twenty-one days, and only one game was canceled. I met with our players outside the stadium to answer their questions, reassure them, and let them know the progress of our negotiations from a management point of view. Many of our veteran players worried they'd get out of shape during the layoff. Steelers player representative Tunch Ilkin asked me if he and some of the other guys could get into the practice field next to Three Rivers Stadium to work out. This was really the only place the players could practice. I told him where he could find the key to the practice field. He got it and when the strike ended, our players returned in pretty good shape.

The strike ended with nothing resolved, especially the issue of player free agency. The NFLPA now took this battle to the courts. Schramm and Culverhouse had won a tactical victory by breaking the strike with replacement players, but I worried that the image of the league had been tarnished, and now we were tied up in court.

At the same time, an adversarial relationship had developed between management and the players. The strike had disaffected many football fans around the country. In Pittsburgh, our fans supported the Steelers. We gave them the opportunity to turn in their tickets for refunds, but of the sixty thousand tickets sold, only five thousand were exchanged. We quickly resold these and actually suffered no loss in attendance. This was not the case in other cities, where some games were played before crowds of as few as fifteen thousand.

The players agreed to come back without a CBA in place, but the issues at the heart of the strike remained and would need to be settled once and for all. Rozelle always maintained the commissioner should not actively participate in player-management negotiations. Rather, he thought he should be an impartial observer. I agreed with him but thought he should play some role for the good of the league. By the time of his retirement in 1989, Pete had come to realize it would be better for the commissioner to shape labor agreements than have the courts do it.

I believe labor relations is the most critical issue facing the league. When Rozelle left, I strongly advocated in favor of Paul Tagliabue, the league's chief outside legal counsel, as our new commissioner. Paul understood that to be effective the new commissioner would have to get fully involved in negotiating a new CBA. The days of impartial observation had passed. I told Gene Upshaw that Tagliabue was a good man and could be trusted to represent the interests of the players and owners.

In 1993, under Commissioner Tagliabue's leadership, a new CBA, including free agency and some revenue-sharing (the players would receive 63 percent of the defined gross income of the NFL), was signed. The new agreement recognized that the NFL comprises players and management. We're all in it together. It's like a marriage.

There has to be give and take. There has to be understanding based on fairness. Whatever is done must be in the best interests of the league.

The burden of responsibility weighed heavily on Pete Rozelle. Though only a little older than I, Pete had aged beyond his years. The constant pressure of lawsuits and hearings—it seemed Pete spent more time in courtrooms than in league offices—had taken its toll. For nearly thirty years Pete had shepherded the NFL through the twists and turns of corporate development. When he took over the commissioner's post in 1960, ten NFL teams played before half-empty stadiums. Now, pro football was a multibillion-dollar business and America's favorite game. He, more than any man, shaped the NFL we know today. I considered Pete not just the commissioner of the NFL but one of my closest friends. We talked almost daily—about television rights, ventures, expansion, public relations, and more. He cared very much about the league and worked tirelessly to ensure its future.

———

When Pete announced his retirement, he formed a commissioner search committee, composed of Wellington Mara, Art Modell, Lamar Hunt, Robert Parins, Ralph Wilson, and me. Pete attended every meeting and guided us through the process. Art Modell came out early with his candidate—Jim Finks. Yes, the same Finks who quarterbacked the Steelers in the 1950s. This put me in a tough spot. I considered Jim a friend, and everybody thought I'd support his candidacy.

But Paul Tagliabue had really impressed me. A lawyer and former basketball player, Paul could handle the business and legal affairs of the NFL, and he had the ability and personality to work effectively in the arena of labor relations. I knew he favored a more hands-on approach with the players and would make a long-term CBA his highest priority.

I told the committee members not to rush their decision. "Look," I said, "we have to see who we have and study the candidates." I told Paul not to pull out, even if the going got rough. I knew it was going to be a tough election. Other candidates emerged, including Willie Davis, the former Green Bay Packers tackle. The committee could not reach a consensus. Pete finally formed another committee and asked me to chair it. This group consisted of Wellington Mara, Art Modell, Pat Bowlen, and Mike Lynn. In short order, we nominated Tagliabue. Modell proposed hiring both Tag and Finks, believing Finks could act as a senior advisor to the less football-wise Tagliabue. I knew this couldn't work, and Tag would have no part of it. I urged the other presidents to take action quickly before we lost our best candidate. After much discussion, on October 26, 1989, the owners finally elected Tagliabue on the twelfth ballot.

In August 1988 Pittsburgh suffered an unprecedented heat wave. For thirty-five straight days the temperature topped ninety degrees. The drought conditions turned the usually green hillsides to straw yellow. The conditions at training camp were brutal. On August 17, while sitting in his office at Three Rivers Stadium, my father suffered a stroke that left him partially paralyzed. Paramedics rushed him to Mercy Hospital, where he was able to talk and seemed to recover. The next morning he had trouble breathing and was moved to the intensive care unit. My brother Art and I stayed by his bedside.

It was hard seeing my father, usually so animated and talkative, connected to a respirator, unable to speak. He communicated with us by blinking his eyes and squeezing our hands until his condition worsened, and he fell into a coma. Dr. Theodore Gelet, my father's longtime physician, explained that the damage from the stroke was so great he had no hope of recovery. At 7:30 a.m., on August 25, I allowed the doctors to remove him from the respirator.

The funeral was scheduled to take place three days later at St. Peter's on the North Side. It was almost one year to the day since our daughter Kathleen had passed away. By order of Mayor Sophie Masloff, all the flags in Pittsburgh flew at half-staff. From across the country, thousands of friends and admirers came to pay their respects. The church overflowed with mourners, and hundreds had to be seated in the basement to watch the service on televisions set up for that purpose. Tony O'Reilly came from Ireland. The ushers stopped him at the door and refused to let him enter the overcrowded church. If my son Art had not seen Tony he would have been turned away. Bishop Donald Wuerl of the diocese of Pittsburgh and Bishop Vincent M. Leonard celebrated the mass. Rooneys came from around the country.

My children were there: Arthur J. Rooney II, with his wife, Greta, and their daughter Meghan; Patricia and her husband, Robert Gerrero, with daughters Laura and Nina; Rita and her husband, Laurence Conway (they had flown in from Ireland where Larry studied medicine); Kathleen's husband, Tom Miller, with daughter Caitlin; Daniel; Duffy; John; James; and Joan.

My brothers were all there: Art Rooney and his wife, Kathleen, with their family, Arthur J. III, and his wife, Christine, and children Michael and Susan;

Tim Rooney and June, with their family, Kathleen and Chris Mara with children Daniel, Kathleen, Patricia, and Arthur; Margaret and Robert Galterio with Erin, Clare, and Molly; Bridget; Timothy J. Jr.; and Cara;

John J. Rooney and JoAnn with family Sean; Mary Jo; Alice and Sean Mahoney with son Sean; Peter; Matthew;

Patrick J. Rooney and Sandy, with their children Patrick J. Jr.; Joseph; Theresa; Christopher; Thomas; Brian; and Molly.

My father's niece Trisha Fiske Jesek, who had been raised with our family, was there. Trish was very much a part of our family. Imagine, one girl in a house with five rough-and-tumble boys—she played sports with us, but my mother delighted in dressing her in pretty clothes. She was as close to Dad as any of us.

My father's only remaining brother, James, was there, as were his sisters Margaret Laughlin and Marie McGinley.

Our NFL friends attended, including Pete Rozelle, Paul Tagliabue, Roger Goodell, Wellington Mara (Giants), Art Modell (Cleveland), Ralph Wilson (Bills), Jim Finks (New Orleans), Tex Schramm (Cowboys), Rankin Smith (Falcons), Bill Bidwill (Cardinals), Ed McCaskey (Bears), Jim Kensil (Jets), Norm Braman (Eagles), Max Winter (Vikings), Al Davis (Raiders), and NFL director of broadcasting, Val Pinchbeck, along with Gene Upshaw, president of the NFLPA.

All the 1988 Steelers players and coaches were there, as well as a number of former Steelers, including Franco Harris, Joe Greene, Andy Russell, Roy Gerela, L.C. Greenwood, and Mel Blount.

It seemed all state, county, and city officials were in attendance, from Governor Bob Casey to Mayor Masloff.

Dad was eighty-seven when he died. Few lived as full a life as he had. A North Side saloon-keeper's son, he had gone on to be a politician, an athlete, a coach, a manager, a promoter, a philanthropist, a community leader, an NFL Hall of Famer, and perhaps the most respected and admired man in all of sports.

But he was also a father. As I sat in the first pew with my four brothers beside me, I could not help but think of our youth and my father's powerful influence on our lives. Though he wasn't always at home, we felt his presence in everything we did. He was a larger-than-life personality, and a force to be reckoned with—in our family, in our community, and in America's sports world. My father's charisma and genuine love of people shone through every aspect of his life. He and I were different, but he instilled in me values that have never failed me—a devotion to our Catholic faith, a love of family, and a commitment to Pittsburgh. Through him I gained my love of sports, and had it not been for my father, the Pittsburgh Steelers would never have been. Through thick and thin, he kept the team in Pittsburgh. And he believed in me and gave me confidence as he passed the leadership of the team on to me.

I saw the greatest tribute to my father in the faces of those who attended the funeral. And there were thousands who lined the streets throughout the North Side—the old First Ward. They came out of their homes and stood at curbsides and street corners as the black limousines of the funeral cortege wound through the narrow streets and passed by familiar shops and parks and hangouts. Some stood silently, others wept. Some came dressed in their Steelers jerseys, and still others held up signs saying "Goodbye Art" and "Thanks Chief." From the backseat of our limousine I saw again how beloved my father really was. These were his people.

Throughout the 1988 season, the Steelers wore an "AJR" patch on the front of their jerseys.

CHAPTER 8

HANDING OFF

In 1989 the Maxwell Football Club honored Chuck Noll with the prestigious Earle "Greasy" Neale Professional Coach of the Year award. The club had been founded by our old friend Bert Bell back in 1937, and both my father and Bert would have approved.

I believe Chuck really showed his greatness the year before, despite our 5-11 record. We were 2-10 at Thanksgiving in 1988, but Chuck rallied the team to three wins over the final four weeks, including an upset of the Oilers in Houston. I thought—our whole organization thought—better days lay ahead.

But that hope certainly didn't seem realistic as the 1989 season began. Our opener against the Cleveland Browns at Three Rivers Stadium snowballed into a 51-0 loss—still the most lopsided defeat in the history of our franchise. Things didn't get better in our second game in Cincinnati against·the Bengals. They beat us 41-10, prompting Chuck to say, "We either just played the two best teams in the AFC, or this is going to be a long season."

That was vintage Noll—he never showed fear or panic. We discussed the situation, and I told Chuck we'd be all right. My confidence in him was unshaken. The following weekend, we pulled off a major upset by defeating the Minnesota Vikings at Three Rivers, and the team stabilized. We won five of our last six games to squeeze into the playoffs as a wild card team. Once in the playoffs, we beat the Oilers in overtime in the Astrodome and came within a dropped pass of beating the eventual conference champion Denver Broncos.

Chuck had won four Super Bowls and was the fifth-winningest coach in NFL history, alongside Don Shula, George Halas, Curly Lambeau, and Tom Landry. That's a pretty elite group. Yet, the Maxwell Club's award was the first time he had ever been honored for the job he did with a team during a single season. He should have been recognized in the 1970s. But he never played to the press the way some coaches did. As Joe Greene said, "I think he's acknowledged when his name comes up, because they have to acknowledge the winning and the tradition and the style of play he put together. That's why the fondness for the Steelers of the 1970s has had such a long life—because we played with a style that was his. Maybe it was because he didn't cater to the media. He was respectful, and that's what he always told us, that the media had a job to do even though it was different than our job, and that we should respect them. He had an appreciation for the media, but he never played up to them, and maybe that's why he's underappreciated."

The "Greasy" Neale award was the highest honor a coach could get—and I thought it was high time.

At the end of the 1991 season, Chuck told me it was time for him to retire. At first I was surprised. He'd been our coach for twenty-three years. That's a lifetime in the NFL. As far as I was concerned, the job was his for as long as he wanted it. I wasn't happy, but I understood his thinking, and in the end I think he made the right decision to leave when he did.

Chuck's departure left us with the hard work of finding a new coach. Of course, every time you change head coaches it's like starting all over again—almost like an expansion club in its first season. That may seem an overstatement, but it's true. Though the culture of the team remains the same—that's something management establishes—a new head coach must rally the team around him, set the tone and spirit, and bring his system to the field and implement it. And working with management and scouts, he must build the team, merging new talent with veteran players.

One thing I've learned over the years is when you hire a head coach you need to have a process. It's not something to be rushed. We came up with a list of potential candidates. High on the list was Joe Greene, who we had hired as the defensive line coach in 1987. Joe had retired as a player in 1981 after thirteen history-making seasons. He was a terrific coach, and I felt strongly we should give him a genuine shot at the top job. We talked to Kansas City Chiefs coach Marty Schottenheimer about his defensive coordinator, Bill Cowher. Marty had played University of Pittsburgh football and knew the kind of guy we were looking for.

Cowher grew up in Crafton, Pennsylvania, just west of Pittsburgh. An outstanding high school athlete, he lettered in football, basketball, and track. At North Carolina State, he played four sports and started as linebacker for three years. As a senior, in 1978, he was team captain and MVP, leading the Wolfpack's defense in tackles. In the early 1980s, Bill played linebacker for the Browns and the Eagles. In 1985, he took over as special teams coordinator for Cleveland and later coached the secondary. Schottenheimer hired him as defensive coordinator for the Kansas City Chiefs in 1989.

We brought Bill to Pittsburgh for an interview. I liked him right off the bat. He was a Western Pennsylvania guy and understood Steelers football. I put great stock in interviews—you can tell a lot about a candidate in the question-answer process. He was a family man, with a fine wife, Kaye, and three little girls. Bill's self-discipline and integrity shone through. I knew he was a good person. This may sound trite, but that's the most important thing to me. When the going gets tough, you need that strength of character to make good decisions. I got the sense he could relate to the players—they would trust him. This trust in the coach is essential in building team closeness.

He was young—only thirty-four years old—but that was a plus. Remember, Chuck Noll was only thirty-seven when we hired him. Cowher also had an infectious enthusiasm. He wanted to win. What's more, he even looked like a Steeler. With his jutting jaw and chiseled features, he reminded me of our old logo, the one that depicted a rough, tough, brawny steelworker walking an I-beam.

Bill didn't have to build a team from scratch. Chuck had handed off the nucleus of a good club. Neil O'Donnell and Bubby Brister were two quarterbacks who had starting experience in the NFL; running back Barry Foster would set a franchise record with 1,690 yards rushing in 1992, Cowher's first season as coach; Gary Anderson had won that playoff game against the Oilers in 1989 with a 50-yard field goal in overtime and was one of the most consistent kickers in the league; and center Dermontti Dawson was just getting started in a career that may someday land him in the Hall of Fame. On defense, Rod Woodson was so good at cornerback that Mel Blount said he was the best at the position in Steelers history. Safety Carnell Lake and linebacker Bryan Hinkle were talented and dependable professionals, and that year's draft added four players who would become starters—offensive tackle Leon Searcy, linebacker Levon Kirkland, nose tackle Joel Steed, and safety Darren Perry.

In 1992, Bill's first year as head coach, the Steelers went 11-5 and won the AFC Central Division for the first time in eight years. Cowher joined an exclusive group of rookie coaches to win eleven games in their first season. Although we lost in the division playoff game to Buffalo, the Associated Press and *Sporting News* named Bill the NFL's Coach of the Year. Dapper Dan Charities also named him Pittsburgh's Man of the Year. "The bottom line was: I wanted it to be a tough football team," Cowher said about the 1992 Steelers. "I wanted to be able to play defense, and I wanted to be great at special teams, because I always thought that being a tough football team was important. I just felt that's how you played the game."

The following year we went 9-7, and in 1994 the team really blossomed under Cowher and his staff. Our 12-4 record energized Pittsburgh and the Steelers Nation. That team did so many good things—it had the best record in the AFC and beat Cleveland three times, including once in the playoffs. But our season ended up three yards short of Super Bowl XXIX when Neil O'Donnell's fourth-down pass from the 3-yard line fell incomplete. San Diego won, 17-13, and went on to play in the Super Bowl.

Then in 1995, after finishing with an 11-5 record and winning our division again, we were back at Three Rivers Stadium playing in another AFC championship game. "Three More Yards!" had become the fans' slogan, and this time we held on to defeat the Indianapolis Colts, 20-16, when Jim Harbaugh's Hail Mary pass dropped into the end zone incomplete. We were off to Super Bowl XXX.

This was a different kind of Steelers team—Cowher had built our offense around the pass instead of the running game. Bill had kept them close, even through the adversity suffered at the beginning of the season when Rod Woodson blew out his knee and didn't play again until the Super Bowl. Again we faced a tough Dallas team, one that had won two Super Bowls over the three previous seasons. The media thought the Cowboys couldn't be beaten. And Dallas came out strong, building a 20-7 halftime lead, largely because our players seemed awestruck at being in the NFL's big game. But our defense dug in and took the game to the Cowboys, pulling within three points, 20-17, by the fourth quarter. We forced a Dallas punt, and during the TV timeout, both Bill Nunn and I noticed the Cowboys defensive players were bent over, their hands on their knees, exhausted. I thought we could put them away if we ran the ball, but we had gotten that far throwing and the coaches thought we should stick to our game plan. We were driving with four minutes to play, when Cowboys cornerback Larry Brown intercepted a Neil O'Donnell pass on our 39-yard line and returned it to the 6. Two plays later the Cowboys ran it in for a touchdown to clinch a 27-17 victory. We had come so close, but the team and the Steelers fans would be denied a fifth Lombardi trophy.

This disappointment didn't stop us. Bill Cowher's teams continued to win. We went to six straight playoffs, which tied an NFL record first set by Paul Brown, and this success awakened the Steelers Nation. The fans and the media talked about "Cowher Power," and wherever we played around the country, thousands of faithful fans greeted us, twirling their Terrible Towels.

Back in Pittsburgh—just two weeks before H. J. Heinz Company chairman Tony O'Reilly broke ground for the new home of the Pittsburgh Public Theater, later named the O'Reilly Theater—an ugly side of America made its presence known in the city. On April 5, 1997, the Ku Klux Klan received a permit from the city to hold a rally in front of the City-County Building on Grant Street. Many local citizens were incensed that the city would close Grant Street, the main thoroughfare downtown, for the Klansmen to hold their demonstration. The situation proved intolerable to Franco Harris, now retired and living in Pittsburgh. Franco knew about discrimination firsthand. Not only had his father suffered racism growing up in Mississippi, but his mother's Italian family had been interned in Nazi slave camps during World War II.

The day before the rally, I received a phone call from Peg McCormick in Mayor Tom Murphy's office. Franco was staging a sit-in on the steps of the City-County Building. She asked if I might come down and talk to him. The mayor believed Franco might be in danger, and his presence might incite the Klansmen to riot. I told them, "I can't tell Franco what to do. He's got to do what he thinks is right." But I agreed to go downtown and talk to him. Joe Gordon drove and dropped me off outside the police barricade that had been erected in anticipation of the Klan demonstrators, who were expected in the morning. The police let me through. I went up the steps to where Franco was sitting, leaning against one of the granite columns. He had food and water, and intended to sit there all night until the Klan arrived the next day. I sat down next to him, and we talked. I told him he was doing a brave thing by being there.

Franco said to me, "I have a hard time letting Nazis take over America." He recounted his mother's experience in a Nazi prison camp. He was outraged that the KKK would come to our town and spread their message of hate. "In Germany, they tried to ignore the Nazis and you know what happened. I'm just saying they can't have Pittsburgh, that's all."

I agreed with him but pointed out that if a riot started with him in the middle of it, the Klansmen would get a lot more press than they deserved. Franco expressed his dismay that the city had even issued the Klan a permit. "Why didn't they just refuse and tell those sheet-wearing cowards to take a hike?" I told him the law protected the Klan's right to freedom of speech and assembly, and they could not be denied.

We talked for quite a while and nobody bothered us. We were alone behind the barrier. I told him Bishop Wuerl and religious leaders of all denominations planned a counterdemonstration the next day, and I asked him if he would consider joining that demonstration instead of confronting the Klan here on the steps. I told him I would go with him. Franco said he'd think about it, and soon after I left he packed up his belongings and quietly departed.

I can't tell you how much respect I have for Franco. He is a deeply principled man, and I admired him for his stand against the Klan. I was reminded of something my father said at the Steelers fiftieth anniversary banquet. He said, "I could never figure out why a person could dislike another person because of his color, whether he was red, yellow, black, or white, or whether he was a Jew or a Protestant or Catholic. I often thought of what God would think of us for thinking in such a manner."

The Klan rally fizzled in the rain the next day. Only thirty-nine Klansmen dressed in robes or storm trooper uniforms showed, and very few spectators appeared. Peaceful counterdemonstrations were held around the city. I did go to the religious rally and spoke against injustice. The largest rally at Market Square, five blocks from the Klan demonstration, drew more than three thousand people. Pittsburgh's not perfect, and we still have our share of racial intolerance, but I was proud of our city that day.

I also was proud to help our community resolve a dispute that was standing in the way of more jobs for the region. In 1999 the H. J. Heinz Company was planning a major expansion of its plant on the North Side, and it needed the adjacent property to build a warehouse and a distribution center. That property was occupied at the time by the Pittsburgh Wool Co., owned by Jeff and Roy Kumer, and the sticking points were the price for the property and the relocation of Pittsburgh Wool Co. The community needed the Heinz expansion because of the jobs it would create, but it also didn't want to lose the Pittsburgh Wool Co. and the people employed there.

I knew the Kumer family personally, and so I became involved in negotiations that also included Heinz executives and representatives of the City of Pittsburgh. After much back-and-forth discussion among the parties, I was able to negotiate a settlement, but not until I convinced the Heinz people to make the Kumers realize that this was the final offer. The Kumers then accepted the deal. Heinz got the property for its expansion, Pittsburgh Wool Co. was relocated to a nearby building, and the Kumers got a fair settlement for their 116-year-old building plus relocation assistance for their five tenants. Pittsburgh Mayor Tom Murphy said at the time, "This is good news for all of us." And it was.

Patricia and I, along with our children Art, Dan, and Duffy went to Atlanta for Super Bowl XXXIV in late January 2000. The St. Louis Rams and Tennessee Titans faced each other in what proved to be an exciting game. But even more exciting for me was the telephone call I got on January 29, the day before the game. Art and I were in a hotel suite near the Georgia Dome interviewing Jerry Angelo, a candidate for Steelers director of football operations.

Super Bowls are a good time to conduct business, because most of the people in the NFL are there—coaches, players, and staff from teams in the league. Tom Donahoe, a former Steelers scout, had been promoted to director of football operations when we hired Bill Cowher in 1992, and even though we enjoyed some fine seasons during the time they worked together, their relationship had deteriorated to the point where a change had to be made. In 1999 the team finished 6-10, our second straight losing season after six straight in the playoffs. Tom and Bill disagreed over many things, especially who had the greater say—the coaches or the scouts—over player personnel. Bill didn't want Donahoe in the coaches' meetings because he thought Tom was a spy. Tom thought Bill was finished as an NFL coach. We went back and forth over this for some time, and then we decided we had to keep the coach. You have to let the head coach do his job. It was a tough decision to make, but I'd been there before and believed it was the right move. And things turned out for the best. Wellington Mara recommended Donahoe to Buffalo Bills owner Ralph Wilson, and Tom later became president of that club.

So in the middle of the interview, the phone rings and it's Patricia on the other end of the line. She said, "Dan, they're looking for you—call Joe Horrigan at the Hall of Fame meeting."

I went into the next room and called Joe. He said, "Dan, I'm happy to say you've been selected for induction into the Pro Football Hall of Fame. There's going to be a press conference in two hours. You've got to be there!"

Of course, I was delighted and called Patricia back right away. Atlanta had just suffered the worst ice storm in memory and you couldn't even get a cab because cars were sliding sideways. Our son Dan and daughter Duffy helped us as we walked the half-dozen blocks on ice-glazed sidewalks, and we arrived just in time for the press conference.

Induction into the Pro Football Hall of Fame is a great honor. It represents the pinnacle of any NFL career, whether you're a player, a coach, or the president of a franchise. I remembered back to the day my father was inducted, and it occurred to me there was only one other father and son to receive such an honor—Timothy and Wellington Mara.

On July 29, 2000, busloads of Rooneys, Steelers, and friends descended on Canton, Ohio, for the annual Pro Football Hall of Fame enshrinement ceremony. The rest of the Class of 2000 included three 49ers—Joe Montana, Ronnie Lott, Dave Wilcox—and Raiders defensive lineman Howie Long. Joe Montana, of course, was a Western Pennsylvania guy, a standout quarterback at Ringgold High School in Monongahela, a town located just south of Pittsburgh. The Hall of Fame hosted a private reception for the inductees, and I got a chance to talk to Joe and the other guys and enjoyed meeting their wives and children.

But I was pleased and thankful when it came time for Joe Greene to present me to the Hall of Fame. When I called Joe to ask him if he would do the honors in Canton, there was dead silence on the other end of the line. Then he said, "I thought you would have Chuck."

Joe and I had a special bond. We'd been through a lot together, and I always believed Joe Greene represented the spirit of the Steelers better than any other player. Here's what he said on the day of my induction:

"When I first met Dan Rooney in the winter of 1969, which was my rookie year, I was young and cocky and aware of my great abilities. With my attributes in mind, I told Dan what I wanted to be paid. I said I wanted to be the highest paid defensive lineman in the NFL. Dan immediately informed me that I was confused. We were sitting across from one another at the table. When I told him how much I wanted to be paid, Dan replied in a loud voice, 'What! We can't pay you that. That's more than Merlin Olsen, Bob Lilly, and Alan Page are being paid. They're all-pro, and you haven't even played a down.' Thus our history began.

"Through thirty-one years of trust and respect, our relationship has transcended that of boss and player. Dan is a best friend. Here's a man of great character and integrity. He loves and confesses God. He loves and cherishes his family. He loves the Steelers organization. He loves the fans in the city of Pittsburgh.

"All of Dan's decisions are very, very, difficult, but they're based on faith. You can read about Dan's devotion to God, his never-ending love and respect for his father, his love and loyalty to his wife of forty-eight years, his love for his nine kids and his fourteen grandchildren, and his love for his four brothers. You can read about the success of the Steelers organization—its championships, the team's competitiveness through three decades of changing dynamics in the business. You can read about Dan's impact on the NFL Management Council, which demonstrates his depth and scope on many, many issues. Dan has always led with humility. When things go as planned, Dan is in the background. When things don't go as planned, he's in the forefront. You can read about Dan's altruism through his service and through his many charitable and civic organizations. But ladies and gentlemen, you cannot read about the great friendship and kindness Dan has shown me and my family. And I know many players who have similar stories.

"When I was a young player, Dan often had to steer me in the right direction. In my youthful exuberance to win, I was in everybody's business. I was always attempting to tell the coaches what plays to call, and telling the players how to play the game. I even had the nerve to tell Dan he needed to get a player signed. Finally, Dan called me to his office and he asked me, 'Joe, do you know what CYA means?' After explaining CYA, he sternly said, 'Joe, take care of Joe.'

"I'm a professional football coach today because of Dan Rooney. In 1987 Dan agreed with Chuck Noll to hire me as a defensive line coach. When Chuck Noll retired, Dan invited me into the interview process to be head coach. Later, Dan told me that I was not going to be his head coach. I was disappointed, but I trusted his judgment. History has proven he made a good choice to lead this team.

"Whenever I've had a special occasion in my life, the times you want your friends to share, Dan or a member of his family has been there. Dan and Pat flew to Dallas for my oldest son's wedding. When he couldn't be at my second son's wedding, his son Dan was there. That means an awful lot. He has also included my family in important events in his life. Dan has not only exhibited kindness toward me, but has followed in his father's footsteps. All the Steelers players are a part of his family. I am most honored and proud to represent the Rooney family, the Steelers organization, all the former players and coaches, the City of Pittsburgh, and the fans representing our boss and our friend to the Pro Football Hall of Fame, Dan Rooney."

When I got up to speak, the first thing I saw was Rooneys—lots of

Rooneys—filling the front rows. Some of the fans whipped Terrible Towels and cheered. I was pretty choked up and wondered whether I'd make it through my short speech. Then my little grandson, Jimmy, who had worked his way through the crowd, stepped up on the stage and handed me a bottle of water. "Here Pop-Pop," he said.

It was a hot and humid Ohio day, and the Hall of Fame organizers cautioned us to limit our remarks to only eight minutes. I read from my handwritten notes—I didn't want to forget anybody, because nobody makes it to the Hall of Fame all by themselves.

"Thank you, Joe. I really appreciate those remarks. Joe is always a champion.

"Are the Pittsburghers still here?

"I too want to thank Canton for really being so kind and great to us. My family is here. They're in this section, that's about half of my family. They go back there. But there are many to thank, and I do so now. I'm not sure that anyone, beyond the league's founders, who gave their time, their savings, their lives to establish the National Football League, should be in the Hall of Fame other than players. Today we had a group of players who brought this game to a new century. Joe Montana, Ronnie Lott, Dave Wilcox, all 49ers. And the Raider, Howie Long. They have been very kind to me. I congratulate them on this most deserved honor. I want to express my appreciation to those who got me to Canton, the Steelers fans of Pittsburgh and beyond. They are the best. I should say, you are the best fans in the world. Your support in good times and tough times has meant much to our success.

"The media everywhere who kept the fire in the Steelers fans and the organization. Those who voted for me, I thank you all, especially Ed Bouchette. The coaches who taught me more about the game than anyone. The Steelers players from the thirties to the present, good people, good friends, they played the game. Kiesling, Dudley, Stautner, Butler, John Henry Johnson, Layne.

"Then came the best team that ever played, the seventies Steelers. There are times, though seldom, when everything comes together. When a group of young men become a special team. Where their accomplishments give them a time in history. Not only winning, but being the best, and doing so with unselfish determination to be the best team. Making the goal together. That happened in Pittsburgh. It was a glorious time.

"It began in 1969 when Chuck Noll, a young coach, arrived with the ideals of commitment to be the best and assembled players with similar desires and convinced them that the goal was possible. Not an easy task, but he never deviated and stuck to the basics. They began to believe that they could be the best. We are not here today to celebrate statistics; we are here to celebrate excellence and the accomplishment of people reaching a level, collectively, to be the best they could be, men of character helping each other to reach the heights of human achievement.

"The first player to be assembled was Joe Greene, a man of intense determination to win. I remember the end of Joe's first year. Not a very successful season. Philadelphia had the lead and had just made a first down with less than two minutes to play. As the Eagles broke the huddle, Joe was so frustrated he picked up the ball and threw it into the stands. Many of you remember that, I'm sure. He does. But I knew right then that things were going to be okay. He went on to dominate opposing lines for a decade, to win games when things were not going okay. One game in Houston, to see if we could make the playoffs, Joe Greene completely crushed his side of the Oilers offensive line. We won a very tough game. Joe Greene, a real Steeler, is a person of integrity, whom I admire as a friend. I am privileged to have Joe present me to the Hall of Fame.

"Later came Jack Lambert, who would not tolerate any less commitment than he had from anyone in the organization. Players, coaches, staff, and, yes, presidents. In 1972, Franco Harris came to the Steelers. Before that time, we never won too often. After he came, we never lost. Franco is a very motivating player in a quiet way. He is probably the most caring individual player I ever met. But there are so many on those teams that brought victory. I could relate heroics on all of them, but time doesn't permit. Remember Bradshaw, Ham, Russell, Webster, Blunt, Rocky, Swann, Stallworth, Shell, L.C., White, Wagner, all of them. They all belong here, because they all deserve to be enshrined in Canton because they were the best of the best. Other teams at times had considered themselves as enemies of the rest. The Steelers respected everyone they played as a tribute to the game. The league had no better champion because they carried the banner with pride and dignity. They were different, different in play as well as conduct. Love for the game, the league. They were all proud of their differences.

"Then our players of the eighties and nineties who were terrific Steelers and accomplished much success. Woodson, Lloyd, Hinkle, Kirkland, Dawson are just a few led by another special coach, Bill Cowher.

"The players and coaches made the Steelers, and I attribute my presence here today to all of them and to my father, Art Rooney. My father, one of the early men who did everything to make the NFL succeed. It is special to join him here. He gave me the understanding of what the league meant. He gave me the commitment to do everything possible to keep it strong and viable. He with Halas, Marshall, Mara, Lambeau, Bidwill, Bell, Carr were the men who forged the league. I wish my parents were here. Mom ran everything in our family, and she would be very pleased.

"Many of our family are here, especially Patricia, my wife. She is the one who keeps me straight. She was there always. She wouldn't let me fail. She's my conscience, counselor, and critic. A thoughtful critic, even when I don't want a critic. Without her, I sure wouldn't be in Canton. Our children, Art, Pat, Rita, Dan Duffy, John, Jim, and

Joan are here. Our daughter Kathleen, who died, is with God, I believe she is here also. Our grandchildren, my children's spouses, I should say, and our grandchildren. My brothers, nephews, nieces, the McGinleys are here as are the Steelers' staff, those not in Dallas for the game tomorrow. I wish you would all stand up, the Steelers players who are here, my family, and everybody. Please stand up.

"I have been very fortunate to have all the support and encouragement. I was in the league with those founders. I knew three commissioners personally. Pete Rozelle was a special friend. We worked on many issues. He was great. He brought the game to modern times. Bert Bell before him was a Steeler who put the television structure in place. And now Paul Tagliabue deals with the complexities of a modern sport. All good people who knew and did what was necessary in their time.

"There are a few men who are members of the Hall who gave me much. Their contribution to the NFL has been substantial. Wellington Mara, the integrity of the league. Tex Schramm, how to get things done for the good of the league—use Robert's Rules when they help, wing it when they don't—Tex, we miss you. Lamar Hunt's concern for the game.

"And thanks to all our friends and owners. Jerry Richardson is here. Pat Bowlen is here. Players who came here this morning. And I thank God for so many things that He has given me and our family. But as has been said, this is a special time to be here. The new century. The return to Canton. All the important men of the game are here, and I thank you especially for making football the greatest sport in history.

"Now I ask you to be watchful, see that the game remains the best. Strong, viable, flexible for the present day. No one can be more interested than youth, you have much to guide you. Your own commitment, how you played the game. The people in the league, players, coaches, owners, staff, and fans. Commissioner Tagliabue provides the leadership for football as America's number-one sport. Gene Upshaw, a Hall of Famer, is committed to the game and wants it to be the best. The television networks, our family, our players, you have my commitment to do whatever it takes. The National Football League, the game is your legacy. Protect it. Don't let anyone tarnish it. God bless you."

———————

Less than a year after my induction, we imploded Three Rivers Stadium. A lot of history went up in smoke that day. I was the last man out of the stadium. It was a kind of walk down memory lane as I strolled through the deserted locker rooms, corridors, and offices. I walked out to the seats on the 50-yard line, and remembered a story my father had told me.

On Saint Patrick's Day in 1936—I was only four years old at the time—the Allegheny and Monongahela Rivers flooded, inundating much of the North Side, including old Exposition Park, where Three Rivers Stadium now stood. My father and some of his buddies found a boat and rowed it across the outfield, the water more than six feet deep. Somehow, while they were horsing around, the boat tipped over and they all splashed into the water. Dressed in light clothes, the other guys easily swam to the bleachers near third base, but my father had on a heavy wool coat and boots which, when soaked with water, weighed him down and nearly pulled him to the bottom. He told me this was the nearest he ever came to death. Had he not been such a strong swimmer he would have drowned right there on the third-base line—just about where I was standing. Imagine how history would have changed. My life would certainly have been different, and the Steelers might never have been.

All of Pittsburgh, it seemed, turned out for the implosion of Three Rivers Stadium. For thirty-one seasons, from 1970 through 2000, it had been our home. Our move to Three Rivers coincided with the beginning of the Steelers dynasty. It was the home of the Terrible Towel, which spawned the Terrible Fan, the Terrible Car, the Terrible Cat, and so many other Steelers traditions. And who can forget the wonderful tailgate parties in the parking lots surrounding the stadium. Diehard fans, in all kinds of weather—sunshine, rain, sleet, snow—they were there, dressed in their black and gold, and painted for war. Fueled on pirogues, kielbasa, nachos, and beer, they fired up our team and tormented the opposition with their deafening cheers, which echoed off Three Rivers' hard concrete surfaces.

> "Here we go, Steelers, here we go!
> Here we go, Steelers, here we go!"

Even in the worst of seasons, those fans never gave up. And when we were winning, they were a vital part of it. Steelers fans are the best fans in the world.

So the fans were there on February 11, 2001, for one last glimpse of Three Rivers Stadium. They watched from the rooftops and windows of Pittsburgh's downtown skyscrapers. Patricia and I decided to stay home. Though our house was only three blocks from the stadium, we watched the implosion on television.

It was both a sad and happy day for me. My son Art and I had worked for years to get state, county, and city support for a new stadium—a football only stadium that would keep us competitive with other teams in the league. Most of the credit goes to Art, who spent countless hours working with the governor, state legislators, and city and county officials to make the financing work. Through his efforts, not only did the Steelers get a new stadium but the Pirates were able to build PNC Park, widely recognized as one of the best baseball parks in the country. The complex negotiations ensured Philadelphia would get new stadiums as well.

We also concluded a precedent-setting partnership with the University of Pittsburgh. The Panthers desperately needed new sports facilities. In discussions with university president Mark Nordenberg and athletic director Steve Pederson, we determined to share facilities both at our new Heinz Field and at the University of Pittsburgh Medical Center Southside Complex. Although the details took a lot of time and hard negotiating—the NCAA wanted to ensure an appropriate separation between professional and collegiate sports—we finally formed a partnership that would benefit the community, the university, and the Steelers.

While Art worked out the business details, I worked on an architectural program that would satisfy the needs of the team. I had learned a thing or two in the years since we had played in places like Forbes Field and Pitt Stadium and training facilities at Latrobe and South Park and Hershey. We paid special attention to the grass, the locker rooms, training rooms, press and television boxes, fan seating, and food concessions. It's a state-of-the-art facility in every way.

Heinz Field is part of Pittsburgh's grand entrance as visitors exit the Fort Pitt Tunnel. What makes the stadium special is the fact that fans can enjoy the city's skyline without leaving their seats. It is fan-friendly, has excellent sight-lines, and features unique amenities, such as the Coca-Cola Great Hall that serves as a tribute to Steelers history. Players always have told me they prefer grass to artificial turf, and so that's what we have at Heinz Field. Even with ten Steelers games, seven Pitt games, and five high school playoff games, the field still plays well—even if it doesn't always look pretty come winter. Brian Opacic, the stadium operations coordinator, does an excellent job in maintaining Heinz Field.

We played our first game at Heinz Field on October 7, 2001, against the Cincinnati Bengals. Everyone—the players, the fans, the media—loved the new facility from the start. It looks out on the Allegheny River and Pittsburgh's beautiful skyline. Whenever our team crosses the opponent's 20-yard line—known in football as the red zone—gigantic Heinz ketchup bottles tip over and do a slow pour.

The Coca-Cola Great Hall is a tribute to Steelers history and allows our fans of all ages to learn about our tradition. The jumbotron features player profiles, short-subject films, and instant replays—all a far cry from the days of Mossy Murphy's marching bands, motor scooter, and gold-sequined baton-twirlers of the 1950s and 1960s.

Those early days seem now like a distant dream. The NFL was still in its infancy when the Steelers joined the league; with the help of guys like Walt Kiesling and Buddy Parker and Bobby Layne and Bill Dudley our team grew right along with it. The 1950s and 1960s were also the days of the great Johnny Unitas.

On September 11, 2002, I got the call that John Unitas had died. The news upset me. We were almost the same age—he was just a little younger. I attended his funeral mass at the Cathedral Mary Our Queen in Baltimore. More than two thousand people filled the pews. The front seats were reserved for family and his many teammates and NFL friends. Everyone was there, from Commissioner Tagliabue to Ravens coach Brian Billick and players Ray Lewis, Peter Boulware, and Michael McCrary. Outside the cathedral a small plane circled overhead with a banner reading in huge red letters "Unitas We Stand." Inside, the wail of bagpipes filled the church. His coffin was covered with white lilies and roses, and beside it stood an easel with a painting of Johnny walking into the sunset in his blue number 19 Colts jersey. His six sons acted as pallbearers, and Cardinal William Keeler, the archbishop of Baltimore, eulogized him, recalling Johnny's glory days at Memorial Stadium. He said, "Johnny Unitas displayed in his NFL career native physical gifts and football intelligence honed by hard, dedicated practice; courage in the face of pain and adversity; grace under pressure; commitment to teammates; unassuming, inspiring leadership . . . these were virtues he carried over to his family, asking his children to give their best, even as he asked it of his teammates."

Commissioner Tagliabue pointed out the truth, "He was mythic . . . he symbolizes football, and more importantly, he symbolizes leadership."

David Modell, Ravens owner Art Modell's son, said, "Johnny U was the father of modern football, so all of us, including my father, who enjoyed participating, owe that to Johnny."

His son Joe remembered his father's reputation as a straight-talking man, including his traditional pregame challenge to his teammates: "Talk is cheap. Let's go play."

And play he did. He was the man with the "golden arm," setting twenty-two NFL passing records, including the seemingly unbreakable record of forty-seven consecutive games with a touchdown pass. He was named MVP three times and was selected for the Pro Bowl ten times. Johnny won three NFL championships, including the overtime victory against the New York Giants in 1958.

As I listened to the testimonials, I thought of the John Unitas I knew—the high school quarterback from St. Justin in his black high-topped shoes and his patented jump pass. I remembered the Unitas who Coach Kiesling didn't give a chance to throw at our summer training camp—he threw instead to my brothers on the sidelines.

I recalled the dispirited Unitas who came before the league's Management Council (CEC), asking for financial assistance when his playing days were long over. Though he was the best quarterback to ever play the game, he played at a time when big salaries were not the norm. He took care of his ailing mother's hospital bills and always paid what he owed. Now he was in debt and needed help. The league had established a Dire Need Fund for retired players, but Johnny didn't qualify under the existing rules. Sitting there in the pew at his funeral I felt we should have done more for him, a man who had done so much to bring the NFL to national prominence. I'll be the first to admit the league could have done more to help Johnny. He deserved better. His funeral marked the end of an era.

The Steelers were less successful in 1998 and 1999. But Bill Cowher didn't lose the team. We now had a good management team in place as well. We hired North Catholic alum Kevin Colbert as director of football operations. Cowher never lost my confidence, and he began to turn the team around. We went 9-7 in 2000 and 13-3 in 2001, the year we went to the AFC championship. We lost to the Patriots, who then went on to win Super Bowl XXXVI that year.

In 2002 we won another division championship, the sixteenth in franchise history. But one of the highlights for me was the return of Terry Bradshaw for a Pittsburgh reunion. Terry had left in 1983 and hadn't been back for a Steelers game in nearly twenty years. Fan and press criticism at the end of his career had hurt him, and he couldn't forget the boos he heard when he'd leave a game injured. Now he was back in Pittsburgh, and we had a good talk—Terry and I had a lot of catching up to do. He attended our game against the Colts and appeared at halftime with his two daughters, Rachel and Erin, before sixty-four thousand wildly cheering fans who welcomed him home. We showed a video tribute on the jumbotron. The crowd went wild with the replay of the Immaculate Reception. The scoreboard read, "Welcome Home Terry." I turned to him and pointed out the obvious, "They love you here."

Terry spoke into an echoing microphone: "That sounds good. That's all right. Keep going. I want to thank the Rooney family. It's been nineteen years since I've been on this playing field. I want to thank their dad, who was my father away from home. I want to thank

Dan Rooney, who signed me on the Three Rivers Stadium field . . . I want to tell all of you that there's no place like home. I think it's important tonight that I let all of you know, you all need your family, you all need your football family, you all need your Steelers family. Though I've probably been an enigma to you, believe me, I have missed you very much. Ladies and gentlemen, it's good to be home." By the end of the speech, those who weren't cheering were crying—some of us were doing both.

———

The year 2003 marked the bicentennial of Lewis and Clark's epic journey of discovery. Captain Meriwether Lewis left Pittsburgh on August 31, 1803, in search of a northwest passage and to explore the Louisiana Territory, an unknown land recently acquired from Napoleon. To commemorate the anniversary, my son Art thought it would be a good idea to focus our family vacation on the Lewis and Clark Expedition. We had always tried to theme our family trips, and now the Rooney family had grown large enough to more than match Lewis and Clark's thirty-three-man Corps of Discovery.

I called the Senator John Heinz History Center here in Pittsburgh for advice on our route and historical background. History Center president Andy Masich and Library and Archives director David Halaas turned out to be experts on the subjects of Lewis and Clark, western history, and American Indians. They really helped us concentrate our energies when they "commissioned" us as the "Rooney Family Corps of Rediscovery." Basing our charter on the document President Thomas Jefferson gave to Captain Lewis, they instructed us to retrace Lewis and Clark's journey west and bring back to Pittsburgh evidence of our discoveries—photographs, water samples, botanical specimens, and artifacts.

We launched our expedition from Pittsburgh on the anniversary of the departure of Lewis and Clark's Corps of Discovery—August 31, 2003, exactly two hundred years to the day—in a replica keelboat, with many of our family members and friends trailing behind in canoes and kayaks.

For three weeks we traveled in the footsteps of the intrepid explorers—by canoe, bus, horseback, and airplane across the continent. To prepare our family, Patricia compiled a reading list, including Lewis and Clark's original journals. In the journals, we learned that the captains had met the Cheyenne Indians in 1804–05 at the Mandan villages in what is now North Dakota. They described them as a "tall, handsome people." Working through our History Center partners, Andy and David, we made arrangements to visit traditional Northern Cheyenne leaders in Montana, the first stop of the western leg of our trip.

We flew from Pittsburgh to Billings, then drove to Pompey's Pillar on the Yellowstone River, where William Clark had scratched his name on the soft sandstone rock, the only physical evidence remaining of the now famous expedition.

We then headed for a little mining town called Coalstrip, twenty miles north of Lame Deer, Montana, and the Northern Cheyenne Reservation. We pulled into our motel, where we found about twenty Cheyennes waiting for us. My first impression was, Lewis and Clark were right, they are a big people—a couple of the men towered over us, their long black hair pulled back in ponytails or braids. At first they just looked at us. They weren't unfriendly, but they weren't smiling either. David introduced us, one by one, beginning with Steve Brady (Braided Hair), a traditional leader and headman of the Crazy Dogs Society. He was very friendly. "Hello Dan Rooney," he said, "*Ha ho.* Welcome to Cheyenne country."

We all went to a restaurant not far away. The wait staff there expected us and had set the tables. But Art's wife, Greta, noticed the Indian kids sat at one table, her kids at another. So she went over and mixed them up, same with the adults. That was a good move.

The next day, with Steve Brady and his brother Otto Braided Hair guiding us, we drove to Lame Deer, the seat of the tribal government. As we drove I saw a church—Sacred Heart Catholic Church—and asked Steve if we could stop. I went inside to the church office and gave the secretary a contribution and my card.

When I returned to the car, Steve turned to me and said, "Dan, the Church has not always been a friend of the Cheyennes. Some Indian people think of it as the house of the enemy. After the whites forced us onto reservations, they tried to destroy our language, customs, and religion. They shaved our heads and dressed us in wool suits. They said they had to 'Kill the Indian to save the man.' They sent us to boarding schools, where we were separated from our parents and forbidden to speak our language or practice our traditional ways."

I was moved—and saw immediately the parallel with the Irish Catholics and their experience with England. And so I said, "You're just like the Irish! Both the Cheyennes and Irish Catholics have been persecuted for their religious beliefs, but both have come through with their faiths strengthened."

Steve and Otto next took us to the home of Douglas Spotted Eagle, a holy man and Keeper of the Sacred Hat. Here we joined other Cheyennes in a traditional sweat lodge ceremony. Once inside the lodge—a frame of willow branches covered with layers of heavy tarps—we seated ourselves on the ground around a pit. Young men carried in red-hot rocks, placed them in the pit, then closed the door flaps. In the pitch darkness Otto Braided Hair poured water over the hot rocks. Intense heat and the scent of sage filled the lodge as Otto and the others began singing songs in their native language. I could hardly breathe. Otto explained the healing powers of a traditional "sweat" and encouraged us to speak our hearts, to share our thoughts and feelings. It was like a confessional.

After about an hour, we emerged from the lodge to find tables of food and drink awaiting us. People from across the reservation had been invited to share this traditional dinner, including the Catholic lay preacher from Sacred Heart, and we spent the evening together, talking and making new friends.

Two hundred years after the Lewis and Clark expedition, after being reduced to poverty and subjected to injustice, the Cheyennes willingly extended their hands in welcome to me and my family. To the Rooneys, they were kind, helpful, open human beings. If history were reversed, would western settlers of European heritage be as forgiving? I hope so.

We continued our trek all the way to Fort Clatsop and the Pacific Ocean. The kids had a great time playing on the beach. We even found a Steelers bar—completely decked out in black and gold—and had a good time meeting the owner and patrons, all citizens of the vast Steelers Nation.

Following our transcontinental trek, we returned to Pittsburgh where the Heinz History Center mounted a major exhibition titled *Rediscovering Lewis & Clark: A Journey with the Rooney Family.* Tens of thousands of people learned of Lewis and Clark while seeing the pictures we had taken on our journey and reading excerpts from our journals. The exhibit provided an interesting contrast with the America Lewis and Clark found in 1803.

At the same time we were enjoying our Lewis and Clark summer, my brother Pat called and suggested that I hand off the presidency of the Steelers. For the past few years, my son Art had taken on more and more responsibility in running the team, just as my father had encouraged me to do. I discussed the situation with my brothers, Art, Tim, John, and especially Pat. It seemed time for Art II to take the reins. I would stay on as chairman, but he would run the day-to-day operations of the franchise. At first I wasn't sure if I was ready to let go. Tim asked me directly if it was okay with me. I assured him—and all my brothers—that Art was the right guy for the job. We all talked about how the business should be run. Art's legal background would serve him well, and today he's doing a terrific job. Of course, I am with him, just the way the Chief and I were, side by side at Three Rivers Stadium.

After the 2003 season it was apparent the Steelers needed to look for a quarterback. Kordell Stewart's "slash" style didn't always get us where we wanted to be. Tommy Maddox played well for a while, but with him at quarterback we'd gotten away from our identity as a tough, hard-nosed team that ran the ball on offense and stopped the run on defense. Our 6-10 record in 2003 earned us the eleventh pick in the first round of the 2004 NFL draft. During the process of evaluating and grading the college prospects, we looked carefully at the quarterbacks. Our staff had concluded that Eli Manning and Philip Rivers were the most polished of the prospects available, but there also was a big, strong, talented kid at Miami of Ohio named Ben Roethlisberger who intrigued a lot of our scouts. Manning and Rivers both were picked before our turn, and so our people seemed to have focused on Shawn Andrews, a big offensive tackle from Arkansas as our likely number-one pick.

But when our turn came, I couldn't bear the thought of passing on another great quarterback prospect the way we had passed on Dan Marino in 1983, so I steered the conversation around to Roethlisberger. After some more talk, we came to a consensus and picked Roethlisberger. Big Ben, six-foot-five, 240 pounds, was quick, tough, had a great arm, and could think on his feet. He was just what we needed.

We started the 2004 season with Maddox as quarterback, but he was injured in our second game—in Baltimore against the Ravens. Ben's first start came in our third game against the Dolphins, which was postponed until Sunday night because of a hurricane. He showed

Commissioner Pete Rozelle presents the Lombardi Trophy to Art Rooney Sr. after the Steelers' Super Bowl IX victory over the Vikings. (COURTESY STEELERS)

Hall of Fame linebacker Jack Ham, 1971–1982, closes on Bengal quarterback Ken Anderson, September 19, 1982 in the Steelers' 26-20 victory at Three Rivers Stadium. (COURTESY STEELERS/MIKE FABUS)

Joe Greene presents
Dan Rooney for induction
into the Hall of Fame at
Canton, Ohio, 2000.
(STEELERS/MIKE FABUS)

Coach Chuck Noll presents
Dan Rooney with Hall of
Fame ring, 2000. (COURTESY
STEELERS/MIKE FABUS)

Pilot Dan Rooney with Beechcraft Bonanza, 2004. (COURTESY STEELERS/MIKE FABUS)

"Rooney Corps of Rediscovery" at the end of the trail, Seaside, Oregon, 2003.
(COURTESY DAN ROONEY)

Dan Rooney and Art Rooney II welcome Terry Bradshaw and daughters Erin and Rachel back to Pittsburgh in front of sixty thousand cheering fans at Heinz Field, 2002. (COURTESY STEELERS/MIKE FABUS)

Dan Rooney with Commissioner Paul Tagliabue and Roger Goodell at Heinz Field, 2005. (COURTESY STEELERS/MIKE FABUS)

Clockwise from top left: running back Jerome Bettis (36), wide receiver Hines Ward (86), nose tackle Casey Hampton (98), and safety Troy Polamalu (43).

(COURTESY STEELERS/MIKE FABUS)

Steelers quarterback
Big Ben Roethlisberger.
(COURTESY STEELERS/
MIKE FABUS)

New Steelers head coach,
Mike Tomlin, 2007.
(COURTESY STEELERS/
MIKE FABUS)

Dan Rooney, quarterback, with Steelers chairman Dan Rooney, 2006.
(COURTESY DAN ROONEY)

Steelers president Art Rooney II and chairman Dan Rooney at Heinz Field, 2006.
(COURTESY STEELERS/MIKE FABUS)

Dan Rooney and NFL commissioner Roger Goodell at Heinz Field.
(COURTESY STEELERS/MIKE FABUS)

Dan Rooney holds aloft the Lombardi Trophy after Super Bowl XL—
the Steelers fifth Super Bowl victory—with Art Rooney II and Coach Bill Cowher.
(PHOTO COURTESY STEELERS/MIKE FABUS)

himself to be a force of nature as well. With a great supporting cast around him, the team was solid.

But what Big Ben did that season is the stuff of legend: he went 13-0 as a starter during the regular season to help us become just the fourth team in NFL history to finish 15-1. But the dream came to an end in the AFC championship game with a 41-27 loss to New England. This was the first time that I ever packed for the Super Bowl. I thought we'd win this one for sure. After the game Hines Ward openly wept for his friend and team leader Jerome Bettis. Everyone thought this would be the Bus's last shot at a Super Bowl. Hines said, "We didn't get the job done. There's a lot of guys who left it all on the field."

Despite the amazing achievement of a 15-1 season, Bill Cowher was subdued after the game. He had coached the team to five AFC championship games—all of them at home—and won once.

The next season, this team had achieved the kind of closeness that wins Super Bowls. If we could keep that going, I thought we could go all the way. But before training camp it looked like things might unravel before we even got started. Jerome agreed to stay on for one more season, but Hines Ward held out. I called Jerome and said, "We need to get this done."

He said, "I agree with you."

"I think we can get it done."

Bettis wasn't so sure—"Hines is tough."

"Here's what I'd like you to do. Get Hines and bring him over to the Latrobe Airport. We'll meet in the back room. Nobody will know we're there." This was not an official negotiation—no agents or management, other than me. Everyone else was at camp, or back in Pittsburgh.

Jerome persuaded Hines to come, and I talked to them both. To Hines I said, "Look, you mean everything to us. We want to get this done."

He said, "Well, I need to get what I deserve."

I said, "You'll get what you should get. You might not be one hundred percent happy with it, but you're going to get what's right."

He said, "You've always been fair."

We understood one another and left with a handshake.

I went back to Art and Kevin Colbert and told them, "You go talk to him and he'll sign. He wants to be here."

For thirteen years Jerome had dreamed of winning a Super Bowl ring. He did everything a player can do—he had run for more than 13,000 yards—and he was a leader on the field and off. Casey Hampton, our nose tackle, said, "Jerome's our guy. He asked us to bring him home. That touched us. That's what we're fighting for." The team rallied around him, from veteran Hines Ward, who signed and came to camp, to Ben Roethlisberger, our phenomenal second-year quarterback.

We went 11-5 for the season and entered the playoffs with a wild card berth. If we were going to get to the Super Bowl, we'd have to win all our games on the road—and that's tough, especially in the playoffs. We opened the postseason at Paul Brown Stadium against a very strong Cincinnati team. The Bengals jumped to a 10-0 lead, even without their starting quarterback, Carson Palmer, who had been knocked out of the game with a torn ACL.

But Ben was poised and in command. Cincinnati built a couple of 10-point leads in the first half, but each time Ben and the offense answered with a touchdown drive. The second of those came late in the first half when Roethlisberger was 3 for 3 for 74 of the drive's 76 yards, plus a touchdown to Hines Ward. Roethlisberger hadn't played well in the 2004 playoffs, but he opened his second go-round in the postseason by completing 14 of 19 for 208 yards with three touchdowns and no interceptions in a 31-17 win.

What a game. Hard-hitting, dramatic, gadget plays, something for everyone—unless you were a Cincinnati fan.

In the AFC divisional playoff, we faced Peyton Manning's heavily favored Colts. Not since the Immaculate Reception have I seen such a heart-stopping, edge-of-your-seat kind of game. Played at the RCA Dome, the noise sometimes seemed as loud as a jet engine.

Now, Manning is a great player, but in this game Ben was the best quarterback on the field. On the game's opening possession, Roethlisberger completed 6 of 7 for 76 yards and a touchdown; the only incompletion was a drop. The Colts punted on each of their opening two possessions before Roethlisberger struck again. On a third-and-10 from the Pittsburgh 39-yard line, he found Hines Ward for 45. Two plays later, he made another strike to Heath Miller over the middle, making it 14-0 with 3:12 still to play in the first quarter.

The game became a fierce back-and-forth battle, and I will always remember Bettis's goal-line fumble; Ben's shoestring, touchdown-saving tackle; and a last-gasp missed field goal by Indianapolis. Final score, 21-18, and what a treat for football fans all over the world.

I always enjoy going into Denver. Even in the thin air of the Mile High City, we felt strong and confident. I talked to my good friend Pat Bowlen, president of the Broncos, before the game. He was confident of his team, too, and I know he fully expected to beat us. We had lost many of these conference championships in recent years, but this time we came into the game in the right frame of mind. Russ Grimm, our assistant head coach, and a great player as a member of the Washington Redskins offensive line known as "the Hogs," helped set the tone early on game day and got the team fired up.

Again, it was Ben who led us. In building a 10-0 lead, Roethlisberger was 7 for 8 for 89 yards and a touchdown, and on the Steelers' other two touchdown drives of the half he completed 6 of 9 for 91 yards and another score.

But it wasn't just the offense that dominated. In helping build that 24-3 halftime lead, the defense limited the Broncos to six first downs and 38 yards rushing while forcing two turnovers. Jeff Reed's 47-yard field goal ten minutes into the game established a positive attitude right at the start. By the end of the game the Steelers Nation made its presence known, swinging Terrible Towels and cheering on our defense as much as our offense. We saw as much Steelers black and gold as Broncos orange and blue that day. Final score, 34-17, and we were off for Super Bowl XL.

By a strange quirk of fate, the Super Bowl would be played February 5, 2006, in Jerome Bettis's hometown—Detroit. Everyone in Motor City seemed behind us. They wanted to see Jerome get his ring as much as we did. The game really came down to three plays. Willie Parker scored on a 75-yard touchdown run, the longest in Super Bowl history. Our cornerback, Ike Taylor, intercepted a Matt Hasselbeck pass on our 5-yard line. And then another of Bill Cowher's patented gadget plays. Randle El took a reverse handoff and threw a 43-yard touchdown to Hines Ward. Roethlisberger became the youngest quarterback to ever win a Super Bowl. And Jerome Bettis held high on the victory stand the Lombardi Trophy. His good friend Hines Ward was named the game's MVP. Bill Cowher had realized his Super Bowl dream, and the Steelers had a fifth championship to bring home to Pittsburgh.

And as I stood there on the podium with my son Art beside me, I flashed back to our very first Super Bowl in 1975, more than thirty years ago. This team was much like that first team. They were young guys who had worked hard for it, who really, really gave it everything they had. Like then, everything came together at the same time— coaches, players, and the entire organization. The first one is special because it was the first. Super Bowl XL is special because, throughout the playoffs, we were on the road and nobody expected us to win eight games in a row. We had the talent, the coaching, good organization, and that intangible thing—team closeness. As Bill Cowher told the media the day after the game, "I said before, in my fourteen years in Pittsburgh, we've had good teams, we've had confident teams, but this was the closest team we've ever had. . . . There are a lot of things that made this group a special group. The coaching staff we had, the best coaching staff, I think, in the National Football League. So I give a lot of credit to them, and it certainly starts at the top with the stability of Mr. Rooney and Kevin Colbert."

I'll never forget the Super Bowl XL victory celebration in Pittsburgh on February 7. Black and gold covered the town. Automobile, truck, and bus traffic came to a halt as fans—families, students, office workers—streamed to the Point by the hundreds of thousands. It seemed the whole Steelers Nation had descended on the Golden Triangle in downtown Pittsburgh. As the Steelers motorcade crawled through the streets, people stretched out their hands to touch the cars and the players, some of whom perched dangerously on the roofs and trunks of the vehicles. Troy Polamalu and James Harrison dove off their truck to body-surf the crowd. The fans—the whole community—came together in their shared joy and pride. They climbed light poles and trees to get better views. They watched from rooftops, fire escapes, and out the windows of towering skyscrapers. Even the horse patrol waved Terrible Towels. Elbow to elbow they packed the square at Gateway Center, where a temporary stage had been erected. Children balanced on their parents' shoulders, and flashes sparkled from the crowd as people held their cameras and cell phones high above their heads, hoping to record even a blurry image of their hometown heroes. The energy of a quarter million chanting, cheering fans echoed off the glass-and-steel buildings and thrilled the players. A half-dozen high school marching bands led the crowd in singing the "Steelers Polka" and "Here We Go." Bettis, holding aloft the Lombardi Trophy, made a heartfelt speech, as did several other players. A sign had been handed to me as we made our way along the parade route. It read simply, "THANKS." When I got to the microphone, I held it up and said, "This sign says it all, and it's for you." And I meant it, too.

For seventeen years, Paul Tagliabue had led the NFL as commissioner. Paul took over at a time when we had serious problems, but he was up to the challenge. We were coming off two strikes, three franchise moves, a decade of litigation, and flat television contracts. We had not expanded in twenty years, had built hardly any new stadiums, had no labor deal, and were facing lawsuits from players. The league needed to revitalize its structure in order to get things done. It had little control over NFL Properties or the Management Council. The commissioner was not in charge of either of those areas.

Paul Tagliabue changed all that.

He took control of league operations, including labor and the business units, and brought in talented new executives to help the owners manage the league much more effectively.

His most important achievement was probably the way he transformed our relationship with the NFL Players Association. He did it by opening a good dialogue with Gene Upshaw. I assured Gene that Tagliabue was a good person and a man who could be trusted. Paul listened carefully to all the arguments on both sides and worked relentlessly to find fair solutions. The result was uninterrupted labor peace during his tenure, which set the foundation for the incredible growth of the league.

In 1993 Paul, Gene Upshaw, Jim Quinn, and I got together and came out with a labor deal that brought not only peace, but also a system (free agency with a salary cap) that made the league more competitive than ever. Every team had a chance to get better and compete for the Super Bowl, not like in baseball where too many teams didn't have the money to compete. Pittsburgh Pirates fans knew every year their team had little chance to reach the World Series. Thankfully, under the NFL system, that wasn't true for Pittsburgh Steelers fans. Our system gave us a chance to win.

Without labor peace, Paul Tagliabue could not have accomplished all the many other achievements that marked his era. Under Tagliabue, we expanded from twenty-eight to thirty-two teams, realigned our divisions and scheduling formula, worked on our revenue-sharing system to make our incomes more even, and signed the largest television contracts in entertainment history.

Paul found a whole new way of involving the NFL in stadium development. He emphasized public-private partnerships, resulting in twenty-four new stadiums. He made sure the NFL continued as a leader in television and new media. Bringing Fox into the NFL television business energized the way our game was presented on TV. Tagliabue also created the first sports league Internet network for fans and the first satellite television subscription service. Then he launched the NFL Network on cable and satellite television.

What he did for the players and the game was just as important—in some ways even more important. He implemented a year-round random testing program for steroids in 1990, way ahead of other sports. He also monitored other drugs that threatened professional football. He created programs to assist players and their families in their lives off the field. All of these programs strengthened the integrity of the league—and integrity is our most important asset.

Paul also made sure the game on the field stayed exciting, and he emphasized player safety. He challenged the Competition Committee to be active and progressive. He also took the game overseas, including the creation of the NFL Europe League, to help the game grow globally. He kept his eye on the health of the game at all levels—from improving our relations with college football, to defending in court our college eligibility rule, to creating the NFL Youth Football Fund with the players' union to support programs for the game at the youth and high school level.

Like Pete Rozelle, Paul was organized. He intuitively knew how things should be handled. Under Tagliabue, the committee system of working through issues flourished. He involved the owners in league business but always offered thoughtful guidance. He put together a terrific staff and professionalized the league.

Jerry Richardson, who chaired the stadium committee, worked with Paul and Roger Goodell. Even though I was also on the stadium committee, those three guys are responsible for the building of some of our nation's greatest stadiums. Teams received up to 50 percent of the stadium cost under the NFL's new G3 loan program. Al Lerner, president of the Cleveland Browns, and I first instituted this program to save the Patriots for Boston. It was originally only for teams in the top-six television markets, but it ended up being used for all clubs that were building or renovating stadiums. The Steelers didn't get money under this plan. We operated under the old system; that is, we borrowed money from the league—money we are still paying back.

Many people talk about NFL commissioners who solved problems. Tagliabue *avoided* problems. He solved them before they arose—that was his brilliance.

In March 2006 Paul called me to let me know he was going to retire. Under his contract, he could step down after the TV and labor contracts were finalized. Paul asked if I would send a letter to all the owners right before the annual March meeting and let them know he was leaving. He would explain his decision at the league meeting.

At the meeting Paul made his formal announcement and, at the same time, he appointed a committee that Jerry Richardson and I co-chaired—Bob Kraft, Al Davis, Lamar Hunt, Woody Johnson, Jerry Jones, and Mike McCaskey. We hired an executive search firm—Korn/Ferry International, headed by Paul Reilly—to help us conduct the search for a new commissioner.

The Korn/Ferry team interviewed league owners to get their buy-in for the process and preliminary ideas about candidates. Findings were kept confidential—no one knew which owner suggested which candidate.

Prior to the annual spring meeting, we split into NFC and AFC groups and gave everyone an opportunity to express an opinion. The plan and the process worked well. Korn/Ferry received, reviewed, and researched almost two hundred applications, which they reduced to about twenty. Our committee screened the applicants and whittled the list down to eleven. After interviewing the remaining candidates, the committee selected a short list of six for the final round. These candidates were a mixture of NFL insiders as well as others outside the league.

On August 7, 2006, we interviewed the five finalists at the Renaissance North Shore Hotel in Chicago—all were articulate and knowledgeable.

Roger Goodell, however, really stood out. He knew the major issues and demonstrated a superior knowledge of the league and its workings—he had, after all, been there for twenty-five years. After only five ballots, the owners elected Roger Goodell, only the seventh commissioner since the NFL began in 1920.

The process allowed the smoothest commissioner transition in NFL history. Jerry Richardson and I were probably the only two people in the National Football League who could have operated and worked together as co-chairmen, a sad—but true—commentary.

Al Davis, who gave us a lot of trouble, questioned everything, argued, and criticized the process. As a result, we scrutinized everything carefully. Al Davis was being Al Davis, but in this case it worked to our advantage because we were more thorough than we might have been otherwise. In the beginning, I wasn't sure about this committee, but I found that each member served well and contributed much to the final result.

At his first press conference as our new commissioner, Roger mentioned three goals: the game, thirty-two strong teams, and innovation. He quickly reinforced what I had known about him all along—he is a man of his word.

He hit the ground running, wasting little time in making good on his promise to visit every NFL team during the 2006 season. He visited thirteen teams in his first month on the job, including the Steelers. And these weren't "preaching" visits. He came to listen. He wanted to know what we thought, what issues concerned us most—now and in the future. He also wanted to know what our players thought.

Roger didn't tell us he had all the answers or suggest what we needed to do. He listened and asked questions to better understand our positions. He took notes. He took it all in and went out of his way to allow each club an equal voice.

Roger made it clear he would have no tolerance for anything that damaged the integrity of the NFL. There's not an owner in any sport who doesn't like to hear that from his commissioner. You want a strong leader, one who will be tough but fair with players, coaches, administrators—even owners—who run afoul of NFL rules.

That sounds pretty good on paper until you become the object of the commissioner's ire, which I did just a few weeks after Roger took office. He hit me hard when I criticized the officials after our game against the Falcons on October 22, 2006.

We were called for a false start on the last play of the game when we were just spiking the ball to kill the clock. The penalty also required that ten seconds be run off the clock. And since just seconds remained to be played, the referee signaled the game over. We lost, 41-38. I hate losing but more than that, I just thought it was a horrible way to end a game. Bad for the fans. Bad for the players. Bad for everyone.

I didn't agree with the call and voiced my displeasure publicly. The commissioner fined me. This was important for Roger to do. Even if

I still disagree with the official's call, I agree that Roger did the right thing by fining me for speaking out. This strong leadership established a precedent that no owner was above the league rules.

I was the first owner to be fined by the new commissioner but certainly not the only person to be disciplined. Roger dealt with several player issues—both on the field and off—and when a few coaches followed my lead and criticized game officials, he handled those as well. In all cases he acted swiftly, but always in the best interests of the league and the game.

We've spent our fair share of time before Congress over the years, testifying on a variety of matters. Most of our attorneys say it's the price of being the most popular sport in America. This year alone, we've dealt with cases ranging from steroid and drug policies to plans for the NFL Network. I'm not going to recount the meetings and hearings on the "Hill," but what impressed me was the commissioner's drive to get out ahead of the issues.

And overall that's the way he operates. He heads off issues by picking up the phone and calling people, or if it makes more sense, meeting face to face. The most important thing is to meet an issue head on.

When we met in Pittsburgh, Roger talked about creating greater transparency between the league office and the clubs. His visits to each team helped move us all in that direction, but I think our October 2006 league meeting brought his idea of open communication into sharp focus. He handled that first meeting brilliantly.

When we next met, we all were very familiar with the issues. Revenue sharing and funding for a joint stadium for the Giants and Jets dominated most of the day-and-a-half meeting. What stood out was the ease with which Roger presided over the meeting, opening up with some brief remarks and moving right into reports and updates on the season. Moreover, he let us—the owners—talk. He said very little but took notes and asked questions. He spoke only to clarify issues or summarize discussions.

One topic, which played out the entire season, was just how good a season we were having. Attendance was up throughout the league. Blackout lifts—a technical term used to describe when games are televised in their local markets—were running at unprecedented levels. We finished the season with record attendance, and what's more, we kept our partners happy. That was true particularly in television where for the first time I can ever remember, each of our broadcast partners showed an increase in ratings from the previous year. It's really quite amazing considering this was the first year of the new contracts with our broadcast partners—CBS, ESPN, Fox, and NBC.

Roger played an important role in the negotiations that resulted in the current deals. He played an even larger role in the creation of the NFL Network, which televised a package of eight games this season, another first. I think the round-the-clock NFL programming on our own network did help drive our partners' ratings.

The Super Bowl caps off the NFL season, but it's also a time when the commissioner undergoes media scrutiny. This is especially true of first-time commissioners.

The commissioner's annual press conference, traditionally held the Friday morning of Super Bowl week, is really something to see. Media from around the world—seven hundred strong—come to ask the commissioner questions about every conceivable topic related to the game.

The point is, this is a big deal. The event is televised live on ESPN and the NFL Network and there's a lot of pressure. Roger did an excellent job. You could tell he was well prepared—he did his homework. He answered more than twenty-five questions during the forty-five-minute event and even looked as though he enjoyed the give-and-take with reporters.

I am confident Roger Goodell will be an excellent commissioner. Every commissioner since Jim Thorpe brought something of value to the league. Each had their own special talent, but the one thing they all possessed was integrity and a love for the game. They committed themselves to the NFL. Roger Goodell possesses that same commitment. We have been blessed with strong, qualified, and honest men to lead us as we pursue America's game.

———————

Coming off of our Super Bowl XL victory we were riding high, expecting a great follow-up season. But the Steelers' fortunes turned in 2006. In June, Ben Roethlisberger crashed his motorcycle on a busy Pittsburgh street. I was in Ireland when I heard the news. I immediately called the hospital and talked to Ben's mother and father. I offered the Steelers' full support. Though he recovered quickly from this accident, in September he was rushed to the hospital for an emergency appendectomy. Charlie Batch filled in at quarterback for the season opener against Miami here at Heinz Field. Charlie threw three touchdown passes to beat the Dolphins, 28-17.

Let me say something about Charlie Batch. Not only is he a talented quarterback, but he really understands the game and Pittsburgh football. And why wouldn't he? He was born in Homestead, just up the river from Pittsburgh, and attended Steel Valley High School, where he lettered in football and basketball. The great thing about Charlie is that he's not just a football player but really cares about this community. He established the Best of the Batch Foundation to assist local youth and hosts Project C.H.U.C.K., an annual youth basketball league in Homestead. I can vouch for the fact that Charlie loves kids. He's been a great help in mentoring my grandson Danny in his development as a first-rate high school quarterback.

Charlie ended up playing in eight games this season as injuries continued to plague Big Ben. Just when he seemed to be regaining confidence, he suffered a concussion in the Atlanta game. Following a loss to the Raiders, the season was pretty much sunk. We ended up with an 8-8 record and missed the playoffs.

All season there had been speculation that Bill Cowher would not return as the Steelers' head coach. This proved to be true. I had talked to Bill and knew he needed a break from coaching. He had achieved his life's ambition with the Steelers. He had a great winning record, 161-99-1, over fifteen seasons, been named Coach of the Year twice by *Sporting News*, and had won Super Bowl XL. He had reached a point in his life where he wanted to spend more time with his family. He and Kaye purchased a house in Raleigh, North Carolina, where their youngest daughter, Lindsey, enrolled in a high school with a good basketball program. Though I was disappointed to see Bill leave, I understood his reasons and wished him and his family only the very best.

The rules for hiring a head coach had changed since we were last in the market. The main thing that was different was the "Rooney Rule," adopted by the league in 2002. I was chairman of the league's diversity committee at the time a report came out called "Black Coaches in the National Football League: Superior Performances, Inferior Opportunities." Attorneys Johnnie Cochran and Cyrus Mehri called attention to the NFL's poor record in the area of minority hiring. They noted that since 1989 only five African-American head coaches had been hired. We suggested that the league require all head coach searches to include at least one minority candidate; that is, you had to at least give an interview opportunity to a minority. This may not seem like a big deal, but since the league adopted this rule, several NFL franchises have hired African-American head coaches. This year both Super Bowl coaches, Tony Dungy of the Colts and the Bears' Lovie Smith, were African American. I know the league takes the rule seriously, and so do I. When the time came for the Steelers to find a new coach, we actively sought minority candidates.

The media figured we would hire an insider, that we had already made up our mind before we began the search process. But that wasn't true. After a series of personal interviews, both inside and outside the organization, we made the decision to hire Mike Tomlin, a thirty-five-year-old African American who had done a terrific job as the Viking's defensive coordinator. Before going to Minnesota, he helped build Tampa Bay's defense into one of the five best in the league. Mike really impressed us in the interview. He was a family man, knew his history, and loved the Steelers tradition. I could tell he was a good person, and he handled our questions with poise and confidence. On January 22, 2007, Mike Tomlin became the sixteenth coach in Steelers history.

I've been fortunate to spend my entire life in professional football. In November 2004, I expressed this in an op-ed piece I wrote for the *New York Times*. I said that I've seen the NFL grow from a struggling operation to its current position of extraordinary popularity. More than a hundred million people watch NFL games every weekend. The league and its teams are admired across America—from Pittsburgh to Seattle—for the quality of our competition and for the charitable and community work performed by our players, coaches, and the larger family of NFL employees.

But this popularity and respect have a downside. There are so many people who want to take advantage of our huge television audience—advertisers, the networks, even individuals within the league itself. That was the case recently when ABC used *Monday Night Football* to promote one of its prime-time soap operas. The promotional video that ABC broadcast at the opening of the game generated an incredibly strong reaction. In the commercial, a star of one of ABC's programs emerged from a locker-room shower, took off her towel and jumped into a player's arms. At the Steelers offices, as well as those of other NFL teams, we were flooded with phone calls and email messages protesting the salacious content. Many of those fans said they were watching with their children and did not expect to see such material, especially on a football game broadcast.

The league headquarters acknowledged that the fans that contacted us were correct. ABC made an error in judgment. The opening was out of place and should not have been part of the broadcast.

I thought it was disgraceful. What seemed most harmful to me was the fact that the NFL player holding the woman claimed, "The team's going to have to win without me." That is not NFL football. The Steelers and the thirty-one other ball clubs that make up the league constitute a team. We play as a team. This promotion simply did not reflect the spirit of the NFL that I've known and been a part of my whole life.

This incident also led to a discussion on a wide range of issues. What does the NFL represent? I believe the NFL represents the game itself. Football is America's sports passion, and the NFL brings families and communities together in a special way. Pittsburgh is feeling great about itself right now—Rand McNally named Pittsburgh America's most livable city in 2007—and the Steelers recently won Super Bowl XL. Our young quarterback Ben Roethlisberger is the toast of the town. The strong character and integrity of our players today are as strong and positive as they were when the Super Steelers of the 1970s won four Super Bowls. The NFL today has a tremendous group of young men representing our teams on and off the field.

Our game represents special values: tough but fair competition on a level playing field, teamwork, an extraordinary work ethic, and advancement based on merit. We represent achievement and excellence based on performance.

Though NFL football is the highest level of America's favorite sport, the roots of the game grow deep in Western Pennsylvania and thousands of other regions across the country. Its values are nourished in urban, suburban, and rural communities; in thousands of football teams, leagues, and organizations; and with millions of coaches, youthful players, and parents.

Going forward, we have to stay true to what we are—the game of football—and not succumb to the pressure of outsiders to be something else. We also need to hold ourselves accountable and speak out when we see another team, player, or official do or say anything that could harm the league's standing with our fans. Our ultimate goal has always been, and will continue to be, to ensure that the NFL is respected throughout America and viewed as an organization that positively influences millions of Americans of all ages and walks of life.

CHAPTER 9

FORWARD PAST

It's TIME TO LOOK TO THE FUTURE. Will these goals stand the test of time?

The Steelers' mission statement: "The mission of the Pittsburgh Steelers Football Club is to represent Pittsburgh in the National Football League, primarily by winning the Championship of Professional Football. The Club should conduct a first-class, profitable operation, as a valuable member of the community."

The Steelers are an integral part of the community. Our success becomes Pittsburgh's success. The Steelers are both an avenue of entertainment and a source of pride. Once a team commits to its community, the community commits to its team. There's something special about Steelers fans: they feel a part of something bigger than themselves—the Steelers Nation. From the time they are old enough to hold a football, their love and knowledge of the game grows.

The year 2007 marks the 75th anniversary season of the Pittsburgh Steelers and my 75th birthday. We have planned quite a celebration for the Steelers 75th season, including throwback uniforms, an exhibit from the Pro Football Hall of Fame, and even a historical marker commemorating the site of Three Rivers Stadium. The fans selected the All-Time Steelers Team, just as we had done in 1982 for our 50th anniversary. A "Legends Team," selected by a panel of experts, honored the top Steelers who played prior to 1970. It's altogether fitting that Joe Greene, one of the greatest Steelers ever, served as the Honorary Captain for the 75th season. How appropriate that Joe's jersey, number 75, coincides with this anniversary.

It's also fitting that our 75th anniversary coincides with Pittsburgh's 250th anniversary. Pittsburghers are a proud people, and while we celebrate the Steelers' past, we also recognize Pittsburgh's contributions to the world—pro football, labor unions, suspension bridges, the jeep, the polio vaccine, and many more world-changing firsts.

As we look back, it's also time to look forward. Pete Rozelle really pushed the league into the television era. Instead of each team pursuing its own individual television deal, Pete consolidated our interests and negotiated as a league with the networks. And maybe even more important than that, before Pete ever began talking with the networks, he pushed the owners into agreeing to split the revenue from television evenly among all the teams. This single policy did more to build the NFL than anything that had come before. It gave all teams an opportunity to be competitive. It's the reason why NFL franchises in places such as Green Bay, Cincinnati, Buffalo, and Pittsburgh could compete with the big market cities of New York, Philadelphia, and Chicago.

Paul Tagliabue followed Rozelle and brought labor peace to the NFL. He maintained that peace through a series of extensions to the original collective bargaining agreement and established a good working relationship with the NFLPA. This labor peace maintained public confidence in the NFL at a time when each of the other professional sports leagues endured a work stoppage. This confidence allowed seventeen teams to build new stadiums, which in turn provided a boon in comfort and entertainment for the fans, while opening opportunities for clubs to increase revenues.

During Tagliabue's term, the league expanded to thirty-two teams—the perfect number because it allows for four divisions of four teams in both the NFC and AFC, with one team from each playing in the Super Bowl. Paul also nurtured the media and marketing opportunities that came with the explosion of the Internet and cable television. The NFL Network contributed to an increase in the league's fan base and sponsorships.

Now it's Roger Goodell's turn. As his first initiative, he took on the task of disciplining players and employees who break the law or are involved in conduct that can damage the league. It's a big job, and a complicated one sometimes, but Roger is committed to making it work.

Roger faces many challenges. The current CBA between the league and the NFLPA is based on sharing revenue, split not only among the clubs but with the players as well. But since 1993, when it first took effect, there's been a growing disparity in the amount of revenue generated by the teams in different markets. It's no longer a level playing field for Green Bay and Buffalo when compared to Washington or Dallas or New England. How will the NFL keep the clubs in the bigger markets with the larger revenue streams on the same competitive field with teams in the smaller markets? And what will be the influence of the CBA? What happens if it is not extended? Can Goodell keep all teams competitive while continuing to maximize revenue? And then, who gets what?

I'm confident Roger Goodell is equal to the challenge. He is capable, intuitive, mentally tough, and at the same time, he possesses vision. Based on his actions thus far, I think it's clear Roger will continue to find ways to handle everything that comes across his desk—from going before Congress to testify about steroids and the league's drug policy; to continuing to meet with players to discuss discipline, pensions, and health plans while bringing together an alliance of those who can help with these important issues; to strengthening the working relationships with Gene Upshaw and the NFLPA.

Roger can do it, but it will not be easy. One of the league's challenges at this time is that most team owners have been, or still are, very successful in other businesses. An "I want what I want *now*" attitude just won't work if the league is to grow and flourish.

NFL owners must understand that WE ARE PARTNERS.

And this partnership does not only pertain to the business of the league; it's a partnership to protect the game and nurture its relationship with the fans. Pat Kirwan, of NFL.com, captured that relationship in this August 3, 2006, report from Latrobe:

"With fourteen thousand fans filling a high school stadium last night, the Steelers showed up in four yellow school buses for a live intrasquad practice and goal-line scrimmage.

"As I stood in the bleachers and watched the buses pull up next to an old steel mill and the players get off with their shoulder pads in hand, I got goose bumps. I was living a dream. For one night, Mr. Rooney . . . turned back the hands of time for me and the Steelers fans. I was allowed to take a peek at how it used to be—and it was awesome.

"It looked like the origins of pro football, a steel town playing another steel town at the local stadium. As the players mingled with their fans, signed autographs and took pictures, Mr. Rooney presented one of the game balls from the Super Bowl to the mayor of the town. In that moment, I finally understood why the Steelers are just different from most teams. There's no way the Steelers players could let these people down, and there's no way the fans could ever turn on the team when times get tough.

"There was a four-year-old boy sitting behind me with his mother, and he turned to her in his Jerome Bettis jersey and told her, 'I'm glad to see coach letting Santonio Holmes catch some punts.' He's too young to understand that much football. At least, I thought a child that young didn't get the game yet, but he and his mom were there to watch some ball. The Steelers fans love football!"

Now we are embarked on a new era in franchise history. Art is the president and will be the driving force behind the Steelers of the twenty-first century. His brother Dan can help Art the way Art Jr. helped me. We have a new coach—Mike Tomlin—who's taking us in new directions but at the same time is showing that he understands the way the Steelers do business. Mike and his wife Kiya are raising three energetic children and are quickly becoming Pittsburgers.

"This is the first situation in the NFL where I have worked that it was not corporate," says Tomlin. "Truth be known, that's what makes it special here. It doesn't matter what business you're in—it's a people business, and people are important here. You hear, 'The door is always open.' Well, here it's not a cliché. There are a lot of things that make this place special, but that stands out when people talk about the Pittsburgh Steelers being a family environment and atmosphere. The business of professional football is competitive, and it's always going to be that way, but to have a pure open-door policy and a willingness to have conversation—both official and unofficial with your people—is something that makes this place special."

During my seventy-five years with the Steelers and the NFL, I've seen a lot of change. Every year brought new challenges and opportunities. Throughout it all, I've had fun and made so many good and lasting friends. My life has been focused on family, faith, and football. I tried to do the best job I could and I try to make a difference. As I look back, I think there's very little I'd change, even if I could. Looking forward, I can see how the past shapes our future. I'm proud to have been part of the story. I've enjoyed my role as colleague to NFL commissioners, especially Pete Rozelle, Paul Tagliabue, and now Roger Goodell. I hope my perspective and love for the traditions of the NFL have been a help to them.

Football is in my blood. In some ways I feel I'm the last man standing, the last of the first generation who knew the founders of the league and who set it on its course to become America's game.

On the day after we lost the 2004 AFC championship game, Jeff Hartings stood in front of a room filled with media and said, "We honestly love each other. I honestly felt that I would rather lose a game like this with this team than win a Super Bowl with a team I didn't enjoy playing with."

I couldn't have said it better myself.

ACKNOWLEDGMENTS

Many friends have helped me along the way. Margaret Vota not only first suggested I write about my experiences with the Steelers and the NFL, but also spent many hours reading and critiquing the manuscript. Bob Labriola of the Steelers organization and editor of *Steelers Digest* gave me the benefit of his knowledge of Steelers games and enhanced the book. Joe Browne, NFL executive vice president of Communications, also read the manuscript and made many suggestions. Patricia Rooney, Rita Rooney Conway, Art Rooney II, Chuck Daly, Trueman H. "Gus" Peek, and Gene Collier also read the entire manuscript and offered helpful changes. My friend and colleague Charles "Stormy" Bidwill encouraged me to continue writing. Joe Paterno, a friend for many years, lent support. I thank them all. They have made it a better book.

My heartfelt thanks also to Commissioners Roger Goodell and Paul Tagliabue for their support and encouragement.

Many within the Steelers organization helped: Tim Carey, Bill Cowher, Mike Fabus, Gerry Glenn, Joe Gordon, Joe Greene, Franco Harris, Danielle Hudak, Sam Kasan, Ed Kiely, Burt Lauten, Dave Lockett, Karen Mercalde, Rebecca Mihalcik, Chuck Noll, Bill Nunn, Tony Quatrini, Jan Rusnak, Andy Russell, Jimmy Sacco, Ike Taylor, and Mike Tomlin.

At the NFL offices I could always call on Pete Abitante, Greg Aiello, Anastasia Danias, Gary Gertzog, and Jeff Pash.

I would like to thank the staff at the Senator John Heinz History Center in Pittsburgh, especially Betty Arenth, Audrey Brourman, Brian Butko, Sherrie Flick, David Grinnell, Jon Halpern, Lisa Lazar, Art Louderback, Jenny Pack, Tonia Rose, Ned Shano, and Bob Stakley. I would also like to express my appreciation to Kaveri Subbarao, an associate attorney at Reed Smith, who offered expert legal advice.

Editor Kevin Hanover and the staff at Da Capo Press provided expert guidance and support throughout the project.

To my co-authors and friends Andy Masich and David Halaas I extend my deep appreciation for their historical perspective and hard work. From beginning to end it has been a rewarding experience.

Thanks to my children and their families—Art, Pat, Kathleen, Rita, Daniel, Duffy, John, Jim, and Joan.

A sincere thank you to my wonderful mother, Kathleen, and my father, Arthur J. Rooney.

My greatest thanks to Patricia, who has always been with me. She made this book possible.

Dan Rooney
Pittsburgh, PA

BILL NUNN

Initially, you resisted the idea of working for the Steelers because you didn't like the way they and the NFL did business in terms of drafting and playing African Americans. Did your opinion of the Steelers change after you started working there?

Nunn: Vast things changed as far as the organization. I'm surmising this, because of the type of people Dan and Chuck were. All of a sudden you started seeing black coaches there. Black people working in the office, sitting at the front desk. The whole structure started to change. To me, both of them were the same type of person. I don't think they see color, and I don't say that about a lot of people. I say that sincerely. When we used to line up the draft board, Chuck wasn't concerned with the dots. There was a time when dots would be put up on the board.

What do you mean "dots"?

Nunn: Just a black dot so you could identify the players. That's the way teams did it. At one time the NFL Scouting Combine identified people by race, and they did it there by using numbers. I said that's illegal. Eventually it was stopped. They had numbers, something like 110 was white and 111 was black, for example. They didn't identify Jews or Italians, it was just black or white.

Can you talk about some of the players of the 1970s, starting with Mel Blount?

Nunn: As sports editor of the *Pittsburgh Courier,* I did an All-America Team every year, and Mel was one of my All-Americans at Southern University. Chuck and I disagreed on him. We both felt he could play, but I thought Mel would have trouble as a cornerback because he was almost six-foot-four. I thought he should have been a safety. Chuck felt Mel could play cornerback. We went back and looked at the film. Chuck was right because of one doggone thing that I hadn't taken into consideration. With the bump-and-run, Mel could jam the receiver at the line of scrimmage so he couldn't get off and get into running his route. You couldn't do that today. Mel was a great athlete.

Terry Bradshaw?

Nunn: Bradshaw—great talent, no question about it. Great arm, marginal touch on his flair passes that you had to have, particularly in the beginning. Great hands to catch. Would have had a lot of balls intercepted early, but the ball was coming so fast that even the defensive players couldn't catch it. Great athlete. Physically had a lot of things.

I'm no coach. I'm not in meetings. I always say it's very easy on the outside to look in, but if you don't know what a guy is supposed to be doing, how can you say he's right or wrong? Early on, Bradshaw had the reputation of being an idiot. That wasn't true. Maybe he wasn't the smartest quarterback, but he did call his own plays. So questioning his intelligence did not hold up.

One of the things about Chuck was that he gave the quarterback a lot of responsibility on the field. As a result, I go along with the Chief's analysis, which was: we won the first Super Bowl despite Bradshaw and the last two of those four Super Bowls because of Bradshaw.

Terry was another guy who came from a small school who needed to be developed. And he wanted to be loved. I didn't like the way he handled the best athletic wide receiver he ever had in Frank Lewis. Frank was an introvert, and he needed the same things that Bradshaw needed, but in a different way. Lynn Swann handled Bradshaw really well, because Swann realized early that since Terry was the quarterback, Terry would be deciding where to throw the football.

When I was a newspaper guy, the first guy that brought that to my attention was Bobby Layne. I was down at the Roosevelt Hotel one Monday and I started asking Layne some questions. "What makes a wide receiver good?" He said, "I'll tell you something, see this guy here?" His name was Jimmy Orr. "You know what makes him a good receiver?" said Layne. "I like him, and I throw him the ball."

I never forgot that. A wide receiver needs to get nice with the guy who's going to throw him the ball. He's got to be able to catch the ball, but if he has talent and there are two equals, the one the quarterback likes the most will get the ball. Swann picked that up early.

Did Dan Rooney ever involve himself in the draft during the 1970s?

Nunn: To the best of my knowledge, and it might not be the case every single time, Dan never interfered. I never saw him interfere with his brother's job. Scouting, personnel, that was Art Jr.'s job. He'd come in and look at some film, and he saw a lot of things when he was looking at films. Dan would make a little remark every now and then. He's a workaholic, and in all probability he would have been a good appraiser of talent himself. I never knew of him interfering with Chuck or Art or the department when it came to that.

Would the process have been as successful if he interfered?

Nunn: It's hard to say. There are different ways of interfering. If you intimidate your employees by sticking your nose in, then it's a difficult situation. If your employees are free to express themselves, then it's something else. It takes a certain type of employee to stand up and say exactly what he thinks. Even if you get torn down, at least you're saying what you think as opposed to what they want to hear. Dan had employees who told him what he wanted to hear, but he eventually got tired of that.

Can you talk about Dan Rooney as a boss?

Nunn: The thing that always impressed me about Dan was that I never heard him complain about illness or any problems. In some ways, we were brought up the same way. I was under my father and trying to prove that I really belonged on the newspaper. I worked for my father, and Dan worked for his father. But even though his father was the boss, Dan worked as hard as anybody.

A lot of times in the off-season, I'd come over on a Sunday. I wouldn't be doing much, so I'd come over and read books. Dan was the same way. I've often wondered if I had the money to control the ball club and everything that he has, if I'd be that tied up with the team, like making all these road trips. It's admirable.

Back when I was negotiating contracts to sign some ballplayers, I'd be fighting with an agent and I'd say, "Look, I can't go any further. This is it." It would be three-thirty in the morning. I'd say, "I'll call Dan Rooney, and he's not going to go any further." The agent thought I was bluffing. But I called Dan, and he would answer the telephone and was coherent right away. At three-thirty in the morning. This happened numerous times. He'd just say, "How are you doing?" I'd give him all the cue words. Then Dan might say, "Take it up a couple of thousand dollars." I'd give the agent the phone and let him speak to Dan, then I'd get back on the phone. I'd hang up and tell the agent, "You won him over. I don't know how you did it. He said take it up $3,000."

Dan's approach was always upbeat. When I ran training camp, Dan and Chuck were both the same. They would want some furniture or other stuff moved, so I'd say, "I'll call someone." But they would just do it themselves.

JOE GREENE

What made Chuck Noll great?

Greene: Taking care of what you can control, and not getting weighed down by things beyond your control. Paying attention to instructions and then asking the right questions all the time. If you don't understand, then ask. Don't pretend you do know when you don't know. Be honest with yourself.

That's the first thing I used to tell the young men I coached. In order to get from A to B, first you have to be truthful with yourself. You have to fess up. If you did something wrong in terms of trying to have success on the football field on a particular down, in order to get rid of that—as Chuck always said, "You have to replace bad habits with good habits"—you first had to know it was a bad habit. A lot of times those things are trivialized by calling them clichés. To us, they weren't. They were a way of life.

Chuck practiced what he preached. That was his lifestyle. Over all those years, he was solid and stable and didn't waver. When you look back at those teams, a lot of us learned well. The questions asked of me right now, you could probably ask twenty other guys on those teams, and the answers would be the same. That's because we got it all from the same guy.

Is Noll's career underappreciated when compared to other coaching greats?

Greene: I think he's acknowledged when his name comes up, because they have to acknowledge the winning and the tradition and the style of play he put together. That's why the fondness for the Steelers of the 1970s has had such a long life—because we played with a style that was his. It was amazing to me that people would confuse Chuck Noll with another football coach named Chuck [Chuck Knox of the Buffalo Bills and the Los Angeles Rams], and that they would spell Chuck Noll's surname with a K. Maybe it was because he didn't cater to the media. He was respectful, and that's what he always told us: that the media had a job to do even though it was different than our job, and we should respect them. He had an appreciation for the media, but he never played up to them, and maybe that's why he's under-appreciated.

What do you mean by "style of play"?

Greene: It was a solid defense that wasn't necessarily spectacular, but it was very difficult to run the ball on and very difficult to throw the ball on. The offense wasn't flashy. We ran the football for the most part, and then with Terry Bradshaw we threw more later on with Lynn Swann and John Stallworth. It was standard football. You run first and you pass second; you pass-protect and you run your routes. It wasn't the West Coast. It wasn't the Dallas Cowboys' shotgun with a lot of motion. It was a two-back offense when a lot of one-back offenses were emerging.

Talk about the 1974 playoffs and finally getting to the Super Bowl and winning it.

Greene: We played Buffalo in the first round of the playoffs, and that's when we really introduced the Stunt 4-3. We were desperate to stop O. J. Simpson, who had put up almost two hundred yards rushing the last time he played against us. The reason we had been losing in the playoffs was that other teams were running the football on us. Miami did it in 1972, and Oakland did it in 1973.

The thing that really, really gave us the impetus and the mind-set and, as Chuck always said, "the refuse-to-be-denied attitude" came on the Monday after we beat Buffalo in the first round of the playoffs in 1974. People on the outside would always hear things like the refuse-to-be-denied attitude and call them a cliché, but to us it was real. Anyway, we were sitting in the locker room over at the stadium, and Chuck said, "You know, the coach of the Raiders said the two best teams in football [Miami and Oakland] played yesterday, and that was the Super Bowl." He said, "Well, the Super Bowl is three weeks from now, and the best team in pro football is sitting right here in this room."

I'm telling you, I think I levitated right out of my seat when I heard that. There was no way the Raiders were going to beat us. It all came from Chuck's consistency, because it was very unlike him to say that. That's why it had so much power. It's almost like it happened yesterday. So during the course of that game we were thinking, "These Raiders don't have a chance."

Just before halftime in the game, John Stallworth caught a touchdown pass in the corner of the end zone with his left hand and the cornerback was holding his other arm. Stallworth somehow crossed over with his feet and stayed in bounds. The officials called him out. At that time we were trailing, but the amazing thing was that none of us complained about it. We could all see that it was a touchdown, but we didn't complain. And when we walked off the field and through the tunnel where all the Raiders fans were lined up, we ran off with the confidence that we're going to beat you. You have no chance. We're going to give you that touchdown.

I had never felt that way—ever. It all stemmed from Chuck: the quiet, steady confidence that he had in us. And that was because he had built it and he knew what was happening. It was all about him.

I've been in locker rooms since then where you get all kinds of speeches and platitudes, and they don't mean a thing. All Chuck said was, play the way you've been coached, and that's what developed the consistency in that football team.

Talk about presenting Dan Rooney for induction at the Hall of Fame?

Greene: When he called me, he said, "I want you to present me." I said, "You don't want Chuck?"

I was almost speechless. After it all sank in, I had a better feeling about being asked to do that than I had about being inducted myself. I think Dan wanted someone from that era to present him, someone he thought could represent the team. I never asked him. I'm definitely assuming. That's one of the greatest honors I've ever had.

What is Dan Rooney like as a boss?

Greene: A great boss. I'll never forget him saying that when you have a big decision to make, let it soak. Think about it. He said that when a team loses it's not always the head coach's fault, and good head coaches are hard to come by. Give them time.

After my rookie year, I made some All-Pro team. In my contract, I had a clause that said if I made a specific All-Pro team—the NEA [Newspaper Enterprise Association] team—I'd get $10,000. I made some All-Pro teams, but not the one spelled out in my contract. Dan wrote me the check anyway.

That's the way he's always been. Starting way back, he always made sure that his players were respected by the organization. We never had issues when we traveled to Super Bowls. And Dan made sure, through the people who worked for him, that we never had issues with travel or hotels or tickets.

Dan was a tough businessman, but he was always fair. He always said that as an owner you may have the upper hand, but that doesn't mean you have to beat the guy down. Give in a little. He's lived that way.

I did things many times—I probably couldn't have played for a lot of teams. But the simple fact is that Chuck and Dan and Mr. Rooney knew they were dealing with kids. They had a way of giving us a helping hand and letting us know it was going to get better. When I had a tantrum and kicked in the door of the equipment room at training camp, all Chuck ever did was come up to my room and say, "That'll be $500." That was it. But I understood, because you can't do that. Through all of my antics, Dan and Chuck felt that my only interest was in winning.

CHUCK NOLL

What made you eventually decide on the Steelers?

Noll: I thought that this probably was the place to come. I talked to Dan Rooney and got a feeling for what he wanted to do. And he liked the thoughts I had, so it worked out well.

Did you talk to anybody from outside the Steelers organization—about the Rooneys, about the Steelers?

Noll: Not really, no. It was just a meeting with Dan, getting his ideas and what they wanted to do, and our ideas meshed.

What we wanted to do was build through the draft. The Steelers had a history of trading away a lot of people before that. My experience, coming up through the American Football League, was in drafting people and teaching the skills to play professional football. That's the way that I knew how to do it, and that's the way Dan wanted to go, so it meshed well.

Did you also talk to Art Rooney Jr.?

Noll: Yes, he was head of scouting. That was something that I was very interested in, because there were a lot of teams that wanted to segregate coaching and talent. I don't think you can do that. I think it has to work together. It has to be a team, completely, not only on the field but off the field as well. I was very comfortable that the Steelers would go in that direction.

Was being on the same page with Dan and Art Jr. what gave you the opportunity to succeed?

Noll: Yeah, no question about it. They were looking for the right way to do things. I came in with some experience of winning, of being with organizations that were successful. They thought, "Hey, this is what made them successful. Why won't it make us successful?" They bought into it, and they were looking for that way to do it.

During that first draft, there was a lot of pressure to draft Terry Hanratty because he was a local guy from Notre Dame. You ultimately, of course, drafted Joe Greene. How were you familiar with Joe?

Noll: Well, I had worked him out specifically. I had known of him, and that was an important thing. He was a young man who had a great desire to be the best. That's what we needed. We needed those kinds of people. He fit the whole profile. Attitude-wise, talent-wise, he could be a dominating player. We needed help in our defensive line. Some people didn't think so, but that's what we needed to be able to rush the passer and control the line of scrimmage.

Was it your philosophy to build the defense first, to focus on the defense?

Noll: Well, before you can win the game, you have to not lose it. That's the premise. So it begins with defense, and defense can set up offense. You can go out there and score lots of points, but end up losing the game because you have no defense. You're running up and down the field, you know, and that may be exciting to the fans. But it's not very exciting when you lose.

With Joe, were there any negatives from a discipline standpoint, where he was kind of a loose cannon?

Noll: No. You know, the thing that he wanted so very badly was to win. And to do what you had to do to win. He went out and played very hard, and expected everybody else to as well. Also, he didn't want anybody holding him. If someone was going to hold him, and the officials didn't call it, well, he lost his temper. That was something that we talked about: that you have to really let the officials call the game. You can complain about being held, but you can't physically take on the other people.

From the standpoint of when he was at his peak, was he the best defensive player you had ever coached?

Noll: He was right there, yes. From an attitude standpoint, there was desire; he'd do whatever you had to do to win. And he was special from a leadership standpoint. Everybody thinks leadership comes from how you talk, but it really doesn't. Leadership on the field from a football player comes from how you perform. If you are a performer, you can be a leader. Joe was an outstanding performer, and led that way.

After that first year, the 1-13, were you convinced the Steelers were still going in the right direction?

Noll: Yeah, I thought we were. It was just a question of upgrading at some different positions. We needed skill positions on offense, which we didn't have the first year. We started off trying to get some defense together, and that picked up a little bit, but not good enough. We still had to get better people.

The next year came the drafting of Terry Bradshaw. The St. Louis Cardinals were offering something like eight players for that draft choice. Talk about that.

Noll: You know, the number of players you're going to get is not going to help your football team. You have to have quality people. So if you trade away quality for less than quality, you're going to be a less-than-quality football team. And what we were after were top-notch players. Terry fell into that category, and that's what we were trying to get via the draft—top-quality people.

Did you figure initially that the learning process would be long with Terry?

Noll: You know, I really had no way of knowing. I knew he had a great deal of talent. He had the ability to throw the football. He had the ability to run with it when he had to. He had all kinds of physical abilities, and it was just a question of being able to use that on the field.

Did he have as strong a commitment to success as Joe Greene?

Noll: Very much so. Terry, without a question, had a great desire to be the best. He worked very hard, physically and mentally. He spent time in the classroom, and watching film, and prepared himself very well.

Lynn Swann and John Stallworth are both Hall of Fame receivers. What were the differences between them?

Noll: John Stallworth probably was a little more physical than Lynn. Lynn was a little more athletic and had the ability to run very well after the catch by making people miss. John Stallworth would break tackles, then run well after the catch. They complemented each other. Both helped the running game, also. In order to have the running game go—to make people respect your running game so you could throw the football—they had to block. They blocked downfield, both of them, very well.

Was there actual competition between them—trying to outdo each other, and each one wanting the ball all the time?

Noll: There's no question about it. If we had thrown the ball to them every time, they would've been happy. The ball had to be spread around, but in order to do it properly we had to make people respect the run. We had to throw it when we were able to slow down the pass rush, so that we would have time to throw it and get open.

What about Franco Harris?

Noll: The first day he came to camp, you could see his ability to make people miss his quickness. His ability to run with the football was something very special. Franco really had great vision. Every good runner I know has that kind of vision, and he had it right from the start. Not only seeing the holes, but seeing the people. You know, a lot of people come in there and they close their eyes when they're running into the line, but Franco had his eyes wide open. He could pick the holes and knew the cuts to make.

What about Rocky Bleier as a complement to Franco Harris?

Noll: Rocky was a guy who was kind of a—I don't want to say an enigma—but a surprise in a lot of senses because he did not appear to be a great athlete. He had better speed than he looked like he had, and he had a great desire to play. He turned out to be an excellent blocker, which also complemented Franco, and he ended up running routes and catching the ball out of the backfield well. At first I didn't think he had that kind of talent, but he developed it by working very hard. He had a great desire to improve in all areas.

So in a sense he was somewhat of a surprise?

Noll: When I was with Baltimore and we played against the Steelers, Rocky was was not someone who we were concerned about at all. But when I got here, and had a chance to work with him and see the desires that he had, and how much he wanted to improve, he was a guy that grew on you.

What about on the defensive side, Mel Blount?

Noll: There was no question that Mel had great abilities from the beginning. He had the size, the speed, the ability to cover. The biggest thing with Mel was making sure that he was on the same page with the rest of the defense and would stay in the pattern of defense. He had a tendency to want to go off on his own and sometimes guess a little bit. We weren't interested in guessers. We wanted to play a good solid defense, where you stayed within the pattern. He adapted to that very well. It ended up being to his benefit.

What about the two Hall of Fame linebackers, Jack Ham and Jack Lambert? George Perles used to say, "There's a lot of Ham in Lambert, and there's a lot of Lambert in Ham." What did George mean by that?

Noll: They were two outstanding football players, there's no question about it. They were talented. Had the ability to cover people out of the backfield. They had the speed and the size. They had the ability to read an offense and stay in pattern and not make mistakes. That was a big part of the whole thing.

When Lambert was first drafted, I think the idea was to play him on the outside. Henry Davis had some problems, and you moved him inside. Was there concern about his size on the inside?

Noll: There was some concern before we saw him in there. After he got in there, we saw his ability to take on blockers, to avoid blockers inside. He had great quickness and recognition to get to the hole. He would stand back there, with the design of the defense, and he could see where the play was going, and he'd beat the blockers to the hole. He had that kind of ability.

What about Ham?

Noll: Jack Ham. From the outset, there was no question he had abilities to play. He had the ability to cover people out of the backfield, which we worked on very hard. He stepped right in there and picked it up without question. He played the run very well. He was a full, complete linebacker.

What about those offensive lines?

Noll: You know, you cannot have an offense if you do not have a solid offensive line. Number one, they have to be able to block for the run, which they did very well. We had good athletes in the line. We were able to not only straight block—you get these big three-hundred-pounders that do that—but we were able to pull and get to the outside. We were able to get a trapping game going, which fit our running backs very well, and it was all because of the agility and the ability of the offensive line. They had quickness. They had the ability to pull and move and run, and all those things came down to being able to move the football on the ground.

We were looking for guys who had quickness and agility. We didn't want the big fat guys who just leaned against somebody and that was the only thing they could do. We wanted to be able to move the football outside, inside, trap, and do all the things that you had to, and still be able to pass-protect.

Mike Webster was probably a good example of that, right?

Noll: Mike wasn't tall enough, he didn't weigh enough, but the thing that he had that made the difference was great playing strength. You could see it on the field. He would come off the ball with great quickness. He would block these guys. I can remember having some films of him against, I think it was UCLA. They had these huge, huge tackles. He just destroyed them. They moved the ball up and down the field. He not only blocked well on the run, but he also pass-protected well.

What about Larry Brown, who started off as a tight end, and then moved to offensive line? You believe he should be in the Hall of Fame?

Noll: No question about it. He was a guy who came in as receiver but did not have the great speed that you wanted there. He had size, and had the desire to be a good football player. He ended up working on the weights and putting on some pounds, and made the move to tackle extremely well. He ended up being a guy who could pull and run. We were able to tackle-trap with him, because he had that kind of ability, and we still used him as a tackle-eligible.

What was the secret of Gerry Mullins' success, to be able to play as well as he did?

Noll: Well, he came in a tight end, an undersized tight end, and worked some on the weights. He got bulked up, and had good physical abilities. He had good movement, that type of thing. We ended up being able to get the maximum out of him when it came to pass protection. We'd work our tight ends on pass protection, because we'd keep them in to block, and he showed abilities there. And offensive line coach Dan Radakovich worked very well with him. He developed into an outstanding offensive tackle.

What do you think of Ben Roethlisberger from an athletic standpoint, and the great success he's had in his two years?

Noll: Well, there's no question he's got the ability and the talent to do it. What you have to make sure of is that you have the supporting cast around him. It looks like they have that: the receivers and the protection. And if you get the running game going along with it, there should be no problem.

What about Rod Woodson?

Noll: He was something special as an athlete. He had the great speed and the size. The big thing with Rod, just like Mel Blount, was to develop the discipline to stay within the pattern of the defense. He had a tendency to want to freelance a little bit, because he had the ability to do that type of thing. On occasion it was a big play, and on other occasions it hurt you. So, to get him to be a disciplined type of player was a big thing.

BILL COWHER

When you got the Steelers job in '92, how confident were you?

Cowher: The first thing I said to my wife was, "If I don't screw this thing up, I can be the head coach of the team where I grew up at my twentieth high school class reunion." And I was a graduate of '75, and I wanted to make it to '95, so I was just hoping I could make it to three years. Everything had happened so fast that, you know, I think when you first get the job it's very overwhelming. I was overwhelmed for the first couple of weeks—I was trying to put together a staff, trying to hire a secretary, all the things that are entailed. But once you get into it, it still comes down to coaching and dealing with people. I didn't really have time to think about whether I could do it or not, because I was doing it whether I liked it or not. I had some success early, and that spawned a little bit of confidence so I could say to myself, "You can do this."

Was there any special philosophy that you had regarding becoming a head coach?

Cowher: I think the bottom line was, I wanted it to be a tough football team. I wanted to be able to run the football and I wanted to be able to play defense. I knew that you had to score points and I knew that you had to throw the ball. But I always thought that being a tough football team was important—I just felt that's how you played the game.

Looking back, fifteen years is an eternity in this profession. What are your thoughts about it?

Cowher: I guess my first thought is that I have an unbelievably supportive wife who sacrificed a lot in raising our kids. I am so proud of each and every one of them. I think, secondly, that I played for an owner who was there for me as a father, as a friend, and as an advisor. As I worked for him, I learned a lot through Dan Rooney. I have so much respect for him.

We had a lot of good players and a lot of good coaches. There are a lot of people, not just myself, that were part of that success. I'll never think it was all done by me, because it wasn't. I was fortunate enough to have a lot of good people around me, and that allowed me to do something that I love. We had some good breaks. We were able to win early, and let's face it—if you don't win early in our profession, you may not be able to survive a couple of bad years. So I may have bought myself a couple of bad years by winning early and getting through that. Then also, winning the championship one year was the best thing about it.

I never came to the job thinking about whether I could make more money somewhere else. I was there because I was brought there to win a championship. Until I had done that, there would always have been a void. I'm not one that's much for change. Pittsburgh was a great place to grow up and it's a great place to raise a family. I was never looking to move from team to team. That never crossed my mind.

Would you say your relationship with Dan was unique relative to the coach-owner relationships in the rest of the NFL?

Cowher: I don't think there's any question about it. I was fortunate. Every year I would look around the league and see some of the things that were being done, and I would count my blessings because of who I was working for. Dan always had the ability to look at the game—for what it was and where it came from. I'm a purist myself, and so from that standpoint, our viewpoints on football meshed. I counted my blessings being able to work for a man like that.

Let's talk briefly about some of your players. How about Jerome Bettis?

Cowher: Just a great player who had unbelievable passion for the game. Very charismatic, great team guy, and the one guy I would say was able to understand the system. Accepted the role, and was one of the few guys I have ever been around that could still be a leader with a limited role. He had that ability and that makeup where the players respected him. I have nothing but the utmost respect for him. He was a guy I could turn to every week, and he was going to be there.

How about Rod Woodson?

Cowher: Probably the best athlete I have ever coached. The guy was an unbelievable student of the game. He had a great feel for the game, and you couple that with athletic ability, without a doubt he was the best football player I coached in my fifteen years.

I mentioned Bettis, Woodson—they're both future Hall of Famers. Dermontti Dawson?

Cowher: Noble athlete. In all the years I watched centers, he did things that I would have never thought a center could do. He was the quickest and fastest and strongest lineman, center that I've ever seen play. You want to talk about a guy that could light up a room; I've never seen a day come when he didn't have a smile on his face. He was a true pleasure to coach.

How about Greg Lloyd?

Cowher: Greg Lloyd was one of the toughest players we ever had. He was self-made. He was explosive and strong-willed, but he could also take a team on his back and lead them. He had demeanor on the field that was second to none.

What about Carnell Lake?

Cowher: Carnell Lake was probably one of the better athletes that I've coached, coming from the standpoint of size and speed. Just a classy guy, too. Salt of the earth. He's a guy that could do it all. He could cover like a corner, he could hit like a safety. He just had that rare combination of size and of speed.

Hines Ward?

Cowher: Oh, the smile. It was so infectious. You talk about a guy that was the complete receiver. You look at receivers today, they are great returners, or they are great with the ball after the catch. They're great at the ball with using their size. I mean, there are guys that can just block. This guy is the complete package. And you want to talk about a student of the game, another guy who is self-made. He blocks, he catches, he runs—he can do it all. To me, his smile, his leadership, and the way he has passion for the game is infectious to a team.

What about Troy Polamalu?

Cowher: He may be second only to Rod Woodson—I just have not been with him long enough. But you want to talk about a guy with feel for the game, a student of the game with athletic ability, he's up there with Rod Woodson. He's another guy who is just a pleasure to be around; he's got that kind of Dermontti Dawson attitude. Every day you're around him he's got a smile on his face. He's a special person—a special football player.

How about Kordell Stewart?

Cowher: Kordell would do whatever you would ask him to do. He was an unbelievable athlete. He could play receiver; he could throw the ball. I like Kordell. I believe in him. Kordell had a way of being able to take over a game. He's a very, very competitive guy. Maybe limited in some of his skills as a quarterback, but you've got to remember how far he took us in the years he quarterbacked for us. For a guy with limited quarterback skills, his competitiveness, his athletic ability, and his will to win took him a long way in the National Football League.

MIKE TOMLIN

What has Tony Dungy told you about the Steelers and his experience here?

Tomlin: So much of how Tony Dungy approaches what he does is based on his experience here. He makes no bones about that. He is very appreciative of the opportunity the Steelers gave him, how he was treated. He talked about the first-class manner in which the organization was run. He came into the league as an undrafted rookie free agent, and the Steelers appreciated the way he approached his work. Tony Dungy was a student of the game as a player, a guy who didn't make mistakes. And he had what I refer to as great football character. He always felt those things were appreciated here.

He always talked a lot about the great people here—Donnie Shell and people like that, to say nothing of the love and respect he has for the Rooney family and Chuck Noll. There are so many stories, and I don't know if I can specifically point to one, but his experience with the Steelers definitely shaped his career and his personal life.

What is the impression of the Steelers around the rest of the NFL?

Tomlin: That it's first class in every way, and that it's run by football people. That's important in today's NFL, that there are long-standing football people in charge who care not only about the business of football but about the game itself. Here, they care about the well-being of the National Football League, and there's always been the feeling throughout league circles that the Rooneys are committed to the overall well-being of the NFL.

And it continues to show, too. Anytime there are decisions to be made or things happen, the Rooneys have always been heavily in-volved—particularly Dan Rooney—even up to the search for the present commissioner. There is a great deal of respect throughout the league for what goes on inside this building.

Are the Steelers perceived as being different?

Tomlin: The Steelers are perceived as different just as Oakland is per-ceived as different, but of course on two totally different levels. It's viewed as a family business, and because it's family, they care about people. They don't ride the emotional roller-coaster, and their long-term success and stability are things that everybody outside of this building admires about the place.

Talk about your first meeting with Dan Rooney.

Tomlin: It was at my interview. I'm a football historian, so what I got from him was what I expected. I had heard he was an awesome guy, but because it was a job interview, I really didn't get a chance to ask him a million questions about his experiences, to hear stories about the significant things that have happened with this organization.

The thing I remember most about the interview itself is that when we would take breaks, either to use the bathroom or maybe get a cup of coffee, he and I might be walking down the hall and he'd stop and start telling a story about a picture on the wall. He is walking, talking, breathing history, and not just Steelers history but NFL history. If you have a love for the game, or are a historian of the game like I am, the time I get to spend with him that's not related to official business is what I enjoy the most, because you get that sense of history. How can you not have an appreciation for that?

I didn't want to rush back from those breaks. And the stories weren't just about football, or about Steelers football. There were aerial shots of Pittsburgh, and he was giving me the history of the city. I'm wired the same way—I'm a history buff. I read history books, biographies, so I enjoyed that time we had.

Because there are only thirty-two NFL head coaching jobs on earth, would you have taken any job that was offered?

Tomlin: I would not have taken any NFL head coaching job just to get one. Some people might think that's a ridiculous statement, but I've always been a guy who enjoyed whatever job I had. I didn't have the mentality of taking any head coaching job, but to be the head coach of the Pittsburgh Steelers, I would have walked here from Minneapolis.

Why?

Tomlin: The commitment to excellence, and the way they go about pursuing excellence. The tradition. The legacy. The high standards. If you're a competitor, all of that is attractive to you. I love the responsibility that comes with being the head coach of the Pittsburgh Steelers. I'd rather have that responsibility than work at a place with low expectations. It's really indescribable, when someone asks you why you feel that way, but being in this business, you know. It's not something that requires a lot of conversation among people in the NFL. You just know.

Many people have misconceptions about the relationships that exist among individual owners. There are disagreements, but on the whole, owners are together for the big picture and realize *we are partners*.

Arizona Cardinals

When Charley Bidwill owned and operated the Cardinals, it was one of the league's better-run teams. Originally the Racine Normals, since they played in Chicago's Normal Park on Racine Avenue, this franchise is the oldest in the league. After Charley's death, his wife, Violet, inherited the team, which she ran for fifteen years. Eventually, her sons Charles "Stormy" and Bill Bidwill took over operations. "Stormy" sold or somehow transferred his stake in the team to Bill. Unsuccessful in Chicago, the team moved to St. Louis and from there to Phoenix, where they play in a unique domed stadium. It's now a successful franchise, and it looks like they're there to stay. Bill's son, Mike Bidwill, now operates the team. They have many former Steelers coaches, including Ken Whisenhunt, their new head coach. We'll see how things go.

Atlanta Falcons

The Atlanta Falcons came into the NFL in 1965 after Pete Rozelle and I went to Atlanta to discuss with Governor Carl Sanders the notion of bringing professional football to Georgia. Believing the team would be good for the economy, Governor Sanders arranged a meeting with Rankin Smith, a successful businessman who was interested in buying the team. During the negotiating period, I made several trips to Atlanta and arranged for the Steelers to play two preseason games there (against the Vikings and the Colts). Smith purchased the team from the NFL, and Atlanta built a new stadium for the football Falcons and the baseball Braves and began play in 1966.

When Rankin died, the family asked if I would speak at the funeral. I was honored to be one of the people to eulogize Rankin, a good friend. His son, Taylor Smith, took over the operation of the Falcons, and today the team has good prospects for the future under its present owner, Arthur Blank.

Baltimore Ravens

The Baltimore Ravens came into the League in 1996 when Art Modell moved the Browns from Cleveland. When the NFL completed its expansion to its present thirty-two teams, a realignment of the league established the AFC North Division, which joined the Ravens with Pittsburgh, Cleveland, and Cincinnati. Steve Bisciotti now owns the Ravens, and he has an organization that includes team president, Dick Cass, a smart and capable lawyer; General Manager Ozzie Newsome, who has done a great job with the draft; and Coach Brian Billick, who has built a strong team that always plays tough football, especially on defense. The Ravens won Super Bowl XXXV.

Buffalo Bills

The Buffalo Bills started as an original AFL team in 1959, and Ralph Wilson has owned the team from the beginning. After appearing in three straight AFL championship games, from 1963 to 1965, and winning the final two of those, the Bills fielded another powerhouse that won four straight AFC championships from 1990 to 1993 under the direction of Coach Marv Levy. Jim Kelly was the quarterback on those teams and was elected to the Hall of Fame in 2002. Ralph is Passionate about league rules and traditions and is not hesitant to speak up on either at league meetings. The Buffalo Bills are in the tough AFC East Division.

Carolina Panthers

The Carolina Panthers, an NFL expansion team, joined the NFL in 1994 as an expansion franchise and (along with Jacksonville) turned us into a thirty-team league. Owner Jerry Richardson, a special friend, and I have similar ideas, especially about the importance of the league and the value of the shield, the NFL logo. Jerry was a receiver who played for the Baltimore Colts when John Unitas quarterbacked there. Jerry, John, and I enjoyed some good conversations over the years. Clearly Jerry and John respected one another. Jerry and his wife, Roz, have a daughter, Ashley, and two sons, Mark and Jon. Mark is the general manager, and Jon handles stadium operations. Jerry and I co-chaired the search committee that elected Commissioner Roger Goodell.

Chicago Bears

The Chicago Bears is one of the oldest teams in the league. Its founder, George Halas, was there at the Hupmobile car dealership in Canton, Ohio, the day the league was born in 1920. George did everything: he played, coached, operated the front office, sold tickets. He was a visionary and his team saw great success. Harold "Red" Grange, the "Galloping Ghost," played for the Bears before his college days were over, even though the University of Illinois, Grange's school, complained. The school asked Halas, also a graduate, to stop NFL raiding of college players. He and the Eagles' Bert Bell responded by initiating the college draft that helped stop players from dropping out of school to join the pros. George's son, George Jr., also called "Mugs," died in 1979 before his parents. George Sr.'s daughter, Virginia McCaskey, owns the team now, and her sons Mike, Ed Jr., and Tim operate the club.

Cincinnati Bengals

The Cincinnati Bengals was the last NFL expansion team before the merger with the AFL. Owner Mike Brown has been a friend for a long time. His father, Paul, an innovator, advanced the pro game most dramatically by introducing a pass-oriented offense not seen before. He brought these innovations from the AAFC when they merged with the NFL for the 1950 season, helping to make NFL football America's favorite game. At league meetings, Mike Brown is often right about things, and he stubbornly sticks to his principles and values.

Cleveland Browns

The Cleveland Browns, one of the original teams in the AAFC, joined the NFL in 1950 along with the San Francisco 49ers and Baltimore Colts. Art Modell bought the club in 1961 and operated in Cleveland until 1995, when he moved the team to Baltimore. I was against moving a team out of Cleveland and away from a loyal fan base, because I believed it was bad for the NFL and bad for the Steelers; it took away our closest natural rival. Filling the void, the NFL built a new stadium near the site of the original Municipal Stadium. Al Lerner, a wonderful man, bought the new club. He was very bright and learned the football operation quickly. I worked on some projects with him, one of which kept the New England Patriots in the Boston area. Al died in 2002. His son, Randy, a smart young man learning the intricacies of football operations, now runs the team. He has brought in people who are trying to build a successful organization, including General Manager Phil Savage and Coach Romeo Crennel.

Dallas Cowboys

Clint Murchison Jr. was the founding owner of the Cowboys in 1960, and his first act was to name Tex Schramm as the president and CEO. Tex had complete authority and ran a first-class operation in every way. The successful Cowboys franchise has gone to eight Super Bowls and won five of them. Tex, another friend, and I worked on many projects: player limits, expansion, World League of American Football, and labor issues. Although we disagreed about the 1987 strike, because we were friends and protégés of Pete Rozelle, we spent much time together.

Murchison sold the team to H. R. "Bum" Bright, who then sold it to Jerry Jones. Jerry has succeeded in promotion and sponsorship, and the teams he built with Coach Jimmy Johnson won three of the franchise's five Super Bowls. He wants to win and does so often. I have worked with Jerry a few times, and he always wanted to get the right results for the league. His plan to build a new state-of-the-art stadium will require considerable funding.

Denver Broncos

In 1961 Gerald Phipps, of the Pittsburgh Phipps family, started the Denver Broncos. The team was not greatly successful, either in the AFL or during its early seasons in the NFL. After renovating Mile High Stadium, Phipps sold the team to Edgar Kaiser, who then sold the team to Pat Bowlen in 1984. Pat, another friend, and I have worked closely together on league issues, and he's been the chairman of the NFL television committee. With quarterback John Elway, his Broncos lost three Super Bowls over a four-year span before winning it back to back in Super Bowls XXXII and XXXIII. They have a new football stadium, and their future looks bright.

Detroit Lions

The Ford family of automobile fame owns the Lions. Bill Ford Jr. and I have always gotten along especially well. Bill runs Ford Motor Company, and I stay in touch with him and try to let him know what is happening in the league. I think Ford does not deserve the criticism he receives. The Lions club has recently built a new stadium in downtown

Detroit and showed it off to good advantage for Super Bowl XL. The Detroit Lions helped to develop Kevin Colbert in the personnel area, and Kevin is now the Steelers' director of football operations.

Green Bay Packers

This club is unusual in the league in that the people of Green Bay own the franchise. Bob Harlan heads the organization as CEO. Green Bay is more like Pittsburgh than any other city in the league, starting with the fact both cities have great fans. Green Bay has been successful. They were the team of the 1960s. Under Vince Lombardi, the Packers won three NFL championships, plus the first two Super Bowls. In the mid-1990s, under Coach Mike Holmgren and with quarterback Brett Favre, the Packers played in two more Super Bowls and won one. The Packers are the best example of how the NFL's revenue-sharing system allows every team—whether it plays in a big city or small—the opportunity to win. Green Bay's future will be interesting to follow and will say a lot about the future of the NFL.

Houston Texans

Bob McNair owns the Houston Texans, the most recent team to join the league in 1999. Bob has been a good businessman whose influence and involvement have set the Texans' direction in the league. I respect Bob even though we have many different opinions at times. Disagreement is okay and can be expected since Houston is one of the largest U.S. cities, and Pittsburgh a smaller market. League members operate differently than regular corporate affiliates. But we are still partners.

Revenue sharing is a contentious topic. Teams at the low end—small markets—believe they should be made whole or equal to the average. Teams at the top want limits on funds distributions to help the lower clubs. Teams in the middle are concerned they will be expected to pay the league a major part of their annual revenue. The concern here is that the league will lose its competitive balance, which is the foundation of the NFL.

Indianapolis Colts

Jim Irsay inherited the Indianapolis Colts from his father who moved the club from Baltimore. That move to Indianapolis helped create the situation that included the Browns moving from Cleveland, but now both of those established football towns have teams again. Jim runs a smooth operation. With General Manager Bill Polian, Coach Tony Dungy, and quarterback Peyton Manning, the Colts won Super Bowl XLI. Jim serves on many league committees and works hard on league issues. Indianapolis has been fair with the Colts, who moved to a new stadium in 2008. When I chaired the expansion committee, Mayor Richard Lugar told me truthfully that the only way Indianapolis could get a team was by importing one from another city. I told him he had to do what he needed to do and that the NFL would do what it had to do.

Jacksonville Jaguars

Because the Jacksonville market is small, Wayne Weaver, owner of the Jaguars, faces problems. Concerned about revenue, he is uncertain about a financial future without hefty revenue sharing. Wayne denies a rumor that the team is for sale. The team is playing well under Coach Jack Del Rio, but the stadium is too big for the market. It is a struggle to sell out, unless it's Steelers vs. Jaguars, or the Florida-Georgia college football game. When the Jaguars began playing in Jacksonville, the city caught the attention of many new businesses that opened in the city. Development of additional league revenue sharing would give the Jaguars a chance.

Kansas City Chiefs

Lamar Hunt started the Kansas City Chiefs when he put together the American Football League. First the team was in Dallas with the

Cowboys, but two teams there was one too many. Lamar and Clint Murchison flipped a coin, and the Cowboys won. So the Cowboys stayed in Dallas, and Lamar took his team to Kansas City. The city built a huge stadium complex there, which serves as a modern prototype, with one stadium for football and another for baseball. The football team is more competitive than the baseball. After Lamar Hunt died in 2006, his son, Clark, took over the team as president.

Miami Dolphins

Wayne Huizenga owns the Miami Dolphins. Having worked with Wayne on a few issues, I have found him to be a stand-up man. He does a thorough job and knows what is right for the Dolphins and the league. When Don Shula coached the Dolphins and Dan Marino was the quarterback, the team went to the Super Bowl only once, but I always knew Dan Marino was a good person and a great quarterback. After Miami beat the Steelers in the 1984 AFC championship game, I thought the Dolphins would go on to win Super Bowl XIX, but they lost to the 49ers. Wayne Huizenga has great ideas and his team should succeed with new coach Cam Cameron.

Minnesota Vikings

Zygi Wilf now owns the Minnesota Vikings. When the club came into the NFL, my father and George Halas were the expansion committee, and Max Winter was the owner and president of the team. Max was well liked by everyone. He and Art Modell entertained the owners during recesses at league meetings. When Bud Grant was the coach and Jim Finks the general manager, the team played well. Later Mike Lynn became the general manager, and the community built a stadium, but it wasn't well thought out in terms of what was good for the football and baseball teams that use it. The Minnesota Vikings have the makings of a successful team and organization but need a new stadium of their own.

New England Patriots
In 1960 the Sullivan family owned the AFL team in Boston, but it was unsuccessful and later moved to Foxborough, Massachusetts. Bob Kraft now owns the New England Patriots. He once threatened to move the team to Connecticut where he could get a new stadium at no cost to him, but things worked out and the team stayed in Foxborough. Coach Bill Belichick was fired for not winning in Cleveland, but his Patriots teams have been extraordinarily successful, with three Super Bowl victories. Bob Kraft is on many NFL major committees, including finance and television. Bob is very intelligent and opinionated, which sometimes gets people upset. Off the field, Bob and his wife, Myra, are charitable people. Their son, Jonathan, is also very involved with the league. He does a good job on NFL issues. Bob and Jonathan let the coach handle the football operations, and with Tom Brady at quarterback the Patriots club should continue to do well.

New Orleans Saints
Tom Benson currently owns the New Orleans Saints. Tom is misunderstood sometimes, but he returned the team to his native New Orleans after Hurricane Katrina. After the hurricane, Paul Tagliabue helped in every way to make New Orleans a viable market for the NFL. In the face of difficulties, the Saints played well and made the playoffs. The team's future seems bright, and Tom wants to stay in New Orleans. But because the city lacks corporate support, the future may also be difficult. Tom knows and recognizes the Saints' situation. Having others in the league come to understand Tom's struggle has helped the team.

New York Giants
Tim Mara was a friend of my father before the Giants or the Steelers were part of the NFL. Jack Mara, Tim's son, ran the business side of the team, and Wellington was the man on the field. All of them are

gone now. John Mara, Wellington's son, now runs the team. Wellington and I were always close. I looked up to him as I would a big
brother. He appointed me chairman of negotiations with the NFLPA,
and we formed friendships with Gene Upshaw. Half of the interest in
the Giants was sold in 1991 to Bob Tisch, who enjoyed his involvement with the team and participated in league matters, especially on
the finance side. The club is building a new superclass stadium with
the New York Jets in New Jersey.

New York Jets

Woody Johnson owns the New York Jets now after buying it from the
estate of Leon Hess who was a tough but fair businessman. A member
of the commissioner search committee, Woody was always helpful.
The Jets are playing good football. The new stadium is going to be
expensive, but the club received $300,000 under the G3 program
from the league. A lot of debt is accruing throughout the NFL, and
that's definitely an issue for the league as it moves forward. Gaining
more experience in the football business, Woody wants to become
more involved with the league and the team.

Oakland Raiders

Al Davis runs the Oakland Raiders, and as many who have dealt with
him have come to say, "Al is Al." He likes to project a bravado image
and wants everyone to think he is a tough guy. We have been on a few
committees together; most recently the commissioner search committee. While Al was negative, his approach forced us to research and be
prepared for his questions in the search. In the end, we worked well. I
always appreciated the fact that Al came to my father's funeral—he
spent the whole day with our family and even watched the Steelers
game with our kids, who really like him. But again, "Al is Al," and he
does things that are questionable, such as his lawsuit against the Steelers, the first time one league team ever sued another. As filed, the suit

was Atkinson, a Raiders player, vs. Chuck Noll. The suit really was Raiders vs. Steelers. The trial was disruptive, which was also intentional. It happened right after we won our first two Super Bowls, but you must realize Al thought the trial was part of the game, part of the attack. However, we prevailed. Davis went on from there to sue the league numerous times, principally about his attempt to move the team to any place he wanted. The NFL won most of the cases but lost the suit that allowed Al to go to Los Angeles. He then returned the team to Oakland and sued that city. Al made life very difficult for Pete Rozelle, who always put the overall interest of the league ahead of any one owner's self interest.

Philadelphia Eagles

Many owners followed Bert Bell, the first owner of the Philadelphia Eagles, and Jeffrey Lurie now owns the team. The Eagles and the Steelers entered the league in the same year, 1933. In 1940, after a switch of the Steelers-Eagles franchises, Lex Thompson owned the Philadelphia team. In 1943, to help the NFL during World War II, the Steelers combined with the Eagles, becoming the Steagles, and the combination helped the league survive. After Thompson, a large number of owners, headed by Bill Green, followed: Jerry Wolman, Leonard Tose, Norm Braman, and now Jeffrey Lurie. Andy Reid coaches the Eagles, a fine team that should continue to do well in the future.

St. Louis Rams

Georgia Frontiere owns the St. Louis Rams, and John Shaw runs the team. Beginning as the Cleveland Rams, the team went to Los Angeles, where it competed successfully. At the time Dan Reeves, who was a real visionary, owned and operated the team. As the West's first NFL team, the Rams were the first to employ Tex Schramm and Pete Rozelle. Reeves was ahead of all the other teams in researching college players for the draft. Then Carroll Rosenbloom acquired the team. On his death his widow, Georgia, inherited the club. John Shaw operates the team and is a proponent of revenue sharing.

San Diego Chargers

The Spanos family owns the San Diego Chargers, and the family members are decent people and very smart. I like Alex Spanos, whose business is real estate home development. As well as building in the West, he now is building on the East Coast. His son, Dean, does a good job of running the team. Dean's wife, Susie, does much for the club in community service. Even after an excellent regular season record in 2006, the club fired Coach Marty Schottenheimer. They have a new staff headed by Norv Turner.

San Francisco Forty-Niners

The Morabito brothers started the team in the AAFC. The team did well when my friend Lou Spadia ran it. At the time, the 49ers had what may have been the best backfield ever in the league. It included Frankie Albert, Y. A. Tittle as quarterback, John Henry Johnson, Joe Perry, and "King" Hugh McElhenny. The whole offense was great; the defense, which could have been better, was okay. Denise York, Eddie DeBartolo's sister, now owns the 49ers. Her husband, Dr. John York, operates the club. Denise and Eddie divided assets after Eddie stepped down, and she took the team. It has a serious problem in continuing to play in the old Candlestick stadium, which was originally built for baseball games. The team is looking to stay in Northern California and may build in Santa Clara where their team offices are.

Seattle Seahawks

Paul Allen, who is interested in getting involved with the team and the league, now owns the Seattle Seahawks, the northernmost NFL team. CEO Tod Leiweke operates the club. The team just moved into a new stadium, which is very functional. The team is very good in part because of the good work done by Coach Mike Holmgren. The Seahawks played a competitive game against the Steelers in Super Bowl XL. Paul Allen has committed himself to fair dealings and success on the field and throughout the organization. I think the team has a good organization and a bright future.

Tampa Bay Buccaneers

The Glazer family owns the Tampa Bay Buccaneers, a family that does things differently but is effective. Joel Glazer runs the team. Recently, the family purchased the Manchester United soccer team. Because the league wants its members close to the football business, the purchase is controversial. I have had some dealings with the Glazers, and everything was fine. Since they purchased the Tampa team, I have had no problems. The club built a new stadium, played in the Super Bowl, and has a bright outlook.

Tennessee Titans

Bud Adams owns the Tennessee Titans. One of the originals of the AFL, the team began as the Houston Oilers. Because Bud could not get a new stadium in Houston, he moved to Tennessee. After playing one year in Memphis, they shifted their games to Nashville and a new stadium a year later. Coach Jeff Fisher has done a good job on the field and is the chairman of the football area of the competition committee. The new stadium has been a big help, and the Titans should do well in the future.

Washington Redskins

The Washington Redskins started in 1933 in Boston and moved to Washington in 1937. George Preston Marshall, a great showman, was the first owner. He formed the Redskins band and composed a song, "Hail to the Redskins." Along with Halas, Marshall was very influential in early league matters. The two men tried to run the league. When Sammy Baugh was the quarterback, the Redskins had a good team; however, the club did not have an African-American player on the team until 1962. Lacking players of color became an embarrassment to the NFL. Jack Kent Cooke, a difficult person at times, then bought the team. When Jack died, his charitable foundation sold the team to Dan Snyder, who operates it today. Coach Joe Gibbs won Super Bowls before retiring after the 1992 season, but he was brought back in 2004 by Dan Snyder. Dan is a good guy, often quiet, but he speaks up when he feels he has something important to say. Sitting on the league's ventures committee, Dan contributes helpful opinions, and he desperately wants a winning football team.